S0-AWZ-819

*out of print
1st edition* *15--*

The White-Headed Eagle

THE MACMILLAN COMPANY
NEW YORK · BOSTON · CHICAGO · DALLAS
ATLANTA · SAN FRANCISCO

MACMILLAN & CO., Limited
LONDON · BOMBAY · CALCUTTA
MELBOURNE

THE MACMILLAN COMPANY
OF CANADA, Limited
TORONTO

Walter & Valerie Reynolds

DR. JOHN McLOUGHLIN

Reproduction of the portrait in oil by William Coggswell now in the State House at Salem, Oregon.

The White-Headed Eagle

JOHN McLOUGHLIN
BUILDER OF AN EMPIRE

BY RICHARD G. MONTGOMERY

AUTHOR OF "PECHUCK: LORNE KNIGHT'S ADVENTURES
IN THE ARCTIC"

ILLUSTRATED

The Macmillan Company

NEW YORK   MCMXXXIV

Copyright, 1934, by
THE MACMILLAN COMPANY.

All rights reserved—no part of this book may be
reproduced in any form without permission in writing
from the publisher, except by a reviewer who wishes
to quote brief passages in connection with a review
written for inclusion in magazine or newspaper.

Set up and printed.
Published November, 1934.

PRINTED IN THE UNITED STATES OF AMERICA
NORWOOD PRESS LINOTYPE, INC.
NORWOOD, MASS., U.S.A.

TO DOROTHY

I am glad to find that you are writing the life of that illustrious pioneer, Dr. John McLoughlin. He deserves the glory of an eternal memory. I do not need to tell you that he was one of the towering personalities of the Far West. He was a lover of man, a lover of justice, a lover of the common people. He had in him something of that sweet compassion that was in the heart of the Christ when the Master said, "I have compassion on the multitude."

After eighty battling years, I still remember this consecrated son of humanity; and he will be remembered by the Far West as long as the hearts of that far land remember the virtue and the valor of heroic men.

I was taken into the cathedral in Oregon City when the good man was lying in state in the hours preceding the descent of his body into the warm embrace of our common mother Earth. It seems only yesterday that some strong man lifted me onto his shoulder that I might look down upon the face of the great dead. It was a moment of sacred silence: it was my first encounter with Death. I did not know the meaning of it then: do I know the meaning of it now?

Edwin Markham

Excerpt from a letter to Richard G. Montgomery.

OF all the heroic figures of the early West, Dr. John McLoughlin was the most remarkable. As a leader, a benefactor, and a Christian, he was unrivaled; and, though his life ended in tragedy, the passage of time has not only enhanced his greatness but placed him within the charmed circle of our national heroes. It seems passing strange, therefore, that the "White-Headed Eagle," in most of what has been written about him, scarcely emerges from the kaleidoscopic background of Northwest history. It was a desire to etch a reverse plate—to bring the doctor into full relief against the already familiar western scene—that prompted the writing of this book.

In building the narrative, original sources were employed as far as possible but, where these were not available, reliance was placed upon standard historical works, many of which have long been out of print. It has often been contended that, until the innermost records of the Hudson's Bay Company are opened to students, the complete story of Dr. McLoughlin cannot be told. However, from such original Hudson's Bay material as I have seen, it is my belief that the ultimate release of these documents will add but little of human interest value to our knowledge of the doctor. True, they will clarify disputed points regarding the establishment of posts as well as the movements of ships and men, and they will undoubtedly open the way to a better understanding of the company's methods and objectives. In a word, they will prove of greater interest to the historian than to the biographer.

Although a search for hitherto unpublished material was not

without result, I am frank to say that my principal aim was to collect, between the covers of a single volume, such information about the "White-Headed Eagle" as has heretofore been accessible only to the more enterprising students of western history.

No one who attempts to write biography can hope to achieve either pure objectivity or complete freedom from personal bias, however sincere his motives may be. I am well aware that much of the political and religious material contained in this study is, by its very nature, controversial. Therefore, where facts were lacking or where reasonable doubts appeared, I was content to advance opinions frankly stated as such.

Many individuals have assisted most generously in the task of gathering data for this work. The list is far too long to include in its entirety, but I should like to mention, in particular, George H. Himes and Miss Nellie B. Pipes of the Oregon Historical Society, Miss Anne M. Mulheron and members of the staff of the Portland Public Library, T. C. Elliott and Pal C. Clark of Walla Walla, Washington, the Misses Elizabeth and Winifred Myrick, great-granddaughters of Dr. McLoughlin, the Sisters of the Holy Names, who permitted an examination of their extremely valuable records, Fred C. Perrine, Mrs. Eva Emery Dye and Monsignor A. Hillebrand of Oregon City, Dr. Walter N. Sage of the University of British Columbia, W. S. Wallace of the University of Toronto, J. A. Gray of Montreal, Louis J. Pelletier of Rivière du Loup, Miss Theressa Gay of Berkeley, California, the Reverend John Laidlaw, Lewis A. McArthur, Judge Charles H. Carey, Mrs. M. Leona Nichols, and Miss Mary Nimmo of Portland.

R. G. M.

CONTENTS

ILLUSTRATIONS

The White-Headed Eagle

CHAPTER I

THE THOUGHTFUL BOY OF RIVIERE DU LOUP

I

TOWARD the close of one of the first spring days in the year 1784, three Montreal merchants sat leisurely around a table on which stood half-filled glasses and a near empty decanter. These three, Benjamin and Joseph Frobisher and Simon McTavish— seasoned veterans of the fur trade—were congratulating themselves upon having accomplished the impossible. For years they had been striving to unite the independent fur traders of eastern Canada into a workable organization, and now their task was completed. It was like a dream come true, and they had good reason to celebrate. Less hardy souls would long since have withdrawn from such a struggle, for their ancient enemy, the mighty Hudson's Bay Company, had long enjoyed exclusive privileges of trade throughout the land. Proud as they were of their newly born child, the North West Company, it is doubtful if any of the trio dared hope he would live to see the day when this youthful enterprise, so modestly conceived, would become a formidable rival of the older and more powerful concern. It was sufficient for the moment that a start had been made. Glasses were refilled while complimentary toasts continued on into the night.

Later in that same year, while these men were wrestling with the initial problems of their infant industry, and while the imperious Hudson's Bay men were receiving their first taste of well ordered competition, an event of signal importance not only to the British fur trade but to the fate of the Pacific Northwest took place in the remote village of Rivière du Loup.

2

On the east bank of the St. Lawrence River, about a hundred and twenty miles below Quebec, Rivière du Loup reposed unpretentiously in its attractive natural setting. In a crude farmhouse close by the village, John McLoughlin was born on October 19 of this epochal year of 1784. As the elder McLoughlin, also John, gazed upon his first male child, he noted a healthy little face with amazingly mature features; there was little else to distinguish him from hundreds of other babies who had first seen the light in Rivière du Loup. Certainly there was nothing to indicate that the serious-looking little fellow, lying so quietly beside his mother, would one day rule like a king at Fort Vancouver on the distant Columbia and prove instrumental in averting a war between the United States and Great Britain. John McLoughlin took one more look, nudged the old French doctor standing at the foot of the bed, and went back to work in his fields.

Good Roman Catholics, John and Angélique McLoughlin turned their thoughts immediately to the baby's christening. There was no resident priest at Rivière du Loup, and so, as soon as the young mother was able to travel, the several-weeks-old John was taken to the town of Kamouraska, some twenty-four miles away, and baptized, according to the parish records of that place, on December 5th.[1] Nor was this the first time that Angélique and her strapping, good-natured husband had made the same journey on the same errand. Their first child, Marie Louise, who was destined to become famous in her own right, had arrived four years earlier, in 1780, and their second, Marie Elizabeth, in 1782.

Good man that he was, there was nothing in the character of the elder McLoughlin to suggest greatness. His father, having emigrated to Canada from his native Ireland at an early age and having fallen in love with the rolling country around Rivière du Loup, had settled down there to lead the uninspiring life of a small farmer. The second John McLoughlin had followed in his footsteps. Working tirelessly from sunup to sundown, he had managed to establish himself sufficiently to ask for the hand of Angélique Fraser, a girl from across the river who was distinctly his superior in intellectual equipment. The very personification of mediocrity, John McLoughlin proved, nevertheless, to be a good husband and father. His greatest charm, an ever ready Celtic wit, he passed along to young John.

The boy's mother, on the other hand, was a truly remarkable woman whose ideas were well in advance of the customary feminine views of her time. In future years, John was to speak of her frequently, and always in the most glowing terms. From her he undoubtedly inherited his aptitude for learning rapidly, as well as his pronounced executive ability.

Of mixed Scottish and French blood, Angélique was the eldest child of Malcolm Fraser, seigneur of Murray Bay, whose massive stone mansion surrounded by an extensive estate was located on the bank of the St. Lawrence across the river from Rivière du Loup. Malcolm Fraser, the influential seigneur of Murray Bay, was a man of parts. Born in 1733, the eldest son of Donald Fraser, he had spent the early part of his life in the military service. For a time he had been a lieutenant in the 178th regiment of the British Army, the so-called Fraser Highlanders; and later, during the French and Indian War, he had been severely wounded at the battle of Quebec. Before he had left the army to settle down to the life of a country gentleman, John's grandfather had risen to the rank of captain in the Royal

Highland Emigrants. The old seigneur was a man of strong character and of high principle. In one way or another he had acquired a thorough education. Indeed he is supposed to have been equally at home in four languages—English, Gaelic, French, and Latin—which was a rare intellectual accomplishment for those days.[2]

One of Malcolm Fraser's sisters had married William Fraser, a distant cousin and a battle-scarred old soldier who, like the seigneur of Murray Bay himself, had seen service during the memorable siege of Quebec.[3] Colonel William Fraser and his wife lived on a pretentious estate over on the Rivière du Loup side of the St. Lawrence where they took a friendly interest in their modest young neighbors, the McLoughlins.

Malcolm Fraser, true to the custom of his day, reared a large family. There were three daughters, Angélique, Julia, and Anne; and five sons, Alexander, Joseph, Simon, William, and John. Although the Scottish seigneur remained a Protestant throughout his life, his second wife, the mother, incidentally, of all his children, was a French Canadian and hence a Roman Catholic. Angélique, like the other children, had embraced the religion of her mother. Of the other Frasers, only two appear to have exerted any considerable influence over John's boyhood. Alexander, the eldest son, entered the fur trade as a young man and rose to a position of power in the North West Company. He was a close friend of each of the three men who had formed this enterprise in the very year of John's birth. The third son, Dr. Simon Fraser, served as a physician in the "Black Watch" regiment of the Royal Highlanders and took part in all the engagements fought by that famous military unit during the Napoleonic Wars, from 1795 to 1803. Each of these uncles was to have a voice in selecting a career for John. Indeed the boy had ample reason to be proud of his Fraser ancestry. They were people to be reckoned with.

3

Amid the pleasant surroundings of the humble Rivière du Loup farmhouse, John grew from a healthy baby into a sturdy little boy. The serious look which the senior John McLoughlin had observed on his son's face at birth persisted, though it was relieved, now and again, by a broad disarming smile. Young John would burst forth with some clever sally, pause a moment or two with wide eyes to study its effect, and then appear lost in thought. "It's the Irish in him," big John would say with a show of pride, but Angélique would only smile to herself. It was the boy's thoughtful look—a look that seemed somehow to promise great things for the future—that interested her. John was the idol of his parents and of his sister, Marie Louise, but not for long was he to remain the baby of the family.

As the years rolled by, the old French doctor found it necessary to call at the McLoughlin farm frequently. David, the second son, arrived two years after John, and then came three girls, Julie, Honorée, and Marguerite. Marie Elizabeth, the second daughter, died in infancy. A sizable family, this. After each blessed event, John's father would go forth into his fields to work with redoubled energy. Feeding so many mouths was not an easy task, as the thrifty Irish farmer and his wife were soon to discover.

Very often, while John was still a tiny tot, Angélique would take him, with Marie Louise, to call at the estate of Colonel William Fraser, close by Rivière du Loup. There, under the great shade trees, the little girl would play for hours at a time with John while the Frasers and Angélique looked on approvingly. After a while, for some reason that is not entirely clear, Marie Louise went to live with her great-uncle for good. It may have been because the Colonel and his wife were childless and felt the need of a young person's company, or it may have been that Angélique and her hard-working husband were having difficulty in making both ends meet. At all events, the old soldier lost his heart to this gifted grandniece and, with the consent of her mother and father, adopted her.[4] For little John the separation was a cruel one though he was still able to see his sister often during the summer months.

Although Malcolm Fraser may have regretted his daughter's marriage to a poor farmer, he was always happy to welcome her back to the palatial home that had once been her own. In his affectionate but imperious manner, the old seigneur insisted that Angélique bring little John with her whenever she came, for, very early, he had developed a strong attachment for the serious-minded boy. Eager as she was to please her father, the busy young mother was not a person to neglect her household duties, and the journey across to Mount Murray, her father's palatial estate, was a long one.

As time passed by, Angélique fell into the habit of leaving first John and later David with her parents for weeks at a time, with the result that both of them came, quite naturally, to feel more at home at Mount Murray than in the modest Rivière du Loup farmhouse. Keenly as Angélique and her husband missed their two boys, they must have been thankful, particularly in bad years, to be afforded some relief in the face of their fast increasing responsibilities. As for the honest Irishman, he soon discovered that, for better or worse, he had married his wife's entire family.

Grandfather Fraser took great pride in his two young wards and arranged personally for their early schooling. Since he was himself a cultured gentleman with an abundance of leisure, it is quite probable that he taught John and David himself, though he may have chosen to place their education in the hands of a private tutor. The subsequent careers of both boys bear ample testimony to the thoroughness of their early training, however they may have acquired it. Wherever John's future travels were to take him—to lonely outposts in western Canada, to Fort Vancouver on the distant Columbia, even to staid old London—he was regarded as a well-educated man with broad human sympathies. It is safe to assume that the old seigneur planted in the receptive mind of his grandson many of those noble traits which were eventually to make him rise far above the men around him.

Then, too, there was Uncle Simon, the fighting doctor, a man of wide experience and of charming personality. To the impressionable McLoughlin boys he seemed a veritable beau ideal. During the doctor's frequent visits at Mount Murray, he taught his nephews the fundamentals of science and inspired them with a desire to study medicine—a desire which, in each case, was later realized. This romantic soldier of fortune remained a powerful influence in the lives of John and David until the time came for him to cross the ocean and cast his lot with the British forces fighting against Napoleon. This was in 1795, and John was eleven—old enough, no doubt, to wish he were going too.

4

There were many visitors at Mount Murray during the happy years John spent there as a boy. Soldiers, statesmen, merchants, and fur traders came to pay their respects to the influential old seigneur; but, of them all, John waited most eagerly for the periodic homecomings of Uncle Alexander, the great North Wester. His was a personality to thrill the soul of any boy who craved adventure! If Dr. Simon Fraser initiated his nephew into the world of science, it was Alexander Fraser, the intrepid fur trader, who brought to him a breath of the great open country. Sitting at the feet of this picturesque wanderer, the boy learned the glowing story of the fur trade in Canada, the most glamorous calling for a young man of that day.

One fine autumn afternoon, when John was a dozen years old, Uncle Alexander invited him to go for a stroll along the bank of the St. Lawrence. The North Wester's purpose was obvious. He fancied he saw, in the tall youth whose stride so nearly matched his own, a prospective recruit for the company. There would be years to wait, of course, but it was not too early to lay the groundwork. A few questions, discreetly put, revealed the fact that John's heart was set on the study of medicine, but Alexander Fraser was not a man to dismiss a whim lightly, once it had taken hold. Indeed he had succeeded, at a most opportune moment and after a long struggle, in luring the famous explorer, David Thompson, away from the hated Hudson's Bay Company into the ranks of his own company. He was a super-salesman, this dashing uncle, and now he was determined to use all of his wiles on young John.

On that memorable stroll, he told the boy about the North West's great rival in trade, the Hudson's Bay Company, whose charter dated back to the time of King Charles II. John listened intently to the story of how the Merry Monarch, in 1670, conferred this grant upon his "dear and entirely beloved Cousin, Prince Rupert, and upon a group of associated gentlemen incorporated as the Governor and Company of Adventurers of England trading into Hudson's Bay." [5] The youth's gray eyes opened wide. A princely gift, he thought, and, to Uncle Alexander's joy, he began to ask questions. He wanted the whole story. His mind was on fire with enthusiasm, however well he may have disguised his emotions behind his serious features.

Alexander Fraser's smile widened. He went on with the tale, relating how the King, not satisfied with having bestowed the charter alone, donated to the gentlemen of the Hudson's Bay Company a vast province called Rupert's Land, named in honor of his fortune-favored relative. He told how the company, eager to grasp everything within reach, had construed its newly acquired territory as extending from Labrador westward across the continent to the Rocky Mountains, and from the northern watershed of the St. Lawrence on up to the line of the watershed of the Hudson Straits. It was, as John had observed, a princely gift.

Immensely pleased, the North Wester continued. He explained that there had been no strings attached to the authority of the company's officers to rule in Rupert's Land save that two elks and two black beavers were to be paid each year to the sovereign and his successors "whenever they should happen to enter into the said territories."[6] Rupert's Land was to have been the proprietary colony of the Hudson's Bay Company, but it was not long before men began to challenge this exclusive claim.

Straightway John wanted to know about these men. Boy that he was, his innate sense of justice rebelled against the very thought of a monopoly so sweeping. He asked more questions, and Alexander Fraser lost no time in following up his advantage. Time was, he explained, when the French had objected strenuously to the Hudson's Bay charter, but the siege of Quebec had driven them forever from the New World. He pointed across the river in the direction of Colonel William Fraser's estate at Rivière du Loup as he related the part John's great-uncle had played in that famous battle—a part, incidentally, which the boy already knew well. Then, with the French gone, there remained only the independent fur traders of Rupert's Land to fight the Hudson's Bay partners; but these Canadians were men of steel. The lad's uncle could tell that part of the narrative with deep feeling since he himself had been one of them. He recalled how, unorganized and without leadership, his comrades in the fur trade had not been permitted to deal with the Indians save at specified villages and government posts.

A scowl stole over John's set features. He, too, was a Canadian, and, with his vivid imagination, he could picture himself, at that moment, in the very thick of the fight. Then came the story of the three men—the brothers Frobisher and Simon Mc-Tavish—who, back in the year of John's birth, had formed the North West Company and, shortly after, had enlisted the services of Uncle Alexander. But that event had marked only the beginning of the struggle for supremacy—the battle was still raging.

The walk was over and the narrative finished. Alexander Fraser, the North Wester, standing at the gates of Mount Murray beside his nephew, had no idea that he had made a convert for his company. The boy had asked a few questions, to be sure, but he had kept his innermost thoughts to himself. That was like him. Little did these two dream—the veteran trader and the serious-minded lad—that the day would come when each would be serving under the banner of the hated Hudson's Bay Company.

5

As John and David grew older, they became so absorbed in their studies and in their many other activities at Mount Murray that they saw but little of their own parents. Infrequent as were the sojourns in the old farmhouse at Rivière du Loup, however, they were always anticipated with great eagerness by both boys. John, in particular, loved the informal atmosphere of the old place, which presented a marked contrast to the exacting conventionalism of the seigneury. Home again, the boy could unbend—he could curl up before the fire, as he had done in the long ago, and listen to the thrilling stories his mother never tired of telling.

For the most part they were tales of brave Scottish Highlanders which Angélique had learned at her father's knee. No doubt John had heard many of them from the lips of the old seigneur himself, but they seemed somehow to take on new life as his mother narrated them. One story that John delighted to tell in future years related the high-handed methods of a certain Highland chief who had fallen into the habit of carrying a yellow cane with which to drive the unwilling of his clan to church. In time, the faith of the tribe had become known as the "religion of the yellow stick."[7] In the Vancouver years ahead, John was to insist upon attendance at divine service so resolutely as to indicate that he may have taken a leaf from the old Scot's book.

Though she saw but little of John and David during their boyhood years, Angélique, remarkable mother that she was, remained very close to them in spirit. Fighting against the discouraging handicap of absence, she exerted such a profound influence upon the early lives of both boys that they were to remember her always with the deepest affection. With the father, however, it was different. When John and David and, more frequently, Marie Louise came home, it seemed to the elder McLoughlin as if they had drifted in from another world though, perhaps without realizing why, he was inordinately proud of them. He could joke with the boys and marvel at their skill with the canoe or at their ability to shoot, but, in conversation, he soon found himself outclassed. Indeed he may have entertained a furtive hope that one or the other would some day follow in his footsteps on the little farm, but when John talked at length of the glamorous Uncle Alexander's life in the fur trade or when David dwelt upon his aspirations to become a doctor, the poor Irishman would shake his head and return to his plow.

For a clan so numerous and yet so centralized, the Frasers got on splendidly together. With the two McLoughlin boys spending most of their time at Mount Murray, with the oldest daughter residing permanently with her great-uncle, and with the children's own parents deprived of their company for long periods, the tribe remained closely welded. As a boy, John could recall only one serious rift in the ranks.

It came about in this manner. Colonel Fraser, the rough and ready soldier, soon discovered that he was unsuited to the task of educating his adopted daughter. Desirous of providing Marie Louise with every advantage, he sent her to the convent of the Ursuline nuns in Quebec. It was but natural for the girl to adopt her mother's chosen faith and, as she grew into young womanhood, she became obsessed with a desire to take orders in the Church. Angélique was enraptured, but, in deference to her father's strong Anglican convictions, she avoided the subject scrupulously while in his presence. Nevertheless, the news was not slow in finding its way across to Mount Murray, and when the old seigneur, who until then had taken but scant interest in his granddaughter, heard of her decision, his anger knew no bounds. It had been humiliating enough for his children to embrace Romanism, but for one of his own flesh and blood to become a nun—that was unthinkable!

For John, the situation was painful in the extreme. Torn between his love for Marie Louise on the one hand and his respect for the old seigneur on the other, the boy, then scarcely thirteen, essayed the rôle of mediator. Although he had attended the Episcopal Church regularly with his grandfather, he could not find it in his heart to oppose the sincere religious convictions of his sister. Even when the old gentleman's ears were closed to the arguments of others, he was in the habit of listening patiently to his favorite grandson; but, in this instance, discussion was cut short. Malcolm Fraser remained obdurate. It was the first personal tragedy in John's life—a life that was to know many before its course had been run.

Across the St. Lawrence, Colonel Fraser and his wife, themselves Protestants, rose to the defense of their adopted daughter. Like most elderly doting foster-parents, they probably found it impossible to deny the girl her one great desire in life. As for Marie Louise, her mind was made up. Oblivious to the storm she had unwittingly caused, she followed her star and, in 1798, joined the Order of the Daughters of St. Ursula in Quebec. She was to fill, at intervals, the office of Superior of the Community with rare talent, justice, and prudence and to attain, ultimately, the title of Mother St. Henry. Long years after, John, proud of having championed so saintly a character, was to have her portrait painted by a noted artist of the time. This picture, amazingly lifelike, hangs today in the community hall of the convent.[8]

6

It was spring in the year 1799, and John was fourteen—not too young, in those days, for a boy to give earnest thought to the future. He was a big chap for his years, straight as an arrow and strong. Long since, he had learned to ride and, with David, to handle a big canoe skilfully in the rough waters of the St. Lawrence. The great world beckoned but, except for an occasional trip with his mother to visit Marie Louise at the convent or an even less frequent journey to Montreal with Grandfather Fraser, John's knowledge of it was confined to the rolling country near Mount Murray. It was a beautiful stretch of land, and the boy loved every square inch of it; but, after all, he was fourteen and he longed to be out on his own.

John and David were inseparable companions. Together they tramped the fields and discussed their plans. At eleven years, David had settled his mind on medicine; but John was less certain. Uncle Simon, the doctor, had gone off to war in 1795, and even Uncle Alexander had seen but little of Mount Murray in the interim; but the examples of these two had hovered in the offing like a pair of magnets, each attracting the lad toward a different calling. One day John would roam through the woods, his gun slung over his shoulder, and imagine himself a gallant fur trader penetrating the wilds of Athabasca. Another time he would sit for hours with his books and, with equal facility, fancy himself a famous physician in some European capital. The more he speculated, the more difficult it became to make a decision.

In his unsettled state of mind, the boy turned to the old seigneur for advice and received, no doubt, a candid opinion. It had been Grandfather Fraser's hope that John would follow one of the learned professions. Fur trading was all right for a rough fellow like Alexander, but it was no calling for his favorite grandson. No, sir, one fur trader in the family was enough. Law might be better, but medicine would do—a man could be a doctor and still be a gentleman! At least one knew where Malcolm Fraser stood.

John listened respectfully, thought much, but said little. It is doubtful if even his close confidant, David, discovered how the old seigneur's advice had been received, so prone was John to consider all sides. There was, of course, one other person he must consult before making up his mind, and so, at his first opportunity, he crossed over to the old farmhouse at Rivière du Loup to lay the case before his mother. Angélique was no stranger to the struggle that had been going on in her son's mind. Respecting the medical profession profoundly, she had, at the same time, enough romance in her soul to idolize her brother Alexander and the adventuresome career he had chosen. Indeed the good woman was as perplexed as John himself, and here he was back home, ready to dump the whole problem in her lap. What could she say to him?

Angélique's sole purpose was to divine her son's real desire, and so, instead of proffering advice, she asked questions—questions adroitly designed to break the deadlock. Responding to his mother's subtle methods, the boy talked at great length and soon found himself expressing a preference. The die was cast. Medicine had won the first round, but the battle was yet young.

Back at Mount Murray, the old seigneur rejoiced, convinced that his logic had carried the day. His grandson would be a gentleman by the grace of God and a doctor by necessity! No expense would be spared to further his education. In his heart John knew that he had reached his own decision, but he allowed the venerable squire of Mount Murray his moment of triumph. At fourteen, John McLoughlin was already a diplomat.

CHAPTER II

THE YOUNG NORTH WESTER

I

WHATEVER medical education John received had necessarily to be crowded into the years between 1799 and 1803, yet there is no record of his activities during this formative period. With so little time available for the attainment of a degree, he could scarcely have tarried long at Grandfather Fraser's once his great decision had been reached, nor was it like the lad, already possessed of a man's will, to delay. Incredible as it seems, therefore, we can only believe that John, not yet sixteen, quitted Mount Murray and, with the joint blessings of the two persons most interested in his future, his mother and the old seigneur, went forth to seek his training. Where he went and exactly when, no one can say.

Tradition has it that near the turn of the century John and David McLoughlin crossed the Atlantic to enter the University of Edinburgh, which boasted one of the finest medical schools of the day.[1] It is difficult to believe that John, even at sixteen, could have journeyed so far from home to study medicine, but that David could have delved into the mysteries of anatomy and physiology in far-away Scotland at the tender age of thirteen seems absurd. Indeed it is highly improbable that John was ever enrolled as a medical student at the Scottish city since the records of the University and of the College of Physicians and Surgeons of Edinburgh are devoid of any reference to him.[2]

Many years later, in 1892, John's youngest son, David, was to cast further doubt on the old tradition by stating in a letter that "my father never went to Paris with his brother David to study, or to Scotland."[3]

The University of Edinburgh records do reveal, however, that John's brother David entered the medical school in 1807 and that he obtained his degree in 1810, some years after John had embarked upon a very different career.[4] Likewise, an interesting collection of letters exchanged between Grandfather Fraser and a Mr. James Ker of Leith Bank, Scotland, from 1809 to 1811, makes frequent mention of David but none at all of John.

"Your grandson, David McLoughlin," wrote Mr. Ker to his Canadian friend, Malcolm Fraser, "left this two days ago for Canada. His uncles have not sent him a shilling for a great length of time and knowing him to be a good, studious young man, neither given to extravagance nor dissipation, but cruelly embarrassed and disappointed by the non-arrival of his uncles' long promised Remittances, . . . I found that if I did not immediately relieve him of some pressing debts, he would run a risk of being thrown into Jail. I have, therefore, been obliged to advance him £120."[5]

The threat of debtors' prison was not for John, however, for while David was being financially assisted by his friends abroad, John had long since obtained his own degree in medicine at home. Medical courses of that day, particularly in the New World, were not only of short duration but of an extremely informal character. It was not uncommon for a young man to select some outstanding practitioner, make the daily rounds of his practice with him, and acquire his professional knowledge purely by the absorption method. Many of these students developed successful practices without ever having obtained a degree from a recognized medical school, and young John, in his eagerness to get an early start, may have been one of them. Two or at most three years would have sufficed to equip him for what he then believed would become his life's work. Whether John actually earned his degree in a medical school or whether he simply learned "doctoring" from some kindly old country practitioner, he soon became Dr. McLoughlin and remained, throughout his long career in the West, a credit to the profession—a skilful surgeon, a resourceful physician, and a man of noble and compassionate character.

His education completed, the young doctor retraced his steps to the old farmhouse in Rivière du Loup to spend a few weeks with his parents. The years away from the family circle had wrought marked changes in his appearance, and the three little sisters, gazing upon him in awe, wondered if this could really be the older brother who had once joined so enthusiastically in their games. Well on the road to the six feet four inches he was ultimately to attain, and commencing to fill out proportionately, Doctor John, towering above his mother, must have seemed to her more like some strange giant than like the serious lad she had reared so tenderly. The thoughtful boy had, in truth, reached man's estate.

Angélique was not slow to discover other changes in this strapping son of hers. She recalled the unsettled state of his mind prior to his leaving home and it must have been with mixed feelings that she now observed his newly acquired poise and self-assurance. They had many pleasant chats together, these two, but mainly they talked of John's experience during the years that had intervened. Each one carefully avoided any mention of the future. Perhaps Angélique still cherished the hope that John would follow his profession in some one of the larger Canadian cities though, with a mother's intuition, she no doubt divined, from the far-away look that came into his eyes whenever the conversation veered dangerously close to the forbidden subject, that he had other plans. To be sure, there were occasional hints that the memory of Uncle Alexander's romantic life in the fur trade was still fresh in the mind of her adventure-loving son. Angélique's affection for her boy was so strong that she was quite content to let him work out his own destiny.

Across the St. Lawrence at Mount Murray, John found a very different situation. Grandfather Fraser, who had aged noticeably in the interim, had not changed in one particular. He was still of the fixed opinion that no grandson of his should lower himself by entering the fur trade. Forthright as always, he launched immediately into a discussion of the matter and discovered, to his dismay, that John's education had not increased his liking for medicine as a career. There were stormy altercations in which, as so often happens where there is strong mutual affection, reason would invariably give way to emotion. John remained unmoved by his grandfather's arguments though, in deference to the old seigneur's earnest convictions, he agreed to give medicine a trial.

It was merely a stop-gap. In his heart he knew that sooner or later the wild country of the little known West would call him just as it had called Alexander Fraser. When and how that call would come he had no idea, but of one thing he was certain—if it were ever to come, he would have to answer it. Yes, and he would still remain a gentleman!

2

It was probably in the summer of 1803 that John, looking more than his nineteen years, left the familiar banks of the lower St. Lawrence, determined to realize his ambition but with no well formed notion of how it was to be accomplished. Little did he realize, as he journeyed up the river to Montreal, that he was putting behind him for all time the happy scenes of his boyhood. For all his impressive height and manly appearance, he was just an overgrown boy, burning with a desire to discover what life had to offer.

It was not without significance that John had chosen Montreal for, located there, was the headquarters of the fast growing North West Company. His purpose appeared obvious—he could carry out his agreement with Grandfather Fraser and still keep his eyes open for an opportunity to enter the company's service. Foresight was always to remain one of his happiest faculties. For a little while he practiced medicine in Montreal; [6] but he was not long in proving what he had long suspected—that a professional career in a well-settled community held no fascination for him. The lad's gray eyes were focused on the West—there was no hankering for city life in his nature.

One may see him in fancy, going about the rounds of his modest practice and accepting small fees when his patients could afford them or leaving, as willingly, with a kindly smile when they could not. Faithful to his work without ever caring for it, he endured the seemingly interminable months in Montreal, hoping against hope that his great chance would come. We can only guess the manner in which the young doctor, so certain now of his own mind, made the contacts which were necessary to land him in the fur trade. It is possible that the North West leaders, ever in search of likely recruits, may have encountered him shadowing their headquarters and, liking his appearance, have invited him into their growing enterprise. Or perhaps Uncle Alexander, still harboring his old whim, pulled timely strings in the lad's favor.

At all events, either late in 1803 or early in 1804, Doctor John joined the North West Company in the capacity of resident physician and received orders to proceed to Fort William, the company's chief depot and factory, located on the north shore of Lake Superior at the mouth of the Kaministikwia River. There is a record of a "Mr. McLauchlin" journeying to Lake

Superior by way of the Kaministikwia route in July, 1804, and this individual, according to Dr. Elliott Coues, was undoubtedly Doctor John.[7] Thus neatly had he reconciled his own ambition with his grandfather's wish—he was a fur trader at last though still a doctor. Medicine, oddly enough, had provided him with an entering wedge.

During the early stages of his career as a North Wester, John's activities were restricted to his duties as resident physician. He was soon to discover, however, that the prosaic routine of doctoring wounded voyageurs or of delivering their numerous half-breed progeny interested him far less than did the actual business of fur trading. John had not been long at Fort William before he came under the personal notice of William McGillivray, one of the company's heads and the man for whom the fort had been named. No doubt McGillivray would have been prejudiced from the start in favor of any nephew of his old friend Alexander Fraser though, quite obviously, the young doctor possessed in marked degree all of the requisites for success in the fur trade—courage, determination, executive ability, and uncommon physical strength. However that may be, the lad was given minor services to perform, outside his medical duties, and these he handled most capably.[8] In this manner, the evolution from physician to fur trader came about rapidly and by natural steps.

Once inside the company's ranks, John made it his business to learn something of how the North West fortunes were progressing. Automatically, Uncle Alexander came to mind. He recalled the thrilling story this favorite uncle had told him on that memorable stroll along the bank of the St. Lawrence. How long ago it seemed! Bit by bit, the new recruit picked up additional information. He knew, of course, that the enterprise with which he had cast his lot was still fighting the grasping Hudson's Bay monopoly. But, as he began to make inquiry, he learned that still another competitor had entered the field—the prosperous X Y Company. Some years before—in 1798—this concern had been formed by certain of the North West partners who had become dissatisfied with the autocratic methods of Simon McTavish—the "Marquis," they called this fire-eating old fur baron. As the years had slipped by, the X Y men had become formidable rivals, and, just recently, they had gained a notable convert in the person of Sir Alexander Mackenzie, the pioneer pathfinder, who, in the early days, had made a brilliant overland dash to the Pacific Coast. Doctor John soon discovered that he would have to fight not one but two respectable adversaries, and somehow we cannot imagine the outlook disturbing him. He craved adventure, and shortly he was to have it in abundance.

3

The young doctor spent most of his early years in the North West Company's service at Fort William [9] though, in his line of duty, he made numerous trips to surrounding posts. One can readily imagine what a striking contrast the primitive life at the fort must have presented both to the quiet atmosphere of Mount Murray and to the fleeting taste of metropolitan activity he had enjoyed in Montreal.

The Fort William that John called home during those years was an extensive settlement—the outstanding interior headquarters post of the company. It has been described as a palisaded village.[10] A stockade, some fifteen feet in height with an overlooking tower, surrounded a spacious square inside of which were located numerous buildings. The principal edifice was the council-house, a pretentious wooden structure, which contained a dining room sixty feet long by some thirty feet wide. Portraits of early North West partners hung on the walls, and these lent a touch of color to the otherwise somber atmosphere of the hall. The young doctor gazed up at these stern faces in awe, particularly at the grim features of old Simon McTavish, the "Marquis." Little wonder, he thought, that the X Y men had bolted! At one end of this great room were the apartments occupied by the principal agents, and at the other, a spacious piazza, surmounted by a balcony. The kitchen was located in the basement, and, adjacent to it, were the servants' quarters.

On either side of the council-house stood two large buildings, slightly less imposing. One provided sleeping quarters for the wintering partners while the other was reserved for apprenticed clerks. In the first of these two long houses was John's narrow bunk, and on the wall beside his pillow he had hung a delicately executed miniature of Angélique. Surrounding the main buildings, within the square, were the lodging-houses of the men, warehouses for the furs, a countinghouse, a doctor's office in which John spent as little time as possible, a powder house, and, of course, a jail. Along one side of the enclosure ran a string of smaller structures which served as stores and workshops where the necessities of life, including generous stocks of liquor, could be purchased. Vegetables were raised in fields outside the stockade, and there, also, were pastures for cattle, sheep, hogs, and poultry. Fort William was a little world unto itself.

To most of his associates at this post—men unaccustomed, in the main, to any evidences of erudition in a youngster—Doctor John must have seemed a strange anomaly. Among the leaders, of course, there were men of similar intellectual equipment, but, at first, the new recruit from Quebec had only a limited association with them. It was with the rank and file that he was thrown, and doubtless, to a young man of his temperate habits, the excessive drinking and roistering all about him must have presented a highly distasteful spectacle.[11] Years later he was to build his own fort on the bank of the Columbia at Vancouver, modeling it after Fort William, but there, ruling like a benevolent despot, he was to set up his own rigid standards of conduct and make them applicable to all. For the moment, John was content to live and learn. So amenable was he, in fact, and so eager to establish himself securely in his chosen career, that the men about him were given no opportunity to suspect that his tastes differed greatly from their own. Indeed he played the game with such finesse that he became a favorite not only with his superiors but, stranger still, with those of his own rank.

In the meticulously penned journals of a few early North West traders, there may be found occasional references to Doctor John during this obscure period of his life. Little more than his name appears in most of the entries, which, granted his youth and relative unimportance in the company's service at the time, is not surprising. We know, for instance, that in August, 1807, he was stationed at Fort Duncan—a small post on Lake Nipigon, north of Lake Superior [12]—and that later in the same year he wintered at Sturgeon Lake not far away. Daniel Williams Harmon, a celebrated North West trader who had risen from the rank of clerk to that of partner, spent the closing months of 1807 and the early part of 1808 at this place with Doctor John.[13] Harmon found the young man "a most agreeable companion," which is probably just another way of saying that he discovered in him a refreshing contrast to the average run of youngsters he had encountered in the service. Even by that time, John had developed a strong will and, with it, the courage to voice his opinions freely though with discretion. If the older man found him agreeable, therefore, his views must have coincided closely with those of the twenty-three-year-old wintering partner.

The fact that John had attained the status of wintering partner by the time Harmon met him at Sturgeon Lake is evidence that he had risen rapidly in the service. The North West Company, at that time, had two general classes of shareholders. There were the eastern partners, mainly merchants of Montreal and Quebec, who furnished the necessary capital; and the so-called wintering partners, the men in the field, who supplied the manual labor and fur-trading experience. The city gentlemen imported goods from England which they exchanged for furs of various kinds to be sold in the London markets. It was the avowed ambition of every young man in the service to become a wintering partner, and this coveted goal could be attained only when the aspirant possessed a natural aptitude for the game plus a capacity for hard work. The whole plan of the company's organization was neatly designed to keep its personnel loyal and interested. To have achieved wintering partner standing at twenty-three was a distinct feather in John's cap.

Like a ship hidden from the sunshine in a belt of fog, John's career as a North Wester between 1808 and 1816 is almost entirely obscured. One must be content, in the main, to dismiss this interval as a period of continuous effort on the part of the youthful fur trader to improve his standing in the company. During all this time he kept in touch as best he could with the various members of his family. As long as he lived and wherever he journeyed, he remained steadfastly loyal to all of his near relatives.

Two events occurred in these years, either or both of which might have urged John to hasten back to Rivière du Loup. One was the death of his father, who had been accidentally drowned in the St. Lawrence on April 28, 1813, and the other was the passing of the doughty old seigneur, Malcolm Fraser, on June 14, 1815.[14] Though it would have required many weeks to receive news of either tragedy and an equally long period to travel home, John's affection for his mother was such that he would have made heroic efforts to be with her during her successive bereavements.

4

In this same hazy span occurred one of the major events of Doctor John's young manhood, his marriage to Margaret McKay. It was on one of his sojourns at the North West Company's isolated Sault Sainte Marie post that he met this comely widow and promptly lost his heart. Up to then the young North Wester, save for one obscure affair, had had no time for romance; but his infatuation for Margaret appears to have been instantaneous and profound. Through the long years ahead, their association was to contain all the elements of a great and lasting love.

It was at Sault Sainte Marie that Margaret, still attractive though well past thirty, had resided since the death of her first husband. Of her early life almost nothing is known. Her father was a fur trader named Wadin, and her mother was either a full-blooded Indian or a half-breed. The historians appear evenly divided between these two alternatives though at least one is positive that the widow of Alexander McKay was "one fourth Chippewa from Red River of the North." [15] Whatever her origin may have been, she was, when John first met her, a picture of loveliness with her straight dark hair, her flashing black eyes, and her slightly coppered skin. She not only was charming but, to a very limited extent, educated for, as a girl, she had attended the convent of the Ursuline nuns in Quebec.[16] There is a remote possibility that John's older sister, Marie Louise, was a student there at the same time, in which case the dark-haired girl from the Red River country may have learned something of her future husband long years before she met him. Doubtless the heart of many a stalwart Scot had thumped in vain until she succumbed to the wiles of the bold-spirited McKay toward the close of the old century.

The name of Alexander McKay is renowned in the annals

of the North West Company. Among other daring feats he had accompanied the pathfinder, Alexander Mackenzie, on his overland expedition of 1789–93. Later, he had joined the Astor enterprise only to be murdered by hostile Indians at Clayoquot Sound on the western end of Vancouver Island when, in the summer of 1811, the savages seized the ill-fated ship *Tonquin* and massacred all hands. Margaret, waiting at Sault Sainte Marie with growing alarm, could scarcely have received news of her husband's tragic death before the latter part of 1811. How long she tarried before accepting Doctor John, who had been pressing his suit with vigor, is an unsolvable riddle, but we can hazard the guess that their wedding took place either late in 1811 or early in 1812. The fact that the first child, John, Jr., arrived on August 18, 1812, offers our only clue as to the marriage date.[17]

Four children, a boy and three girls, had been born to Alexander McKay and his wife at their Sault Sainte Marie cabin. When John married Margaret, he adopted these children as his own. The boy Tom, who, as a lad of fourteen, had gone west with his father, was to become a picturesque character in the subsequent history of Oregon and a worthy stepson to John McLoughlin. The girls married early and remained in the East.[18]

One wonders whether John, despite his admiration for Margaret's charm and innate wisdom, may not have thought twice before taking a wife with Indian blood. Such marriages, however, were the order of the day. They were, in fact, the only ones. Those early traders knew only too well that white girls could not stand the rough life at far-flung outposts whereas Indian women and half-breeds knew no other. Margaret, with her Indian heritage, could follow the doctor wherever he went, and he could not have found anywhere a more loyal or helpful companion. Indeed she was to prove a model of self-sacrifice and wifely devotion.

Since, at that time, there were no clergymen at the various trading posts of the North West Company, John and Margaret were united by the simple service then in vogue. Many years later, one of these marriage certificates was brought to light. Appealing in its plainness, the document reads as follows:

In presence of the undersigned witnesses I Archibald McKinlay a clerk in the service of the Honbl Hudson's Bay Company late of Scotland and now residing at Ft. Vancouver Columbia River do voluntarily and of my own freewill and accord take Sarah Julia Ogden daughter of Peter Skene Ogden to be my lawful wife and the said Sarah Julia Ogden also, voluntarily and of her own freewill and accord take the said Archibald McKinlay to be my lawful husband.
Witnesses
    ARCH'D McDONALD
    ALEX C. ANDERSON
Ft. Vancouver
June 1840   ARCH'D McKINLAY
                                             SARAH JULIA OGDEN
                                             JOHN McLOUGHLIN
                                             C F H B Co.[19]

Such was a wedding ceremony in the heyday of the fur trade! Although the document quoted above records a marriage much later than Doctor John's in point of time, it is, nevertheless, the same general form as that which North West and Hudson's Bay traders alike had used prior to the union of the companies in 1821 and, for that matter, as far back as men then living could remember. We can picture Doctor John and Margaret standing side by side in the semi-gloom of a candle-lit cabin— the groom towering above the bride—and the two of them, in the presence of some grizzled chief factor, affixing their signatures to a parchment upon which this primitive wedding ritual had already been inscribed. Simple, impressive, and sincere, this form of marriage was as sacred to those who entered into it as if a clergyman had officiated, and it is unfair to the early traders to look upon their marriages as mere subterfuges because they were not blessed by the Church. Had the Archbishop of Canterbury himself tied the knot, the young doctor would not have considered himself more securely bound.

Notwithstanding the fact that Margaret was nine years John's senior, she proved, from the very first, a devoted and understanding companion. Undoubtedly she accompanied her husband on some of his journeys throughout the Lake Superior country, but most of her time, in the years immediately following her marriage, she spent at Fort William. She had, it appears, ample reason to do so for, by 1821, four children had been born: John, Eliza, Eloisa, and David. John, as we have already noted, was born in 1812. Eliza's birth year is not known, but Eloisa arrived in 1818 and David in 1821. Such a sizable brood, augmented as it was by Margaret's own four from her previous union, must have kept the youthful fur trader busy planning and providing.

We have already suggested that Doctor John, at the time of his marriage, was no stranger to romance. Indeed his experience with women, however limited it may have been, had netted him a half-breed son named Joseph.[20] Whether or not the child was illegitimate is a moot question and one which most writers on the early West have, for reasons of their own, evaded. Proof lacking, one must be content to speculate upon probabilities. Surely the doctor's character, as revealed by his own high sense of morality, would suggest a previous marriage.[21] It should be remembered, too, that the marriage relation, in the main, was held in high respect by the factors, traders, and clerks of the North West Company, and the reasons for this attitude were practical as well as ethical. Certificates of marriage were invariably sent, with the annual report of each post, to the company's heads in the East. In this manner, those high in command were able to maintain a rigid moral tone among their subordinates in the field, and they made it a practice to promote only those whose conduct in marital affairs was above reproach.[22]

It is true that there were occasional instances, among the North Westers, of temporary liaisons, but the doctor, throughout his life, was to frown upon them. Years later, at Fort Vancouver, he was not only to set an example of marital fidelity but to compel every man who had taken an Indian wife to treat her exactly as if the Church and State had sanctified the wedding.[23] Even if one is inclined to discount the future chief factor's lofty sense of moral values, it seems certain that his standing in the company would have suffered had he entered into an illicit union, particularly when a half-breed son remained as damning evidence. The boy Joseph, it would seem, was legitimate in the same sense as were his half-brothers and half-sisters.

5

The middle part of 1816—an eventful year throughout Rupert's Land—found Doctor John at Fort William, happy to spend a few weeks with Margaret and the two babies between fur-trading expeditions. He was then thirty-one—a tall, commanding figure with a strong face, handsome after a fashion, and with thick dark hair, already graying, that hung to his shoulders. In the service of the company he had risen rapidly, having attained the rank of chief trader and having become solidly intrenched in the good graces of the all-powerful McGillivray. He was also on excellent terms with Kenneth McKenzie, then in charge of the fort. Whether by coincidence or design, the new chief trader was present at Fort William in time to participate in momentous happenings.

This period constitutes an important chapter in Doctor John's career, and in order to understand it fully we must go back a few years to the origin of the Hudson's Bay Company's Red River Colony. In 1811, while the doctor was becoming acquainted with

Margaret down at Sault Sainte Marie, the Earl of Selkirk received a grant of land from the Hudson's Bay Company for the purpose of establishing a colony in the Red River country. It was a vast domain extending from Lake Winnipeg southward into American territory. Lord Selkirk's ambition had been to induce a large number of Scotchmen to settle there permanently though, in his invitation to prospective colonists, he had included Irishmen, Scandinavians, French Canadians, and half-breeds.

It was but natural for the ambitious North West Company to dispute Lord Selkirk's claim since it not only infringed upon their main route of travel from the St. Lawrence to the Northwest but actually included one of their principal pemmican depots. Doctor John, among others, had raised his voice in vigorous protest. Well did those North Westers know that if colonization were permitted, the buffalo would soon disappear, and they would, in consequence, be forced to move their pemmican depot to a less favorable place or haul their supplies at great expense from distant points. They proposed to do neither, with the result that, soon after the founding of the colony, a civil war broke out between the rival factions of the fur trade which was soon to develop into a bitter, bloody struggle.[24]

Lord Selkirk, however, was not easily discouraged. In the face of well organized opposition, he persevered until his colony had become reasonably well established. The fires of hate and jealousy smoldered with occasional flare-ups until 1816, when hostilities began in earnest. The climax came when both forces found themselves in the woods near the Red River Colony. William McGillivray had hurried to the spot with several of his most trusted men, including Doctor John and his uncle, Alexander Fraser. Fighting broke out near their camp before they were prepared for it, and in the engagement that followed —the so-called battle of Seven Oaks—Governor Robert Semple of the Red River Colony and twenty of his men were killed.[25]

This battle was nothing more than a deliberate and brutal massacre perpetrated by half-breeds who, though allied with the North Westers, had acted entirely on their own initiative and without the approval of McGillivray. Although the doctor and his associates were to be held responsible, they had taken no part in the bloody business of Seven Oaks and were not to learn of it, in fact, until several hours later.

Realizing that trouble was in store for them, McGillivray and his men rushed back to Fort William to defend the post. McGillivray himself was in favor of placing all blame on the Indians, but Doctor John, always sympathetic to the race from which his wife had sprung, retorted that "there was not an Indian took part in the massacre." He knew well enough that French Canadian half-breeds had committed the crime, and he was not disposed to let innocent red men suffer. Far better, he reasoned, for the North Westers to assume full responsibility. The doctor's view prevailed.

Smarting under the sting of defeat, Lord Selkirk repaired at once to Fort William with a well-armed force. The defenses proved entirely inadequate, and, on August 13, Selkirk seized the post, capturing the Honourable William McGillivray in the bargain. Without a moment's hesitation, John and his superior, Kenneth McKenzie, offered themselves to the invader as bail for their chief. The wily Hudson's Bay leader refused bail and, instead, arrested both young men who had so unselfishly, though perhaps too hastily, surrendered themselves.[26]

Lord Selkirk was a man of action. On the spur of the moment, he charged Doctor John, McKenzie, and a number of others with complicity in the murder of Governor Semple. It was, of course, a ridiculous charge, in the light of what had already transpired, but all was fair in the fur trade. Fate, however, decreed that Doctor John was not to be haled into court so easily. While crossing Lake Superior, the canoe in which he was traveling capsized, with the result that most of its occupants, including McKenzie, were drowned. More dead than alive, the accused chief trader was fished out of the water and, with great difficulty, revived. Almost invariably, when a youngish man with graying hair undergoes a severe shock, there is born a legend to the effect that it has turned white overnight. Tradition makes this claim [27] for John, but, since such cases are contrary to medical experience, the sudden transformation of his long locks from black to white must be put down as fiction.

Following this narrow escape from drowning, the doctor, unable to proceed, was permitted to land and rest for a time at Haldimand "in the house of one Grover, a tavern keeper, where he was treated with great kindness." [28] Since he was reported back at Fort William on August 16, 1817, he must have been allowed a rather considerable amount of liberty for one awaiting trial on charges of murder.[29] Earlier in that same year, the fort had reverted to the North Westers in accordance with the terms of a Royal Proclamation, and Doctor John had been appointed its chief to succeed his late companion, Kenneth McKenzie.[30] Restored to health, granted new authority, and happy with his small family, he had no intention of getting back into the Hudson's Bay clutches until the atmosphere had cleared.

Nevertheless, in spite of the fact that it would have been a comparatively simple matter to evade trial, the ambitious chief trader, now in supreme command at Fort William, was so determined to clear himself that he journeyed voluntarily to York Factory, where his case was heard on October 30, 1818.[31] It was sheer bravado but entirely consistent with his character. Just how long the trial lasted is not known, but the jury, after a short deliberation, brought in a verdict of "Not guilty." This speedy acquittal may have been facilitated by a temporary truce which had been patched up between the companies, but, even with this fortunate turn of events in his favor, John displayed real courage and not a little foolhardiness in throwing himself needlessly upon the mercy of his rivals. To vindicate himself was worth any risk.

Doctor John was coming on. The thoughtful boy of Rivière du Loup had indeed become an influential North Wester. Not yet thirty-five, he had escaped Davy Jones's locker as well as the hangman's rope. Even if they did so unwittingly, the Hudson's Bay men, considering their own future interests, displayed good judgment in sparing his life.

CHAPTER III

To London

I

FOLLOWING his exoneration, Doctor John returned to Fort William to spend the holidays of 1818 with Margaret and the children. He had seen little enough of them during the preceding months of that year—so little, in fact, that the baby, Eloisa, who had arrived in February, cried when this great giant of a man took her tenderly in his arms. With her fair skin and dancing blue eyes she was a strange contrast to the swarthy tribe of McLoughlins, but, from the first, she was the doctor's favorite.

Joseph had grown tall and silent, and it pleased the returned chief trader that Margaret had accepted the lad as her own. Eliza had become a beautiful child, the image of her mother, and John, now six, was beginning to develop a strong will. There was no happier family at Fort William, and the doctor, weary from his travels, hoped he might linger indefinitely in its midst. But this, he knew, was not to be.

By that time he had taken his place as one of the leaders of the North West cause; and he knew that, as the chief of Fort William, he would have to assume a large measure of responsibility for the company's future fortunes, good or bad. The temporary truce between the rivals had already been canceled in spite of the fact that the litigation leading up to it had cost each adversary in excess of fifty thousand pounds.[1] Early in 1819, Doctor John realized that there could be no lasting peace in

35

Rupert's Land until one or the other dominated the field. A North Wester first and always, he resigned himself to the impending struggle though he shuddered when he contemplated the price of victory.

Back in 1817, even before the impotent armistice, Sir John Sherbrooke, Governor General of Canada, had issued a Royal Proclamation commanding peace. He might as well have saved his ink and paper. Aside from complying with a few of the most obviously innocuous demands of this order, neither faction had taken it seriously. William Williams, who had succeeded the unfortunate Semple as governor of the Hudson's Bay Red River Colony, had denounced it as "damned nonsense" and had declared emphatically that he "would drive every Nor' Wester out of the country or perish in the attempt." The North Westers, on their part, had hailed the manifesto with equal disdain.[2] Then, as a breathing spell, had come the truce; but its life was short. Doctor John, more foresighted than most of his associates, deplored the resumption of hostilities. Though he was to remain a lover of peace throughout his life, his chance to act as peacemaker had not yet arrived.

In his travels through Rupert's Land, the doctor had ample opportunity to observe at first hand the ruinous results of this unbridled competition. He saw the fur prices paid to the Indians rise to levels which rendered profits out of the question. He saw the red men, whom he admired deeply, demoralized by rum which they were often forced to accept in payment for their furs. Resolutely he set himself against this practice, and, wherever he was in charge, it was prevented or at least discouraged. Unfortunately, he was but one of many leaders, and the others —certainly most of them—entertained no such scruples. He saw game recklessly wasted. Well did he know that furs reached prime condition only in winter, and that the results of hunting and trapping pelts out of season were disastrous; yet, all around him, he witnessed these abuses. In spite of anything he could do, he saw the hitherto rigid discipline of the men under him grow lax. Waste, extravagance, and corruption abounded everywhere.[3]

Against these overwhelming forces of destruction, Doctor John fought with all his great strength, but, save in his immediate vicinity, he was utterly unable to stem the tide. Although he looked upon the future with grave foreboding and found himself entirely out of sympathy with the methods practiced by his company, no man could accuse him of disloyalty. He fought fairly, but he was still a North Wester. If there were fleeting moments when he regretted having given up medicine, no one —not even Margaret—knew about them.

2

By the early summer of 1819, the struggle for supremacy had resolved itself into a mad scramble for the possession of Athabasca, a rich fur-producing area lying far to the northwest of Lake Superior. For many years the North Westers had held sway over this territory. It had, in fact, yielded some of their finest furs, and they were not inclined to let it go without a fight to the finish. But the Hudson's Bay men, mindful of the prize that lay beyond their grasp, were equally determined to wrest it from their rivals; and, with rare wisdom, they selected Colin Robertson, a fighting Scotchman of unusual ability, to lead their forces.[4] Blood was spilled freely on each side. For a little while, the result hung in the balance, and then, quite suddenly, the North Westers began to give way. Robertson, employing French woods runners in place of Scotchmen and Orkneymen, pressed them so hard that, by midsummer, they were ready to sue for peace. It was indeed high time, for the relentless struggle between the fur companies had at last attracted the attention of the British Parliament in far-away London. In June, 1819, that august body began its consideration of the civil warfare in Canada.[5]

Things had come to such a pass that both companies were rapidly heading for ruin. Reluctantly, the more moderate leaders on each side—and Doctor John was one of them—came to realize that only through union could the fur trade be saved. Nevertheless, there remained two prominent individuals, one in each camp, who opposed any thought of alliance so bitterly that there could be scant hope for a peaceful settlement so long as they occupied influential positions. One was Alexander Mackenzie, the grizzled, stubborn old North Wester, and the other was Lord Selkirk, whose experiences in the Red River Colony had doubtless embittered him for all time against his enemies.[6] Doctor John and his more liberal-minded colleagues knew how difficult it would be to circumvent these two determined old lions. Even with Parliament aroused, affairs had apparently reached a stalemate.

Among the many recruits who joined the North West Company during this troubled time was a lad fresh from Scotland named James Douglas. Chief Trader McLoughlin was on hand to greet the sixteen-year-old boy when he reached Fort William on August 6, 1819.[7] Remembering his own early days in the service and especially the friendly help McGillivray and others had given him, the doctor took young Douglas under his wing and set about to educate him in the fur trade. Doubtless the boy's arrival at that particular moment provided Fort William's chief with a pleasant diversion from the vexing matters that had been weighing him down through that harrowing summer. At all events, the youthful Scot responded in a most promising manner and soon began to develop a real capacity for the business. Well born and thoroughly schooled, James Douglas was exactly the type to appeal strongly to a man of the doctor's tastes. Shortly, the chief trader of thirty-five and the apprenticed clerk of sixteen became fast friends. Long years after, Doctor John was to demonstrate his confidence in this protégé by placing him in a position of great responsibility; and no name was to be linked more closely with his own than that of James Douglas.

Toward fall, the North West leaders gathered at Fort William to discuss the remote possibility of uniting with the Hudson's Bay Company. To some, such a course seemed suicidal; to others, the only way out. It was a very stormy conclave. Though diverse opinions were freely expressed during the after-dinner conversations at the council-house, it soon became apparent that a majority favored union as the only alternative to complete annihilation. Doctor John sided with the majority, not because he professed any love for the Hudson's Bay Company but solely because he hoped to see the fur trade restored to its once prosperous state. Most of all, he insisted upon a union that, in its terms, would be fair to his associates, the wintering partners. Pounding the table, threatening, pleading, and reasoning, he gradually won additional converts for the cause; but the victory was an empty one. Before him, as before the others, there loomed the dual vision of the obstructionists, Mackenzie and Selkirk. The outlook seemed hopeless.

Soon, however, outside forces began to rally to the support of the doctor and those who sided with him. Public opinion throughout Canada against the useless and ruinous warfare had at last risen to strengthen the hands of an already aroused Parliament. Then, too, the loss of Athabasca had removed one of the principal reasons for further strife.

Things drifted apace until 1820, when, happily, two events occurred which smoothed the way toward union.[8] Early in that year, as if Providence had intervened on behalf of the unionists, Alexander Mackenzie and Lord Selkirk died within a few weeks of each other. With this last obstacle removed, the time for action had arrived, and no one realized it more keenly than Doctor

John. Immediately he began to lay his plans. They were well formulated by the time the North Westers assembled for their annual meeting at Fort William late in July.[9]

Word had reached the doctor that the Hudson's Bay fighter, Colin Robertson, having learned that the North Westers were about to propose a merger with his company as a result of their failure in Athabasca, had decided to go to London. His purpose appeared obvious. Flushed with victory—no doubt justifiably— he hoped to convince the Hudson's Bay Company's General Court that union was now unnecessary since he had vanquished the North Westers on all fronts. On all fronts! So that was the game! Doctor John's fighting blood was up! Athabasca was not the whole of Rupert's Land, and the warrior's boasts had taken in too much territory. It required no stretch of the doctor's imagination to picture the terms his partners would be likely to receive if Robertson's views were to prevail.

Grimly determined to block his adversary, Doctor John, after extended conferences with his superiors in Montreal, obtained permission to carry the fight of the wintering partners to London in person. Angus Bethune, an old-timer in the service, was selected to accompany him. Eager as he was to serve his friends and, incidentally, himself, the doctor could not have undertaken the voyage with any great enthusiasm. Not only did affairs at Fort William require his attention, but he had become a stranger to his own family. Nevertheless his sense of duty prevailed, and, after a hurried farewell to Margaret and the children, he departed with Bethune for New York, there to catch the next ship London-bound.

3

It would be interesting to know what impression the Yankees made on the young chief trader from Lake Superior. It was his first visit to their country, and little did he dream, as he roamed the streets of New York in that fall of 1820, what misery these southern neighbors were one day to cause him. At the moment, however, the two North Westers could think of nothing but the all-absorbing problem of effecting a satisfactory settlement abroad, and within a very few days they set sail.

No sooner had they boarded the vessel than, by one of those odd twists of fate, they were greeted, with mixed curiosity and condescension, by none other than Colin Robertson himself! One wonders which of the three was the most surprised. After a moment or two of awkward embarrassment, Doctor John broke the ice with characteristic abruptness by requesting the Athabasca warrior to introduce Bethune and himself to the Hudson's Bay Company's officials upon their arrival in London. It was a bold thrust and almost more than the none too quick-witted Robertson could stomach, though he probably missed the sly wink that was exchanged between his enemies. But Doctor John intended this sally as more than a jest. Whether Robertson realized it or not, he was offering a challenge.

Throughout the long voyage these three managed to preserve the outward amenities in spite of the fact that they exchanged their irreconcilable views freely and frankly. Outnumbered two to one, it is likely that Robertson experienced some difficulty in restraining himself, especially when the doctor reminded him, as he did with tantalizing regularity, how little of Rupert's Land had actually been subdued. At all events, the Hudson's Bay fighter was no match for Doctor John. Forgetting discretion in his wrath, Robertson let slip certain bits of information which the doctor would not otherwise have acquired until the time of the hearings in London. As for the chief trader from Fort William, his trump cards remained carefully guarded, and whenever the impetuous Bethune, foaming with rage, seemed to be on the point of dropping some hint which Robertson could use, Doctor John would suavely switch the conversation into less dangerous channels. Unwittingly, the Athabasca fire-eater made it possible for the two North Westers to plan a most effective campaign.

In one of his letters to the Hudson's Bay Company, written some time later, Robertson related an amusing incident that took place on the voyage.

"Wine went around freely," he wrote, "and subscriptions were opened for the ship's hands. Our friend, the Nor'wester, Dr. McLoughlin, had put down his name. I took the pen to put mine down, but seeing Bethune, the other Nor'wester, waiting, said to Abbé Carrière:

" 'Come, Abbé, put down your name. I don't want to sign between two Nor'westers.'

" 'Never mind, Robertson,' says the Abbé, 'Christ was crucified between two thieves.'

"Mr. McLoughlin flew into a dreadful passion but, being a good Catholic, had to stomach it." [10]

This anecdote, if correctly reported, would indicate that Robertson was not as lacking in wit as we have pictured him, but it reveals, also, how completely he had misread the victim of his quip. It is true, of course, that he had a violent temper which, on occasion, could make the rafters tremble; but, with his jovial Celtic nature, one doubts that he could have become seriously annoyed over a situation so obviously humorous. Indeed it would seem that the cocksure Robertson himself was the real butt of this bit of pleasantry in view of the rebuff his own bold design was to meet in London.

On this memorable voyage, the doctor found in Angus Bethune a most congenial traveling companion. Long a North Wester, Bethune had once been stationed at Fort George on the Columbia River,[11] whither Doctor John himself was eventually to go. Little did he dream, as he listened to his friend's spirited account of conditions in the Far West, that when his turn came to make the long dash overland, he would go not as a North Wester but as a Hudson's Bay chief factor. Plowing her way wearily across the Atlantic and bucking heavy weather a good part of the time, the ship was bringing the ambitious fur trader nearer to the scene of his first great triumph.

4

Doctor John's first glimpse of the Old World brought back vivid memories of Grandfather Fraser, who, on many a winter evening in the long ago, had fired the imagination of his favorite grandson with tales of the country across the ocean. How clearly it all came back! He must see it for himself now—later, there would be no opportunity. The merger could wait a little. Immediately after disembarking at Liverpool, he allowed himself a brief holiday before reporting to the General Council in London. Traveling through England and Scotland, he picked out, with boyish enthusiasm, the landmarks which for so long had been realities in his mind. In spirit, the old seigneur guided his steps.

All too soon it was over, and the doctor, refreshed and eager, found himself in London ready to fight the battle of his fellow North Westers. He lost no time in meeting the exalted tycoons of the Hudson's Bay Company—Joseph Berens, the governor; John Pelly, the deputy governor; Nicolas Garry, Benjamin Harrison, Andrew Colville, and other prominent personages. Somehow we like to imagine that Colin Robertson, still in high glee over the incident which had occurred aboard ship and still secure in his lofty illusions, may have been the one who, with proper condescension, presented the tall Canadian to these dignitaries. Such a scene seems so perfect a prologue to the ensuing drama that we cannot resist its possibility, however remote. Whatever may have been the manner of his presentation,

Doctor John made an instantaneous and favorable impression. No doubt the Hudson's Bay chiefs recognized, in this white-headed giant from America, a man providentially sent over to assist them in the difficult task of solidifying the opposing factions. It was not long before the doctor was sitting in the councils, giving, rather than seeking, advice.

Through the closing months of 1820 and well into the early part of 1821, the General Council labored. Engrossed as he was in all the proceedings, Doctor John found time to cross the Channel to visit David, who had become one of the leading physicians of the Continent. As the two brothers reminisced in Paris— the brilliant practitioner and the modest fur trader—doubts again assailed John's mind. Had he, after all, chosen wisely in relinquishing the life David was leading? Certainly no one seeing them together would have selected John as the one to go down in history as the greater personage. David was to go further, much further, in medicine; but John—the silent fur trader—was to build an empire!

The Paris interlude concluded, Doctor John was again a familiar figure in the London councils. Through the weary months these determined men carried forward their contest. There was frequent disagreement on both sides, and, on a number of occasions, it appeared likely that the deliberations would come to naught. Uppermost in the minds of all, however, was the disquieting thought that if some sort of merger were not effected voluntarily, the British government, through Parliament, would intervene.[12] From the point of view of shrewd business men, this would be leaving entirely too much to chance. Such a threat, hovering over the meetings, served as a timely prod to remind both the Hudson's Bay leaders and their determined Canadian adversaries that it would be better to yield a little than to lose much. It was, in fact, one of the principal arrows in Doctor John's quiver, and, time and again, he shot it straight to the mark. At length, on the 20th of March, 1821, the long and bitter struggle came to an end.

A hush fell over the room in which the General Council was assembled as the governor, Joseph Berens, rose with the final draft of the union in his hand. Doctor John, seated well to the front, his gray eyes fixed steadfastly upon the fateful document, nudged Bethune at his side and waited expectantly. Nervously adjusting his spectacles, Governor Berens, after a final look into the faces before him, some friendly and some hostile, began slowly. Himself thoroughly familiar with all the points of the merger, having wrestled with them for days, Doctor John knew that many of the men in the great room were not. As he glanced about him, he speculated. The votes of these men would settle the issue once and for all, and well he knew that his whole future hung in the balance. There were occasional bursts of applause and not a few audible objections as the reading progressed, but, in a little while, it was over. A vote was taken, and the union was a fact. Henceforth there would be peace in Rupert's Land!

On the whole, the doctor was well enough pleased with the terms agreed upon though, in later years, he was to find fault with them. With the passage of time, the objectionable features of the merger, from the point of view of the field partners, were to loom larger, but at the moment, and with so many conflicting interests at stake, it was surprising that the various factions were able to reach a settlement at all. In the circumstances, the resulting union reflected credit upon the good faith of the British and Canadian leaders who, on that spring day of 1821, proved themselves big enough to cast aside personal differences for the common good. Greater men than these had labored less fruitfully.

Because of its greater age and prestige, the Hudson's Bay Company retained its own name in the merger; but the North

Westers wrested some noteworthy concessions. Indeed it was the Canadians who suggested the plan of union finally adopted. It was they who named the first governor of the united companies. It was they who insisted that the new enterprise be given judicial jurisdiction over the territory involved—a concession Parliament had been refusing the original Hudson's Bay Company for a hundred and twenty years! The doctor and his wintering partners had not been asleep.[13]

One of the basic elements of the merger was the so-called Deed Poll. Doctor John, among others, had waged a dogged fight to achieve it though he had hoped, all along, for better terms than those finally allowed. According to the provisions of this important covenant, the most distinctive feature of the old North West Company's field structure was retained—partnership status for the field officers. Such profits as the new company might earn were to be divided in the proportion of sixty per cent to the proprietors and forty per cent to the wintering partners. The forty per cent was to be divided into eighty-five equal shares, two of which were to go to each chief factor and one to each chief trader. Seven of the eighty-five shares were to be held by the company as a retiring fund.[14] Only in this one particular—the division of the profits—were the doctor and Bethune disappointed. They had frankly hoped for a larger share.[15] Bethune, especially, may have experienced a bitter pang of regret over the disappearance of the North West name after so many years of association with it. As against these minor failures to attain their highest aspirations, the Canadians could point to some brilliant triumphs; and, everything considered, they had good reason to be proud of the work they had done in London. As for the doctor, his future standing in the company was assured.

Although the assembled dignitaries had accomplished much, their task still remained unfinished. Well did the wiser heads among them realize that it is one thing to strike off a document pleasing to the eye and quite another to render the terms of such a document workable. The crying need of the moment, of course, was a man who, as governor of the Hudson's Bay Company in Rupert's Land, could bind up old wounds quickly and securely. All agreed that the prospective governor should be a young man of recognized ability, of limitless tact, and as free as possible from deeply ingrained prejudices against either faction. The older Hudson's Bay leaders were insistent that he should be a Britisher in preference to a Canadian, but Doctor John and his colleagues, willing enough to yield this point, were nevertheless determined, remembering the preponderance of Scotchmen within their ranks, that he should be of Scottish origin.

To find an individual possessed of all these qualifications seemed, at first blush, a quest impossible of attainment. Certain it was that William Williams, the incumbent Hudson's Bay governor, could not measure up. Not a few expressed regret that Doctor John, ideally suited for the place otherwise, had been too closely associated with the North Westers. How nearly he escaped the appointment, no one can say; but one fact remains certain—had he been selected, the subsequent history of Oregon would have run a vastly different and probably a less tranquil course. Scores of men were considered, only to be found wanting in some important requirement. It remained for Edward Ellice, a North Wester, to nominate George Simpson, a Hudson's Bay man, for the post and for Doctor John to join heartily in the chorus of seconds that followed his nomination. The General Council, weary of their labors, experienced little difficulty in agreeing upon him.[16]

And who was this man of destiny whose sudden selection had broken a deadlock of many days? While his future was being decided in London, George Simpson was rapidly becoming acquainted with the ways of Indians and fur traders in distant

Athabasca. A hard-working Scot with a good background and with unusual educational advantages, he had attracted the favorable attention of the London Committee and had, in the spring of 1820, been sent out to learn the practical end of the business. Following a brilliant record of service in the field, he had, in November of the same year, been appointed governor "locum tenens" in place of the incompetent Williams, then under indictment in the Courts of Lower Canada for his alleged actions during the inter-company warfare. Throughout the winter of 1820-21, while the General Council was struggling with the merger question in London, George Simpson, ignorant of his proximity to high responsibility, remained quietly at his post in Athabasca. Through Ellice's nomination in the spring, however, this twenty-nine-year-old Hudson's Bay trader was promoted to the governorship, jointly with Williams, of the united company's territories in North America, with special charge of the department of Rupert's Land including the far western department of the Columbia. Indeed he had become, for all practical purposes, the actual field chief for the entire enterprise. Strangely enough, a former adversary had unwittingly opened George Simpson's way to a notable career! Only a few years were to elapse before he was to become Governor-in-Chief of all the territories of the Hudson's Bay Company in America.[17]

We have no means of knowing whether or not Doctor John had met Simpson prior to this time. They had been the bitterest of opponents—these two—and Rupert's Land was a vast domain; still, it is likely that their widely divergent paths had crossed on more than one occasion. By reputation, at least, they must have been well known to each other. At all events, the doctor acquiesced readily in the appointment of the man who was to be so closely, and eventually so unhappily, associated with him. He knew the vexing problems at home as did few others gathered around the council table, and he was quick to recognize, with Ellice, that George Simpson possessed just the right combination of sound judgment and external affability to smooth over old difficulties and reconcile men to a new order. Long since, Doctor John had mastered the art of diplomacy. If he was to be a Hudson's Bay partner, his enthusiastic support of the man who would be his superior would do him no harm. His ardor, no doubt, was fired by expediency.

5

A scant few months after the terms of union had been agreed upon by the two factions, the British Parliament, well pleased with the turn events had taken, expressed its approval by granting to the united Hudson's Bay Company a license of exclusive trade, sweeping in scope. This license was incorporated in an Act of Parliament passed in July, 1821, and it granted exclusive trading rights for a period of twenty-one years not only in that part of British North America lying between Rupert's Land and the Rocky Mountains but also in the remote Oregon country.[18] With the avowed purpose of strengthening the union still further, Parliament made the grant specifically to the "adventurers trading in Hudson's Bay" and to Edward Ellice, William McGillivray, and Simon McGillivray, the three leading proprietors of the old North West Company.[19] This public recognition of the foremost parties to the union was unquestionably a wise move on the part of a government gratefully relieved of a vexatious problem. Both factions were placated. By one bold strike, Parliament not only had approved the amalgamation officially but had conferred upon it a bounteous grant— a gift almost without parallel in history.

Vitally concerned as he was with all these developments, Doctor John did not remain in London to see them consummated. His labors ended, he turned his thoughts toward home. On the very day that the terms of union had been settled— the 20th of March—he and Bethune began to investigate sailing dates. They learned that the ship *Amity* was scheduled to leave

Liverpool for New York on the 6th of April. With little more
than a fortnight left on English soil, the doctor completed his
study of the Hudson's Bay Company's personnel and organization, taking advantage of every opportunity to ingratiate himself with the company's officials at their Fenchurch Street headquarters. Berens, Pelly, Colville, Garry, and others plied him
with questions about Rupert's Land and sought his advice concerning a number of appointments still pending. When the day
arrived for Doctor John to board the Liverpool stage with Bethune, he had become an influential personage in the minds of
these men and had earned, as a direct result of his efforts in
London, the title of chief factor. This tall Canadian would bear
watching, they agreed; and, in future years, they were to demonstrate their confidence by granting him concessions allowed no
other man of his rank in the service.

On the dock at Liverpool, the new chief factor was surprised
to find Nicholas Garry waiting to embark with him on the
Amity.[20] Garry, who was soon to be named deputy governor
of the Hudson's Bay Company, was being sent to Fort Williams to assist George Simpson in the task of reorganizing the
company's affairs in North America. It is apparent, from
Garry's references to the doctor in his journal of the voyage,
that the two got on splendidly. Doctor John recalled that in the
somber London offices of the company Garry had been a good
listener, but now, on shipboard, he was quite willing to talk.
From him the doctor gathered valuable information regarding
the company's plans and aspirations—useful bits that not even
the leaders had divulged.

6

It was evening, the first night out. Pacing the deck of the
Amity as she plowed westward through the choppy Irish Sea,
Doctor John took stock of himself. Soon his years would num-

ber thirty-eight, and most of them had been given, loyally and unselfishly, to the North West Company. They had been years of uphill fighting, he had grown gray in the service. Whatever success he had attained had not come easily. Now the company—his company—was but a memory, and he would have to take his chances with the older concern that had absorbed it.

The night grew blacker, and the sea rougher. The doctor walked on, alone with his thoughts. True, there had been brave talk in London about the brilliant future of the merged companies and about the shining opportunities awaiting former North Westers. He had not been misled by his contact with the mighty—he knew he would have to start over again, building from the ground up. At heart, Doctor John was still a North Wester, and, in a moment of doubt, he wondered if he could ever be anything else. At length, as he continued his silent stroll, Margaret and the children came to mind. His thoughts drifted across the Atlantic to the little cabin at Fort William and to the future he had planned for himself and his family. No, there would be no turning back.

The ship's clock sounded eight bells. It was blowing a gale. Suddenly one of the *Amity's* officers appeared, ordering the lonely walker inside. Yes, he would go in now—his mind was at rest. He'd go right on fighting. He would become a good Hudson's Bay man just as he had been a good North Wester!

CHAPTER IV

Opportunity

I

The early summer of 1821 found Doctor John back at his old post, travel-weary and still somewhat skeptical of the future. These periodic separations from his family had become more annoying as they had grown more frequent. Indeed they had caused him to yearn, with mounting eagerness, for the time when he could enjoy his own fireside for more than a few fleeting weeks without interruption. At thirty-eight, he told himself, one had the right to hope for that much even in the fur trade. But, for the moment, the doctor's hope could not be realized. Although he had gained immeasurably in prestige as a result of his activities in London, his new rank of chief factor had not yet been confirmed. Until it was an accomplished fact, his activities would of necessity be confined to the field—scarcely a rosy outlook for one who had done much to cement the union. Even so, his goal seemed somehow nearer.

In the little cabin at Fort William, Doctor John found an anxious but delighted family awaiting him. He crossed the threshold, kissed Margaret, greeted the older children, and then gathered Eloisa into his big arms. It seemed only yesterday that he had left them, and yet, in the very next moment when he became fully aware of the vivacious young lady of three nestling close to his heart and smiling up with unmistakable Irish mirth, he realized, with a sudden pang, that he had been gone a long time—nearly a year. But the biggest surprise of all was saved until the last, when Margaret led him into a small adjoining room where the newest baby, who had been born in February, lay peacefully in his crib.[1] Advancing cautiously on tiptoe and shading an oil lamp with his hand, the doctor peered down with pride and curiosity into the tiny face of David—the boy in whom his greatest hopes were later to be placed. It was a joyous homecoming. John, Jr., Eliza, and even the tall, silent Joseph crowded around for news of the land across the sea, and the doctor, always a good story-teller, spent long evenings before the open fire, surrounded by open mouths and pairs of eager, bulging eyes. From her vantage point in a far corner of the room, Margaret would inspect the scene with motherly pride, sewing while she listened.

Well as he understood and appreciated his wife's sterling qualities as a mother and home-maker, Doctor John was scarcely prepared to find that she had turned sleuth. During his long absence, she had picked up valuable bits of information concerning the company's affairs, and these she had assembled, with unsuspected ingenuity, into a succinct and unbiased account of what had actually happened. At first incredulously, and then with open admiration, he heard her story. In the main, it had to do with the wintering partners.

Even before the doctor had returned in company with the new deputy governor, Nicholas Garry, news of the merger had trickled into Fort William. Few of the wintering partners had been pleased with the terms of the union, but it was the passing of the sacred old North West name in particular that had caused widespread annoyance and no little wonder.[2] In Margaret's presence, these men had spoken their minds without restraint, little suspecting that she comprehended the issues involved, and never dreaming that she would pass along such an accurate summary of their views to the doctor. Had it not been for her grasp of the situation, he might not have learned how things stood until a much later time, for the wintering partners were naturally loath to air their grievances before their old associate, who had suddenly risen to power, and especially before his little known and less admired Hudson's Bay companion, Garry. To complain was not the way to curry favor. At all events, Doctor John, thanks to the resourcefulness of his dark-skinned helpmate, was permitted to know the real state of affairs almost as soon as he reached the fort, and was hence placed immediately in a strategic position to plan his campaign of conciliation.

Sympathetically disposed toward his old comrades in their disillusionment, yet fully aware of the advantages offered them by the Hudson's Bay Company, the doctor was uniquely qualified to assist Garry and Simpson in the none too easy task of reconciling the former North Westers to their altered status. He was, in fact, one of the few leaders who could appreciate both points of view. With infinite patience and never failing tact, he explained to the wintering partners the reasons why it had become inevitable to make certain concessions to the Hudson's Bay Company. During this trying period, Doctor John, in the difficult rôle of good-will ambassador, swung around the circle of Rupert's Land, assuaging wounded feelings, making, no doubt with his tongue in his cheek, rash promises, and winning converts to the new order on every hand. Everywhere success attended his efforts, and there is no doubt that both Simpson and Garry leaned heavily on his rare organizing talent during the initial stages of realigning the field structure of the company. Without his help, harmony might have been indefinitely deferred.

Such service could scarcely go unrecognized, and, before the end of 1821, Doctor John received confirmation of his chief factorship from Governor Simpson.[3] He was, at this time, a

man of striking appearance, looking somewhat older than his
thirty-eight years. Six feet four inches in height and solidly
built, he was indeed a person to be remembered, once seen.
His snow-white hair, parted in the middle, descended to his
shoulders like twin waterfalls, and his steel-gray eyes, deep-set
beneath a brow of classic symmetry, looked out with firmness yet
with unbounded human sympathy.[4] Even a stranger with no
knowledge of the doctor's ancestry could surmise, after the
briefest glance at his features, the Scotch and Irish blood that
flowed in his veins. The firm mouth and long upper lip be-
trayed the Scotchman, while the hearty laugh and ready wit
proclaimed the Hibernian half of him. The elemental grandeur
of his appearance was emphasized both by his stately bearing and
by the black clothes he wore on almost every occasion. With his
courtly manners and eager affability in conversation, he was
an outstanding figure among the traders at Fort William.[5] It
is little wonder that George Simpson was quick to recognize in
him a natural leader of men.

2

But the new chief factor chafed at the bit. Throughout the
closing months of 1821 and well into the early part of 1822, he
remained, largely against his own wishes, a supersalesman for
the Hudson's Bay Company and an officer without portfolio.
He longed to be back where he belonged—back in the executive
end of the fur-trading business—but so indispensable had he
become to George Simpson that that harassed leader dared not
release him from the work of reorganization he had been carrying on so effectively. Toward the end of spring in the year
1822, however, the governor felt sufficiently assured of the
merged company's impregnability to return the overworked
doctor to active field service. Accordingly, he was sent to assume
command of Fort Frances on the Lake of the Woods, a small

though by no means unimportant post a hundred miles due west of Fort William.[6]

Obviously, the appointment was merely a stop-gap designed to keep the doctor's mind at rest until an opening more nearly suited to his rank and ability might arise. Disappointed as he must have been with his new post, the ambitious chief factor, remembering his decision to become a "good Hudson's Bay man," settled down to bide his time. His loyalty to his chief as well as to the company had been unquestioned from the moment of the merger, and it is obvious that he trusted implicitly in George Simpson's oft-expressed desire to do the right thing by him. Meanwhile, he could only work hard and wait.

Two uneventful years ran their course—none too quickly, we imagine, for the restless doctor. During this time he accomplished nothing of sufficient importance to find its way into contemporary records. We can see him in our mind's eye, fretting over his lot and mourning his increasing years but performing his routine tasks in such a manner as to prepare himself for the great opportunity he fervently hoped would not be long delayed. With high hopes he attended the annual Hudson's Bay councils of 1822 and 1823 at York Factory, only to be returned to Fort Frances for further stretches of fitful suspense. Again there were moments of doubt—moments during which his mind reverted automatically to brother David's brilliant professional life in France and to the career he had himself forsaken; but his faith in George Simpson remained unshaken.

At length, in July, 1824, the doctor was summoned, along with the rest of the company's chief factors and chief traders, to the annual council which was assembled at York Factory, a large and impressive distributing center located on the left bank of the Hayes River some five miles from Hudson Bay.[7] Once more he set forth with every expectation of obtaining a major appointment. It seemed high time—he was forty, and twice he had met failure. Gathered at York Factory he found the leaders of the amalgamated Hudson's Bay Company in America—Governor George Simpson, Angus Bethune, James Leith, George and James Keith, his old rival Colin Robertson, and a number of others, many of whom had been familiars of his North West days. We can only surmise the anguish it must have caused Athabasca's proud warrior to realize that the rugged North Wester had become, like himself, a chief factor of the Honourable Hudson's Bay Company, although he probably took comfort in the knowledge that his ancient enemy had been kept languishing at Fort Frances for more than two years. Robertson's gloating, however, was not to last much longer.

Early on the morning of July 10th, Governor Simpson called the crucial session of the council to order. Soon the doctor would know his fate. With his customary patience, he listened to his chief's recital of the year's accomplishments in trade and to his various proposals for the coming twelve months. He admired George Simpon's tireless energy as well as his thorough grasp of the company's many problems. Indeed he was proud that he had supported such a man in London, however much he may have bemoaned his forced isolation at the Lake of the Woods. After what seemed to Doctor John an eternity, the docket was cleared of routine business. At last the great moment had come, and the governor, fully cognizant of its import to those present, stepped forward to read his prepared list of assignments for the ensuing year. The chief factor from Fort Frances held his breath.

"To Athabasca," began the governor, "I assign Chief Factor James Keith and Chief Traders Hugh Fairies and Robert McVicor. To McKenzies River," he continued, "Chief Factor Edward Smith and Chief Trader Alexander R. McLeod." On he read through the long schedule of appointments, and the doctor noted with revived hope that a new man had been chosen for his old post at the Lake of the Woods. One by one the company's field officers were assigned their places until, at length, there remained but one station to be accounted for. The doctor's name had not been read. Suddenly the governor paused in the midst of a deathlike silence while Doctor John leaned forward in his chair, his heart pounding. "To the Columbia," resumed Governor Simpson, in his clear, even voice, "I reappoint Chief Factor Alexander Kennedy and, to serve with him, I assign Chief Factor John McLoughlin."

The Columbia's new chief sat transfixed. Had he heard aright? Was it actually he, John McLoughlin, who had been chosen to serve in the company's vast western empire? His mind in a daze, he scarcely heard the remainder of the governor's appointments to this district—the three chief traders, John W. Dease, John McLeod, and Peter Skene Ogden.[8] Governor Simpson had finished—the list was complete. At last the doctor was to have a post worthy of his competence. In the midst of the hubbub around him, he rose to his majestic height, bowed his head, made the sign of the cross over his heart, and, oblivious to his surroundings, gave thanks to Almighty God.

3

George Simpson had already accomplished much within the three busy years of his incumbency. A prototype of the modern widely traveled captain of industry, he had visited most of the outlying districts of the vast area over which he held sway. The Columbia, to which Doctor John had been assigned, was, in fact, one of the very few departments the energetic governor had not as yet inspected. Aided by the doctor and a handful of others, he had, through his strenuous efforts, won over all but the most skeptical of the old North Westers. He had drastically reduced the company's personnel by weeding out such employees as seemed better suited to farming than to fur trading, and these he had transferred to the growing Red River Colony. Under his able management, fur prices had been standardized, waste had been reduced, and even the liquor traffic—the greatest hindrance of all to satisfactory trading relations with the Indians—had been brought under control.[9]

In spite of the significant part Doctor John had played in the successful accomplishment of this pretentious program, he was not only ready and willing to acknowledge the guiding genius of his chief but eager to serve him further in distant fields.

The governor lost no time in acquainting his new appointee with the plans he had made for the immediate future. They were characteristically Simpsonian—brief, clear, and irrevocable. Having decided to make the hazardous journey overland to the Pacific in company with Doctor John, he announced his intention of setting forth immediately upon the arrival of a ship bringing important instructions from England. The governor prided himself upon his ability to travel swiftly, and perhaps it was with a slight tinge of braggadocio that he suggested it might be well for the doctor to get a head start. At all events, the Columbia's new field officer was instructed to leave York Factory for the West as soon as he could complete the necessary preparations. It was understood, of course, that the governor would follow the moment his ship arrived, but, with the vessel long overdue, he was growing anxious. He realized how unwise it would be to attempt the overland passage too late in the season.

During the days immediately following the adjournment of the annual council, Governor Simpson discussed with Doctor John the details of the Columbia situation as he understood them. It was a part of the general plan to have the doctor relieve Chief Factor Kennedy, who expected to return East in the spring.[10] Nothing could have indicated more completely George Simpson's high regard for Doctor John's ability as a trader and organizer than this particular appointment, for, out in Oregon, there remained some knotty problems to be solved. The governor's cordial feeling toward his chief factor at that time can scarcely be reconciled with the enmity which was soon to spring up between them, and which, with the passing of years, was to assume the proportions of an open breach.

The doctor, as it happened, was not unfamiliar with the general condition of the company's interest in the Pacific Northwest. He knew that Astoria, which had been founded at the mouth of the Columbia in 1811 by the American capitalist, John Jacob Astor, had fallen into the hands of the North Westers in 1813, and that its name had been summarily changed to Fort George. The War of 1812 and the treachery of Duncan McDougal, one of the Astor partners, had combined to bring about the surrender. Doctor John knew, also, that these early North West traders had accomplished little of a constructive nature at Fort George, partly because of their inability to establish satisfactory relations with the Indians and partly because, with a few exceptions, capable men had not been sent there. He was aware of the covenant entered into, in 1818, between Great Britain and the United States, under the terms of which vessels and citizens of both nations were to be allowed free access to the Oregon country for trading purposes until 1828. He knew, too, that since the Americans, thoroughly discouraged, had made no further attempts to establish trading posts on the Columbia, Fort George remained in the actual possession of the British. Following the merger of 1821, the Hudson's Bay Company had fallen heir to the post.[11] No doubt the doctor had gleaned much of this information from Angus Bethune on the voyage these two had made to London before the union.

The imminent problem facing the company—a problem which, in the main, Doctor John would have to solve—was clearly stated to him by Governor Simpson, who, canny Scot that he was, had been laying his plans with an eye toward profits. Up to that time, the Columbia department had proved a liability, and it was the shrewd governor's purpose to unite it with New Caledonia to the northward, thus reducing administrative costs and, at the same time, bringing all the territory west of the Rocky Mountains within a single Hudson's Bay Company jurisdiction. He hoped also, by this method, to present a united front to the United States in the vast area then settled, in theory at least, under joint occupancy.

George Simpson made it clear to Doctor John that his aspirations for the Oregon Country depended, for their realization, upon a vigorous and enlightened local leadership—a leadership which would develop the fur trade to its ultimate possibilities, create friendly relations with the Indians, and establish, eventually, schools and missions.[12]

It was a gigantic undertaking that he proposed, and it was significant that, from his able staff of chief factors, he had selected Doctor John as the man best equipped to attain these ambitious objectives. If the doctor was a bit nonplussed by the magnitude of his assignment, there was no hint of it in the alacrity with which he embraced this great chance to win his spurs. With profound respect he listened to the views of his chief, but with characteristic wisdom he refused to commit himself. There would be ample time to form his own opinion later.

On July 27th, just seventeen days after receiving his coveted appointment, Doctor John started on his long journey with two light canoes and fourteen men. He was embarked, at last, upon an adventure that could measure up to his dreams! His instructions were to follow a route which ran from York Factory via the Hayes River and Norway House to Lake Winnipeg and thence up the Saskatchewan to Cumberland Lake. Passing through the Frog Portage, he was to travel by the English and Beaver rivers until he reached the waters of the Athabasca via

Portage La Biche, arriving eventually at the Columbia upon whose broad bosom he could paddle down to the Pacific and Fort George. It was just such an expedition as he had imagined in the long ago when, as a silent, sensitive lad, he had wandered the fields near Mount Murray. The great unknown beckoned. Margaret's second husband stood well to rival the exploits of her first.

The governor had had a double reason for sending along so many men under the doctor's charge. In the first place, the Snake River Expedition, which had been sent out by the company some time before, would be needing reinforcements; and, further, there were other posts along the route which would be requiring new hands to replace those scheduled to leave in the spring.[18] Supremely self-confident, Governor Simpson had issued these instructions merely as a gesture. He fully expected to overtake the doctor in ample time to execute them himself.

As for Doctor John, the start of his long trek across America had been tinged with disappointment. Once he had become aware of the speed he would have to maintain to keep up with the swift pace Governor Simpson was certain to set, he had reluctantly decided to leave his family behind. The probability is that he had not even been able to see them before his departure. What with extended conferences and elaborate preparations for the overland journey, he could scarcely have sandwiched a side trip to Fort Frances into the scant seventeen days at his disposal. Another prolonged separation from his own people had begun.

Meanwhile, at York Factory, the governor was waiting for his ship with mounting impatience. Days became weeks, but still no sail appeared on the horizon of Hudson Bay. At last, on August 17, George Simpson, fearful of further delay, set forth on his eventful trip—a trip, by the way, which was to break all existing records for speed.

It had become an obsession with this ambitious executive to wipe out Doctor John's head start and overtake him at the earliest possible moment. It was the first suggestion of rivalry between them—the first ominous warning of a bitter antagonism to follow. On Sunday, September 5th, at Ile à la Crosse, Governor Simpson, with just a trace of swagger, wrote in his journal, "the Dr. is still Eight Days ahead of me and does not expect I can overtake him before he reaches Nez Percés on the Columbia, but in this he is mistaken as we shall assuredly be up with him if no accident happens before he can reach the Athabasca River." [14]

The racing governor was as good as his word for, on the morning of September 26, he overtook the astonished doctor and his party while they were breakfasting on the bank of the Rivière la Biche. A note of contempt enters his account when he remarks that "we came up with the Dr. before his people had left their Encampment altho we had by that early hour come from his breakfasting place of the preceding day." [15] He then describes the doctor in terms far from flattering, stating that "he was such a figure as I should not like to meet in a dark night in one of the bye lanes in the neighborhood of London, dressed in clothes that had once been fashionable, but now covered with a thousand patches of different colors, his beard would do honor to the chin of a Grizzly Bear, his face and hands evidently Showing that he had not lost much time at his Toilette, loaded with Arms and his own herculean dimensions forming a tout ensemble that would convey a good idea of the highway men of former days." [16] Perhaps it is just as well that the author of this descriptive bit kept his diary under lock and key!

Nevertheless the doctor must have experienced a small degree of satisfaction when, a few days later, the governor, still boasting of his speed, was forced to delay the expedition because of his own illness. "Being extremely unwell for some time past," he wrote, "I was recommended by Dr. McLoughlin to lay by the remainder of the day in order to benefit by his professional skill which I accordingly did and experienced much benefit therefrom." We can picture Doctor John ministering solicitously to his ailing chief but perhaps getting a measure of quiet gratification out of the incident. He was intensely human.

4

At Jasper House in the heart of the Rockies, where the party arrived on the evening of October 10, the doctor met with an unexpected surprise. Waiting there was his stepson, Thomas McKay, who had come up from the Columbia several days before with letters for the governor from Chief Factor Kennedy and Chief Trader Ogden.[17] Tall and straight and bronzed by the weather, Tom McKay looked the Indian far more than did the doctor's own sons. An able guide and trapper, he had already become a veteran of the Far West, this copper-skinned young man of twenty-eight who was so eager for news of his mother. It had been a long time since Doctor John had seen his stepson, and it is to be regretted that Governor Simpson, usually so quick to record interesting details, failed to pen an account of their reunion. At all events, they enjoyed a fleeting visit together while the party remained at Jasper House throughout the 11th, making preparations to negotiate the difficult Athabasca Pass which lay ahead.

Tom had brought word that two canoes were waiting on the bank of the Columbia to convey the expedition down to Fort George. George Simpson was not a man to be caught unprepared. After counting noses, he realized that another craft would be required, and so, on the morning of October 12, he sent the doctor's stepson and a small detachment of men ahead to build one. Later in the day, the governor, Doctor John, and the rest of the expedition followed Tom McKay's trail through the mountains.[18] Weary days followed, but on the 19th, the doctor's fortieth birthday, the entire caravan reached the western end of the treacherous portage in safety.[19]

On the 27th they arrived at the junction of the Columbia and Spokane rivers, where they met Peter Skene Ogden and a party of trappers who had come up from Fort George en route to various interior posts. Tom McKay, his shipbuilding duties completed, was with them. These men brought optimistic reports of the company's progress on the lower Columbia which Governor Simpson, who had been otherwise informed, took with his customary grain of salt.[20] Scarcely hearing them, Doctor John looked down upon the great, swift river rushing past him—a river which, though he little dreamed it then, was to figure prominently in the drama of his life in the West. He felt strangely attracted by the Columbia's exhaustless strength and rugged beauty. In that moment, it had become his river.

The very next morning the governor, with Doctor John, Tom McKay, and Chief Traders McMillan and Ogden, turned southward on horseback to visit Spokane House, one of the company's important inland posts. After a brief inspection of the fort, the party returned to the Columbia, and once again the governor's intimate diary reveals a sly dig at his new chief factor. "We started to rejoin our Craft on the morning of the 30th," runs the entry, "and after a hard ride got to the Forks the same Evening, the Dr. quite knocked up being unaccustomed to such violent exercise." [21]

On the 31st they began their wild dash down the turbulent Columbia. They traveled rapidly, stopping at Okanagan, Fort Nez Percés, and other places and keeping a sharp outlook everywhere for hostile Indians. Tom McKay, who knew the country and the natives as did few others, served in the double capacity of guide and peacemaker. We can imagine with what pride Doctor John saw his energetic stepson lead the way across the portages, pass around the calumet and man his big canoe over the rapids. On they sped. At length, on November 9th, they reached the end of the trail at Fort George. Governor Simpson had made the dash from York Factory in eighty-four days, cutting the time of previous record by more than one-fourth.[22] Not only had he outdone his predecessors, but he had brought his men through without mishap.

5

Doctor John appraised Fort George with mixed feelings. Though he had labored long to obtain a worthy appointment, he could scarcely have been favorably impressed with his new surroundings. The fort, which was located about a hundred yards from the bank of the Columbia, was circumscribed by palisades and furnished with bastions. The entrance, situated on the river side, opened into a large square court. On the west side of the enclosure were located stores and warehouses, and on the east side, houses for the men and shops for the mechanics. To the rear were placed the mess hall and the apartments of the officers. About eighty acres of land had been cleared, and, on these, potatoes were cultivated. The woods behind the fort supplied pasturage to a few head of cattle. Situated on a sandy beach, a little west of the fort, was an Indian village consisting of a dozen or more huts.[23] That was Fort George, and that was all of it.

No doubt the doctor, at the very moment of his arrival, had a premonition that this tiny outpost of the far-flung Hudson's Bay Company was not to become his permanent western headquarters. There was little enough at Fort George to inspire dreams of empire in one of his boundless ambition, and, with his trained eye, he was quick to comprehend the inherent drawbacks of the location. For the time being, however, he was a

FORT GEORGE

From an etching made by Lieutenant Warre of the Warre-Vavasour Expedition in 1845.

proud chief factor with a charge of his own. Little else mattered.

Doctor John was equal to the weighty responsibilities which were so soon to be thrust upon him. Had an attendant Providence been guiding his path, his preparation, in point of early training and company experience, could not have been more wisely directed. Fate had provided the materials, his own strong will the tools—what he might hope to create remained for the future.

CHAPTER V

The Columbia's Chief Factor Scores a Point

I

The chaotic conditions prevailing throughout the Columbia department were extremely distasteful to the systematic and businesslike mind of Governor Simpson. "Everything appears to me," he wrote on the very day of his arrival at Fort George, "on too extended a scale except the trade." Then, following this ironic sally, he continued, "when I say that that [the trade] is confined to Four permanent Establishments the returns of which do not amount to 20,000 Beaver and otters altho the country has been occupied upwards of Fourteen Years I feel that a very Severe reflection is cast on those who have had the management of the Business, as on looking at the prodigious expenses that have been incurred and the means at their command, I cannot help thinking that no economy has been observed, that little exertion has been used, and that sound judgment has not been exercised but that mismanagement and extravagance has been the order of the day." [1]

George Simpson's denunciation of what he found has a surprisingly modern ring. Indeed, a chain store executive of our own time would have difficulty in finding more forceful language with which to reprimand the manager of a lagging branch. Having placed the blame where it undoubtedly belonged, the governor next proceeded to announce the Colum-

68

bia's "new deal" in a sweeping statement that suggests a typical campaign promise of the present day. "It is now however necessary," he concluded, "that a radical change should take place and we have no time to lose in bringing it about."[2]

From the very first, Governor Simpson shared Doctor John's view that Fort George was of no practical value as a western headquarters. These two, together with the other chief factor, Alexander Kennedy, discussed the situation at great length around the mess-hall table during those first few November evenings. Although Kennedy was scheduled to leave in the spring and was, as a consequence, less vitally concerned, he agreed entirely with his colleagues. Thus it came about that Fort George's doom was sealed shortly after the coming of its new management.

Though the reasons favoring an early change of location were varied, the international situation supplied perhaps the most urgent spur to action. In spite of the fact that the company's predecessor, the North West Company, had purchased Fort George from John Jacob Astor's Pacific Fur Company, the United States had, through the covenant of 1818, forced the Hudson's Bay men to relinquish exclusive rights to the post. For all that the British found themselves in possession of the fort at the moment, it was, in theory at least, the joint property of both nations. Both George Simpson and the doctor were shrewd enough to realize that, with the coming of American settlers—a perpetual threat—they might have serious trouble on their hands. Of that they had a plenty as things stood. Far better, they reasoned, to select a site less open to dispute. If, as then seemed likely, the Columbia should be decided upon as the boundary line between the two nations, it would be wise to choose a location north of the river. Again there was complete agreement.

In addition to these grave handicaps, Fort George was too far from the seat of the company's interior operations and, further, it provided but scant facilities for agriculture. Once ocean-going vessels had negotiated the bar of the Columbia, argued Doctor John, they could easily proceed upstream to some point more favorably situated both from the commercial and from the agricultural point of view.[3]

While admitting the truth of this contention, Governor Simpson astonished his chief factor by opposing the Columbia altogether. Entertaining a more comprehensive vision of the company's future operations in the West, he had already concluded that "the principal Depot should be situated North of this place [Fort George] about Two or Three Degrees at the Mouth of Fraser's or as it is sometimes called New Caledonia River as it is more central both for the coast and interior trade and as from thence we could with greater facility and at less expense extend our discoveries and Establishments to the Northward and supply all the Interior Posts now occupied." [4]

We marvel both at the governor's business acumen and at his audacity! He was well aware of the law which vested British trading rights to China exclusively with the powerful East India Company. He hoped, a bit naïvely, to prevail upon the Hudson's Bay leaders in London to wrest two important concessions from their East India rivals. First, he wanted permission to dispose, at Canton, of the furs taken by his company on the west side of the Rocky Mountains, and secondly, he wanted leave, in exchange for his privilege, to carry cargoes of Chinese produce to the west coast of South America to be sold there. He might as well have suggested that the British capital be moved to Athabasca! Indeed it required hardihood to offer such proposals in the face of the strenuous fight the East India Company had been making in Parliament to guard its exclusive monopoly.

The governor was more than courageous. Staking everything

on the remote possibility of obtaining these concessions, he favored the Fraser River site as the one best situated for carrying on trade with China. Then, too, in the absence of definite information to the contrary, he supposed it to be a point of easier access from the east than the Columbia. However wild the scheme, it had been logically planned. The only difficulty was that it involved too many *if*'s. Unmindful of these, George Simpson was content, for the time being, to toy with his daring project, which, we must admit, was worthy of the ingenious mind that had conceived it.

But the governor's bold plan left Doctor John cold. Already he had grown to love the Columbia to such a degree that he was not backward in expressing his personal desire to see the company's western headquarters located permanently at some point along its friendly banks. Although there can be little doubt that his romantic attachment for the great river influenced his judgment, it would be grossly wrong to conclude that his reasons for favoring it were founded exclusively on sentiment. He was quick to discern its strategic advantages from both the political and the commercial point of view, and, after all, he could not overlook the fact that it was a bird in hand. Then too, Doctor John knew, from personal experience, something of the obstinacy of London merchants. It is, in fact, quite likely that, even then, he appreciated the utter folly of his superior officer's dream. In age, he was George Simpson's senior by eight years—in practical field experience, the discrepancy between them was even greater.

The struggle was on in earnest. Each man was sincere in his convictions, and each was determined. It resolved itself into a clash between iron wills though Doctor John realized only too well that, in the normal course of events, the decision would rest with his chief. Little did he suspect that forces beyond the control of either would soon settle the matter in his favor.

2

The months following the expedition's arrival at Fort George were busy ones. With the governor definitely committed to the Fraser River site and with the doctor enthusiastically champion- ing the Columbia, each, in his own way, set about to prove his case.

So certain was Governor Simpson that his own pet project would ultimately triumph that he willingly and, in the circum- stances, magnanimously granted Doctor John permission to sur- vey "his" river from its mouth eastward as far as the foothills of the Cascade Range. The zealous chief factor, eager to find a suitable spot for the western depot, lost not a moment in organ- izing a scouting party. Tirelessly he raced his swift canoes up and down the river, and, not content with these investigations or perhaps merely to convince himself that the Columbia need not fear competitive locations, he made several trips northward into the interior, penetrating more than a hundred miles.

His intrepid spirit rose to the occasion, and he set a pace that would have done credit even to the racing governor. Upon the completion of this journey, which had taken him over ground never before traversed by white men, he drew a rough map of the entire region and presented it to his chief.[5] Unfortunately this chart, the result of many weeks of untold hardships, has not been preserved.

It is significant that not a line appears in Governor Simpson's scrupulously complete journal regarding his new chief factor's important explorations—particularly so, since Doctor John must have recommended, in his report, the exact location which was later to be chosen. We can only conclude that the governor's singular reticence was caused by his rigid opposition to what the doctor had proposed—an opposition based, of course, upon his own preference for the northern site.

But George Simpson, on his own account, had not been idle. Even before the doctor's departure, he had dispatched a party of forty men, under Chief Trader McMillan, to investigate the possibilities of the Fraser River and make an early report. Tom McKay, Doctor John's stepson, was among them. "Altho the Season was extremely unfavorable for such an Enterprize," wrote the governor, "I entertain sanguine hopes that he [McMillan] will accomplish the object of his mission with credit to himself." [6] Indeed this expedition had not returned when the chief factor brought in his glowing account of the Columbia, and the probability is that Governor Simpson, waiting anxiously for McMillan's report, could think only of what news that worthy officer might bring him.

Time, the great settler of controversies, eventually forced the governor to abandon his dream though several years were to elapse before the London Committee of the Hudson's Bay Company was to decide, once and for all, against bringing furs of the Columbia department to market in Canton. [7] For the moment, however, Simpson refused to give up hope—even when the McMillan party, after an extremely hazardous excursion, returned with an unfavorable report regarding the fitness of the Fraser River for a permanent station. Nevertheless, it was imperative, in the best interests of the company, that Fort George be relinquished as soon as possible, and so, with great reluctance, the governor began to listen more sympathetically to Doctor John's description of a location he had found some ninety miles up the river at Belle Vue Point.

For a little while the chief hesitated; then, with characteristic suddenness, he made his decision. It was, of necessity, a compromise—the post would be moved up the river in the spring where temporary quarters would be established pending further exploration of the northern country. Doctor John had won the first round.

3

Thirty-two years earlier, in May of 1792, Captain Robert Gray of Boston had sailed his stout little ship *Columbia* over the bar of the previously undiscovered river—the first navigator of any nation to enter its broad but frequently fog-bound mouth. He had not, however, ventured more than twenty-five miles upstream.[8] Later that same year, Lieutenant Broughton of the Vancouver expedition had not only duplicated the Yankee skipper's feat but had penetrated up the river to the distance of a hundred miles. To many of the prominent landmarks of either bank he had given names of his own selection, including Belle Vue Point near the mouth of the Willamette River, and Point Vancouver some ten miles farther east.[9]

Although the Britisher had trailed the American, he had been more thorough in his investigations. As a consequence, both nations, before the dawn of the nineteenth century, were claiming the Columbia—America, by right of discovery; Great Britain, by virtue of more extended exploration. The controversy had continued until the ratification of the treaty of joint occupancy in 1818 which, instead of settling matters, opened the way for further dispute.

When Governor Simpson finally brought himself to agree with Doctor John that Belle Vue Point offered the best available location for the new settlement, he decided, with his customary foresight, to name it Vancouver in honor of the famous British navigator who had visited the Northwest Coast some thirty-two years earlier. Though the governor was a loyal Britisher, something more than mere patriotic sentiment prompted the choosing of this name. Notwithstanding the fact that Great Britain had given up hope of holding permanently any territory south of the Columbia, she was determined, if humanly possible, to maintain her authority over all lands lying to the northward. No less a personage than George Canning, Secretary of State for Foreign Affairs, had intimated as much in a letter to the Hudson's Bay Company's field chief.[10] Thus, by selecting a strategic site on the north bank of the river and by giving it a thoroughly British name, both George Simpson and the doctor hoped to add a certain prestige to the none too secure claim of their government. It was, to say the least, a shrewd bit of diplomacy.

Vancouver offered marked advantages of location. Doctor John, in the course of his investigations, had discovered that the channel, up to this point, would accommodate ocean-going vessels comfortably. It was, in addition, the natural terminus for inland voyages, and it furnished an especially well-situated starting point for parties traveling up the Willamette valley or overland to Puget Sound. On a fertile plain that sloped gently to the river's edge, Vancouver afforded unlimited possibilities for agriculture and pasturage.[11] This was highly important, since the governor had warned his chief factor that he expected the settlement to become practically self-supporting.

James Keith, one of the doctor's predecessors at Fort George, had once been asked by the London Committee whether or not produce could be raised on the Columbia. "No," had been his emphatic reply, "if you stop supplies from beyond the mountains, you will have to ship provisions round Cape Horn. This is no agricultural country."[12] As Doctor John's trained eye appraised the unmistakable quality of the soil surrounding Vancouver, he must certainly have experienced a feeling of contempt for Keith's colossal blindness: here, beyond doubt, was the garden spot of the Northwest. In the years ahead, the chief factor's faith in it was to be rewarded abundantly.

The early months of 1825 found him busy superintending the construction of the new depot at Belle Vue Point. Securely built with rough lumber cut from the huge trees near by, stores, warehouses, workshops, magazines, and quarters for the officers began slowly to take form. Governor Simpson, who still regarded the post on the Columbia as a mere stepping-stone to his greater plan, ordered the work to proceed rapidly. No doubt he hoped, in this manner, to guarantee the temporary character of the settlement; but if such was his purpose, he misread the man he had placed in charge. Whatever the doctor built was constructed with a view toward permanency. George Simpson might ride his hobby, he allowed, but Vancouver must be a credit to the company.

4

While the work progressed, Doctor John divided his time between Vancouver and Fort George. His frequent journeys up and down the river by canoe afforded him an excellent opportunity to win the friendship of the natives along the way. He understood the Indians as had none of his predecessors, and, from the very first, they regarded him as their friend. Gazing in awe upon his striking figure, topped by the imposing mane of snow-white hair, the Chinooks early dubbed him "White-Headed Eagle." [18] For a generation this fitting title was to endure in the minds of the red men of the Oregon country as a symbol of power and justice. Endowed by nature with a kindly feeling toward all humanity, the doctor found much in the native life to correct, and, very early in his career on the Columbia, he determined to bring to the Indians an understanding of Christian principles. This he was able to accomplish—even before the advent of the missionaries—through a rare combination of force, benevolence, and lofty example.

Although slavery among the neighboring Indian tribes had begun to decline before Doctor John reached the country, it was still far from extinct. Far worse, however, was the barbarous practice of sacrificing human lives upon the death of an influential chief. It was not uncommon for one or more of these unfortunate slaves to be killed in order that they might accompany their late master on his last long journey into the unknown.[14] When, early in his career as chief factor at Vancouver, news of a few such cases were brought to his attention, the doctor's blood boiled! Through tactful though strong-willed intervention, he succeeded in ameliorating the evils of slavery. This one man, single-handed in a savage country, settled a great human issue which, some thirty-five years later, was to cost the lives of hundreds of thousands of brothers in arms down in the civilized United States of America!

One of the first Indians Doctor John grew to know well was Comcomly, the one-eyed chief of the Chinooks, whose villages were located on the Columbia opposite Fort George. He was a picturesque character, this sterling old redskin, and for many years his relations with the whites had been more than cordial. Chief Comcomly's daughter had, in fact, married Duncan McDougal, the turncoat Astor partner, who had surrendered Astoria to the North Westers. As a consequence, the old man became thoroughly disgusted with his son-in-law, but so mercurial was his own temperament that, upon completion of the post's transfer, he set sail, against McDougal's wishes, to pay a visit to the victorious British ship *Raccoon* then lying at anchor in the harbor. Black, the vessel's commander, completely disarmed Comcomly with his gracious and flattering reception. When the native leader left the ship, he returned to his Chinook village with an old flag, a laced coat, a cocked hat, a sword, and a high opinion of the erstwhile hated "King George" men. On the very next day he sailed proudly across to Fort George, dressed in full uniform and flying the Union Jack.[15] From that day forward, the one-eyed Comcomly had remained unflinchingly loyal to the British.

Between the sympathetic chief factor and the high-minded red man, there developed a friendship unique in the history of the West—an interracial alliance that was to smooth over many a situation which might otherwise have been dangerous. Each recognized in the other a natural leader of men, and, until the chief's death in 1831, this close bond was to continue with increasing warmth.

Another Indian for whom the doctor formed an early and lasting regard was Chief Casseno of the Multnomahs, a son-in-law to Comcomly. Governor Simpson described him as the most intelligent Indian he had ever met, and it is apparent that Doctor John shared this estimable opinion from the first moment he set eyes on the young warrior. Casseno's tribe lived on the south shore of the Columbia, almost dirctly opposite Vancouver and close to the present site of Portland. He, like his illustrious father-in-law, had become much attached to the British, and his frequent attempts to imitate them were as sincere as they were ridiculous. With significant emphasis, he maintained that he was "not an American but a Relative and subject of King George."[16]

Keeping a close watch on the rising settlement across from his native village, Casseno visioned an active and profitable trade looming on his very doorstep. Crossing over in his big canoe, he chatted affably with Doctor John, assuring him of undying allegiance to the Hudson's Bay Company and intimating that he would not be likely, with such excellent commercial opportunities at his very doorstep, to carry his valuable furs many miles eastward to trade with the Americans, who were then operating on a limited scale in the vicinity of the Snake River. Such promises must have been welcome to the ears of the new chief factor, upon whose shoulders would soon fall complete responsibility for making the Columbia department turn in a profit to the company. Doctor John was to count heavily upon the assistance of these two red men—Comcomly and Casseno—in bringing a wise and efficient dominion to the Oregon country.

The doctor's stepson, Tom McKay, had married a princess of

the Chinook tribe, and their eldest son, later to become Dr.
William McKay, recalled, as a little boy, the kindly feeling of
all Indians for the "White-Headed Eagle." [17] Other white men
before him had enjoyed partial success in their dealings with the
natives, but none had earned their whole-hearted respect and
admiration. It remained for him to introduce a new era of peace
and interracial understanding.

One of the first and certainly one of the most vexing problems
faced by the new chief factor was that of restricting the use of
alcohol among the Indians. He soon discovered that the Chinooks were much the worse for the indiscriminate drinking of
spirits, though, from Chief Comcomly, he learned that this had
not always been true. Prior to the founding of Astoria, the
Chinooks had been a temperate tribe. Old Comcomly, ruling
his people with an iron hand, had stood firmly against "fire
water" until the arrival of the North Westers, in 1813, had
forced such quantities of it upon the natives that he had no
longer been able to control the situation. Indeed Comcomly had
once reprimanded his son-in-law, McDougal, for giving rum
to the chief's own son, Cassius, known as the "Prince of Wales."
This prince, it seems, had, upon a certain occasion, staggered
home to the Chinook village in such a state of inebriety that
his royal father had turned militant prohibitionist on the spot.[18]

We can imagine with what joy Doctor John welcomed the
coöperation of a native imbued with such principles, for, if the
liquor traffic on the Columbia could not be controlled, the fur
trade would inevitably suffer. No doubt Comcomly, on his
part, hailed, as equally providential, the arrival of a white leader
whose views on alcohol coincided with his own. A hundred
years before prohibition was to be acknowledged a failure in
civilized America, these benevolent despots enforced it successfully in the wilds of British Oregon. No "pussyfooters" were
they—their battle was waged on broad economic grounds!

5

Doctor John, who had already escaped one drowning on the rough waters of Lake Superior, came perilously close to another on the Columbia. One day, quite early in his Fort George experience, Governor Simpson set out across the river with a party to explore Baker's Bay and Cape Disappointment on the north shore. "Chief Factors Kennedy & McLoughlin with Thos McKay clerk," wrote the governor in his all-inclusive journal, "accompanied me in an open Craft called the Gun Boat; previous to starting I made no enquiry in respect to the state of the Craft or rigging, abilities of the Crew or dangers of the voyage conceiving that all was right as a matter of course but we had not got a mile from the wharf when owing to the crazy condition of our Vessel it became necessary to Bail with Buckets &c, she was so unmanageable that we could not regain the Shore our rigging so rotten that the Sails came down by the run and so ignorant were we of the River that we touched a sand bank but fortunately drifted off otherwise we must have perished among the breakers; we exhausted our strength at the oars in order to get ashore but to no avail as we were drifting rapidly past Point Adams towards the Breakers at the Bar of the River, when the Tide providentially turned and brought us up under the Lee of Chinook Point where we landed and returned on Foot to the Fort." [19]

In spite of the governor's penchant for interminable sentences, sadly wanting in punctuation, he succeeded in recording a thrilling account of an adventure that came near costing his own life as well as three others. Tom McKay, no doubt, should have been familiar with the vagaries of the great river. Indeed, he may have been, but it was probably no simple matter for a mere clerk to dissuade a strong-willed governor.

Weeks stretched into months with Governor Simpson working manfully to bring order out of chaos at Fort George and with Doctor John spending a good part of his time at Vancouver. Gradually these two were speeding up to a new tempo the company's activities in the Far West. The doctor was learning in a rough school, but the lessons were not wasted. From the first he had shared the governor's view that Fort George had been grossly mismanaged, and that radical changes were imperative. George Simpson could not have chosen a better man to entrust with his sweeping reform program on the Columbia. At length, toward the middle of March, 1825, Doctor John came paddling down to Fort George with the gratifying news that the new post, though far from finished, was at least ready for occupancy.

No one was happier than the governor. It was high time for him to be returning East though, naturally, he had not wanted to quit Oregon until the transfer to Vancouver had been completed. As a matter of fact, he was pleased and, in a measure, relieved for quite another reason. It seems that Lady Calpo, the squaw of a powerful Chinook, had been imploring the governor to take her daughter, the princess "Chowie," for his wife. The ambitious mother's arguments had grown so insistent that the harassed Simpson, anxious to maintain both the good will of the Chinooks and his bachelorhood, was finding it exceedingly difficult to hold out. Actually, he may have been sorely tempted, for not only was the young lady attractive, as Indian belles went, but the dowry was to have consisted of a hundred prime beaver skins. As an added inducement, Lady Calpo had not been insisting upon a permanent union. Nevertheless, the governor had resisted the proposal with such tact that no one—not even the prospective bride—had become offended.[20] Great as was his genius for diplomacy, he must have felt a burden lifted from his shoulders when the doctor's canoe slid up on the sandy beach.

On Wednesday, March 16, the governor, Doctor John and the entire party, except ten men who were to remain temporarily at Fort George, started up the river in four heavily laden canoes. With tears dimming his one good eye, old Chief Comcomly bade them farewell while the rest of the Chinooks, including the fair princess "Chowie" and her disillusioned mother, stood by, sadly waving their good-byes to the "King George" men. The graceful canoes were soon out of sight.

On the evening of the second day, they reached Chief Casseno's village on the south shore of the Columbia near the mouth of the Willamette, where they were received cordially and presented with a generous catch of fresh fish for dinner. With Casseno at the time was Cassius, the eldest son of old Comcomly. Both chiefs implored Governor Simpson to take their sons East with him to be educated at the Missionary Society's School in the Red River settlement; but the ever cautious governor, again with consummate tact, refused on the ground that the lads were too young and too frail to undergo the hardships of the overland journey. Privately, to Doctor John, he explained that he did not care to assume such a heavy responsibility until the company's position in Oregon was more firmly intrenched.[21]

Early the next morning, Friday, March 18, the governor's party arrived at Vancouver. The chief executive appeared well pleased with the new fort. "I have," he wrote, "rarely seen a Gentleman's Seat in England possessing so many natural advantages and where ornament and use are so agreeably combined."[22] This was hardly what one would expect from a man who was supposed to be mourning the failure of the Fraser River expedition; but, at all events, it was a high tribute to Doctor John's foresight and organizing ability. If the rift between these two had grown apace since their arrival on the Columbia, there was no outward evidence of it as the time for their parting drew near.

At sunrise the following day, Governor Simpson summoned his entire party—gentlemen, servants, and Indians—to the flagstaff. Breaking a bottle of good English rum over the pole, he christened the post with these impressive words: "In behalf of the Honble Hudson's Bay Co. I hereby name this Establishment Fort Vancouver God Save King George the 4th." Three rousing cheers went up from the men while the governor, in order to do full justice to the occasion, dispensed "a couple of Drams to the people and the Indians." [23] At nine o'clock, Governor Simpson, accompanied by the retiring chief factor, Alexander Kennedy, and a dozen or more men detailed for duty at various interior posts, started on his homeward journey.

6

The doctor stood on the river bank with the bright spring sun playing on his flowing hair. He watched the canoes until they disappeared around a bend in the river. For a moment or two more he stood there, alone with his thoughts—great thoughts of empire. Then he turned and walked slowly back to the fort he had built. The White-Headed Eagle had come into his own, and, for better or worse, he was, at last, the undisputed King of the Columbia.

CHAPTER VI

The Beginnings of Empire

I

GOVERNOR SIMPSON's departure left Doctor John in sole charge of the vast Oregon country. Well may the forty-one-year-old chief factor have wondered at its extent, for he could name a score of contemporary sovereigns ruling over kingdoms insignificant by comparison. This far-flung empire extended from the present northern boundaries of California and Nevada to the Alaskan border, and from the Rocky Mountains westward to the Pacific. Vancouver had become, for the time being, its capital.

The White-Headed Eagle must have been similarly bewildered when he turned his thoughts to the subjects over whom he was to rule. Proud and warlike, these Indians, except for a few friendly tribes, were as prone to quarrel among themselves as with the whites. Scattered throughout the Oregon country, which they naturally regarded as their own, they presented a grave problem to the Hudson's Bay men who had come to trade with them.

When the Indians came to realize that the Britishers sought to exploit the land rather than to settle upon it, their hostility lessened, but at the outset they were both suspicious and belligerent. With only a handful of helpers—officers, employees, and servants of the company—Doctor John set about to rule his empire—a task from which most men would have shrunk.

Notwithstanding the weighty responsibility and almost limit-less authority he was ultimately to acquire, the doctor, through-out his career in Oregon, never rose above the rank of chief factor. However, as the years passed, men fell naturally into the habit of addressing him as "Governor," convinced that no other title could do justice to his position in the company. Governor, officially, he never became.

Doctor John's duties, from the beginning of his reign, were clearly outlined. In him was vested complete responsibility for developing the fur trade. From Vancouver he was to dispatch brigades of trappers and traders northward, eastward, and south-ward into the rich interior. He was to strengthen all existing posts and to create new ones as the need arose. After the furs had been collected, he was to send them, properly dressed, to London, where they would be sold at a handsome profit and con-verted into beaver hats to be worn by the King and his bosom companion, George (Beau) Brummell, who set the fashions for gentlemen of fastidious taste. Indeed, the fur trade was the main objective—the *raison d'être,* as it were—of the company's activities in the Northwest; and the ideal Hudson's Bay chief factor was the man who could have eyes and ears for naught else. Around this one consideration were eventually to develop both the grandeur and the misery of the doctor's steward-ship.

Although the covenant of 1818, under which the company had established its posts in Oregon, allowed citizens of Great Britain and the United States free access to the country, the Hudson's Bay leaders through Governor Simpson had given strict orders to Doctor John to discourage colonization. Here, indeed, was an anomaly. Traditionally, the English had been the world's most sedulous colonizers; yet, sitting in their London councils, the tycoons of the Hudson's Bay Company demanded that Oregon be exploited but never settled!

There can be little doubt that Doctor John understood the mandate of his superiors. What these dignitaries failed to comprehend from the first, however, was that the good doctor possessed not only the kindly instincts of a human being but also the prodigious ambitions of a born ruler.

From 1825 onward, a disquieting thought haunted the doctor's mind. What would he do if hungry colonists—British or American—were suddenly to appear demanding land, food, and shelter? Would he remain blindly loyal to the letter of his company's policy, or would he follow the promptings of his humane nature? Fortunately, both for the history of the country and for the chief factor's standing in the company, he was not to be put to the test until after seventeen years of faithful service had been rendered.

2

During those first busy months at Vancouver, with practical problems waiting to be solved, it is not likely that the White-Headed Eagle found much time in which to ponder remote possibilities. He understood what was expected of him and set about, vigorously and thoroughly, to put his orders into execution. Turning his attention to agriculture, he planted potatoes in the fertile fields to the rear of the fort and sowed two bushels of peas which he had brought up the river from Fort George. This was the only produce available for cultivation at the time, though by the fall of 1825, he had received from York Factory a bushel each of spring wheat, oats, barley, and Indian corn as well as a small quantity of timothy.

With infinite patience the doctor watched over this precious grain, and when at last he saw it break through the ground, he must have thought of his skeptical predecessor, James Keith— the man who had been so positive that nothing would grow on the Columbia! With the exception of the Indian corn, the grain flourished, though until 1828 the crop was not large enough to enable the doctor to discontinue the importation of flour! [1]

He took great pride in his new establishment. Throughout the remainder of 1825, he continued to improve the buildings and grounds, though he was by no means certain that the location was to be permanent. Indeed, it presented certain difficulties from the very beginning. The original settlement had been placed some distance back from the river because of the Columbia's tendency, during the spring and early summer, to overflow its banks. It was an irksome task both to carry water to the fort and to transport furs and supplies from the boats. [2] In spite of these drawbacks, the doctor put forth every effort to make Vancouver secure and habitable. It remained his headquarters until 1829, when he built a new post on higher ground about a mile to the westward and much closer to the river.

Since no accurate description of Doctor John's original fort can be found, we can only surmise its character. The chances are that he built it along traditional Hudson's Bay Company lines, using the familiar Fort William as his pattern. It is known that he placed the various buildings inside a stockade which enclosed two acres of ground, and that he erected a picket wall of large and closely fitted beams, placed upright and supported by stout buttresses. [3]

Even by that time the doctor had established such amicable relations with the Indians that elaborate defenses were unnecessary. He may have gone so far as to build bastions at the four corners of the fort, but if he did so, he could scarcely have expected them to serve as more than gentle reminders of the white man's power. Human kindness had rendered gunpowder unnecessary. Intercourse with the natives was indeed so friendly that, within a surprisingly short time, a village populated by Indians and half-breeds as well as by the company's servants began to rise close by the fort. [4]

Meanwhile, Fort George had been reduced to a mere lookout station. Contact was maintained through Chief Trader Donald Manson, an able Scotchman, whom Governor Simpson had stationed there. He was expected to keep the Chinook and Clatsop tribes friendly, to give notice of the arrival of ships, and to assist these vessels over the Columbia's bar. In Manson the chief factor had complete confidence.

Doctor John, in his dealings with the Indians, set a standard which must have seemed as extraordinary to some of his own men as it did to the natives themselves. Like a father firm yet kind, he punished the Indians when they erred, and rewarded them when they acquitted themselves well.[5] Though an inborn sense of fairness dominated his every act, he was still an able trader. In reality, he had the happy faculty of driving a good bargain for the company without cheating the red men.

At first the Indians were puzzled by such unheard-of tactics on the part of a Hudson's Bay Company official, but soon they responded enthusiastically. Even their conduct toward one another showed signs of improvement, and as for the whites, they could at last travel up and down the Columbia in perfect safety. A new era had dawned, and with it had been realized the company's fondest hope—an appreciable pick-up in the fur trade.

One of the most potent factors in bringing about this marked change was the doctor's wise and timely regulation of the liquor traffic, in which he was aided by the sagacious Comcomly. So determined was he to maintain this policy that, on one occasion, he purchased outright the entire cargo of a Yankee ship in order to keep the spirits on board from getting into the hands of the Indians.[6] Years later, some of this "fire water" was found cached away in the cellars at Vancouver. Oddly enough, Doctor John's high-handed methods seemed only to augment the respect in which he was held. Not a single uprising of any moment occurred in the vicinity of the fort during the White-Headed

Eagle's long reign—sufficient justification, it would seem, for his benevolent despotism.

In due time he became the first white arbiter of Indian disputes. An opportunity to play this rôle came in August, 1825, when hostilities broke out between old Comcomly and his ambitious son-in-law, Casseno. It was a situation that demanded prompt action for, with these two powerful chiefs warring on the Columbia, the fur trade stood in grave jeopardy. With characteristic diplomacy, Doctor John induced his old friend Comcomly to come up to Vancouver and discuss terms. As evidence of his good faith, the venerable chief brought with him, at no small risk, a sizable lot of high-grade skins from the Chinook village. When Casseno realized that the doctor would go to any length to protect Comcomly in his peaceful trading journeys through hostile territory, he saw that nothing could be gained by prolonging the warfare. Moreover, he dreaded the thought that his rivals would be gaining favor with the British at his own expense, so, with excellent grace, he capitulated.[7] The doctor's rare knowledge of Indian character had not only terminated a troublesome feud but had increased his popularity with both antagonists. No chief factor before him had scored such a triumph.

During the early years at Vancouver, visitors were few, but any traveler or trader who chanced to find himself in the vicinity would make it a point to call at the fort and partake of the good doctor's hospitality which became famous throughout the West. The White-Headed Eagle received such persons with the utmost cordiality though, in his treatment of them, he drew a fine distinction. As guests they were royally entertained, but as rivals in trade they were subjected to the most ruthless competition.

Illustrative of his attitude is a letter he wrote to the Governor and Committee of the Hudson's Bay Company in London on October 6, 1825. "I consider," runs the communication, "our object ought to be if there is strong opposition on the coast as this year to allow them to exhaust themselves; as they have only this market for their goods they will sell for what they can get, while having an extensive inland trade we would be certain of disposing ours and would be always ready to take every advantage of the market." [8] Such a declaration would have done credit to a Gould, a Vanderbilt, or a Rockefeller!

At any cost, Doctor John was determined to defend his company's supremacy in trade against all comers. Across the jolly mess-hall table at Vancouver, he might chat affably with the independent fur trader within his gates, showering upon him every courtesy; but in the gray dawn of the next day he would marshal against that same individual every commercial weapon of his mighty organization. Nor could any one accuse him of double dealing for, with a twinkle in his eye, he would announce to his astonished guest, even as he refilled his wineglass, exactly what he intended to do. Unless the stranger happened to be a rank novice at the game, he would pack up and depart, carrying with him a high personal regard for his host but leaving behind his fur-trading aspirations. During the doctor's administration of affairs on the Columbia, no independent trader succeeded in building up a profitable business—few attempted to do so.

3

Important and exacting as were the many duties imposed upon him, the versatile chief factor was, necessarily, most deeply concerned with the preservation and extension of the fur trade. In the vast Columbia department where he was personally responsible for the company's commercial interests, there were four major posts—Spokane House, Thompson's River, Fort George, and, of course, Fort Vancouver. The Thompson's River depot served a temporary outpost at Okanagan while Spokane House maintained two tributary stations, Flathead House and Kootenae

House.[9] Another post of some importance was Fort Nez Percés, later to become Fort Walla Walla. In spite of the strategic location of this settlement, Governor Simpson had expressed some doubt as to the ability of his company to retain it since it was situated on the south bank of the Columbia and hence might ultimately be acquired by the United States. He had even displayed similar doubts regarding the entire Snake Country.[10]

With this sweep of territory to supervise, the doctor realized only too well how much depended upon his personnel. The same council which, at York Factory in the summer of 1824, had assigned him to the Columbia department had, in addition, made the following appointments: J. W. Dease, chief trader, to Fort Nez Percés; Peter Skene Ogden, chief trader, to Spokane House; Alexander Ross, clerk, to the Snake Country; John McLeod, chief trader, to Thompson's River; and James Birnie, clerk, to Okanagan.[11] Although Governor Simpson made certain shifts after his arrival at Fort George, the council's selections were nevertheless significant since these were the very men upon whom the doctor was to lean most heavily in the development of his great project. The only important name absent from the original group was that of James Douglas.

Although the new western field chief felt complete confidence in all of these officers, it is doubtful if any one of them remained closer to him than the picturesque and resourceful Peter Skene Ogden. The eldest son of an eminent jurist of Quebec, Ogden had been educated to follow in his father's footsteps. Like Doctor John, however, he had proved too venturesome by nature for the sheltered life of a city barrister and had heeded, in preference, the glamorous call of the fur trade. His service with the Hudson's Bay Company had taken him to the West at an early date, and he was already in charge of the Snake Country when the doctor arrived in 1824. Indeed he passed down the Columbia in company with Doctor John and Governor Simpson on their first journey to Fort George.[12] With his amiable disposition, his fund of humorous stories, and his capacity for hard work, he soon became a favorite with his superior officers. Next to the doctor himself, Peter Skene Ogden was the most successful of the Hudson's Bay men in dealing with the Indians.

With a smattering of legal training, Ogden had carried into the wild western country a primitive though equitable method of dealing out justice. Ross Cox, an Irish clerk once connected with the Astor expedition, recorded, in his interesting book of reminiscences, a revealing statement credited to the legally trained fur trader. " 'My legal primer,' remarked Ogden, 'says that necessity has no law, and in this place, where the custom of the country, or as the lawyers say, the "lex non scripta" is our only guide, we must, in our acts of summary legislation, sometimes perform the parts of judge, jury, sheriff, hangman, gallows and all.' " [13]

No one could have described more accurately Doctor John's own conception of fundamental justice as revealed by his policy toward the natives, and hence it is little wonder that the White-Headed Eagle turned to Ogden not only for friendship but for sound advice. If John McLoughlin was early Oregon's Æsculapius, then assuredly Peter Skene Ogden was the country's Rhadamanthus.

One of Governor Simpson's first official acts in Oregon had been to send Chief Trader Ogden on an important mission to Flathead House. There he was to join forces with Alexander Ross in refitting the Snake Country party for active duty in the rich hunting grounds near by.[14] This sojourn in the wildest country of the Northwest was destined to be a long one fraught with innumerable perilous experiences. In fact, throughout the first year and a half of Doctor John's rule at Vancouver, this intrepid pathfinder remained in the field trapping and trading, and it was not until July 17, 1826, that he returned to the western headquarters post, to be warmly welcomed by his chief and highly commended upon the success of his efforts.

An exact statement of the returns of this expedition was made by the doctor in a letter dated August 8, 1826, and addressed to John McLeod. "Enclosed," he wrote, "is a copy of the Snake Expedition A/c current; . . . 2740 Large Beaver w't 4285 lbs. 837 small Beaver w't 551 lbs. 114 Large otter 9 Small Otter 3 Misquash 12 Beav'r Coating apparent gain £2,533–18." [15] No wonder Ogden's chief was pleased with what he had accomplished.

4

During his first eight years at Fort Vancouver, Doctor John was the only man connected with the establishment who possessed any knowledge of medicine. As a consequence, he was frequently called to render medical aid. At first his responsibilities in this regard were not heavy. As time went on, however, the Indians, who, of course, had had no opportunity to develop immunity against certain diseases imported by the whites, began to contract these ailments in increasing numbers. We can readily believe, therefore, that the doctor's practice became, within a comparatively short time, a heavy burden. Making no distinction between the whites and the natives, he extended every kindness to the ailing, and this broad-minded attitude went far toward building the legend of the White-Headed Eagle. Humanitarian that he was, Doctor John soon came to realize with a pang that other matters required his whole attention. Probably no man ever regretted his human limitations with greater sincerity! However, with customary foresight, he instructed one of his ablest clerks, George T. Allan, in the art of caring for the sick long before any of the regular Hudson's Bay Company physicians arrived at the fort. [16]

Although the chief factor supervised all of his early cases

personally, his decision in this regard appears to have been one of choice for, during the first year of Vancouver's existence, at least one other medical man visited the post. Dr. John Scouler, an eminent physician who had received his degree from the University of Edinburgh, spent some time there in 1825, having come on a journey of scientific investigation with the young botanist, David Douglas. These two scientists reached Fort George as passengers aboard the Hudson's Bay Company ship *William and Anne,* which had been cruising up the coast on a fur-trading expedition,[17] and Doctor John, upon receiving word of their safe arrival through one of Manson's scouts, hurried down the river to welcome them in person.

On April 19, just one month to the day after he had assumed full charge of affairs on the Columbia, the busy chief factor headed upstream with his two distinguished guests. His keen interest in all branches of science made him a particularly sympathetic host, and David Douglas, who had been sent out by the Royal Horticultural Society of London, speaks highly, in his journal, of the reception accorded him. "I showed him [Doctor John] my instructions," writes the enthusiastic young botanist, "and informed him verbally the object of my voyage, and talked over my pursuit. In the most frank and handsome manner, he assured me that everything in his power would be done to promote the views of the Society."[18] Very soon young Douglas was to appreciate his host's ability and willingness to make good this friendly offer.

Knowing the doctor, we can readily appreciate what satisfaction this unexpected contact with the world of science must have brought him, cut off from the association with cultured men. During the months that followed, he extended countless courtesies to his guests and made it possible for them to visit, in safety, every section of the country within his jurisdiction. Douglas, in particular, proved a diligent worker, adding to the botanical vocabulary of the time names of over one thousand plants.[19] The stately Douglas fir stands today as a silent reminder of this young scientist's efforts in early Oregon. The Douglas journal is of tremendous scientific importance since it contains a minute record of the visiting botanist's discoveries; but it is of even greater significance as a human document. Page after page reveals the author's indebtedness to the resident chief factor.

"Having resolved to devote a season in the interior parts of the country skirting the Rocky Mountains," wrote Douglas, in his diary, "Dr. John McLoughlin, who was unremitting with his kind attentions, allowed me to embark in the spring boat for the interior with two reams of paper, which was an enormous indulgence. Rather than go unprovided in this respect, I curtailed the small supply of clothing." It would be difficult to say which was the more remarkable—the scientific ardor of the young botanist or the thoughtful generosity of the White-Headed Eagle.

Douglas, however, was not alone in his praise of the chief factor, as Dr. Scouler's journal so emphatically discloses. "This morning," wrote the other visiting scientist on April 16, 1825, "I had the pleasure of being introduced to Dr. John McLoughlin . . . From him I experienced the utmost politeness & to his Kindness was indebted for some curious specimens of the rocks of the Rocky Mountains."[20] Like Douglas, Scouler conducted extensive research during his stay in Oregon, and, as a result, a number of the plant species of the region still bear his name.

There is no evidence that he assisted Doctor John in the routine medical work at Vancouver though he must have had ample opportunity to do so between his various sallies into the wilds. No doubt the modest visitor, somewhat awed by the determination of his genial but autocratic host to handle things

in his own way, shrank from proffering his services. But if
Dr. Scouler had any reticence about practicing medicine in the
chief factor's presence, he became bolder out in the great open
spaces, where he took a keen interest in studying the diseases
of the Indians.[21] He appears to have been happiest when puz-
zling over symptoms—with cool, scientific abandon he could
stand over some dying native and record his orderly impressions
in a notebook; but Doctor John was the man to set a broken
leg, amputate a foot, or apply a timely dose of physic and then
weep unabashed for the poor heathen who writhed in pain before
him.

5

Thus passed into history the first year at Vancouver. It had
been a year of varying fortunes but, in the main, a year of
progress. Step by step the doctor was building an empire in the
wilderness, but, with the crude tools and unskilled workmen
at his disposal, the headway was slow. When Douglas and
Scouler arrived, for instance, the best the chief factor could
provide for them in shelter was a tent; a little later, he was able
to offer them a rude hut constructed entirely from bark.[22] "As
my lodgings were not of the most comfortable sort," wrote David
Douglas, referring to the bark cabin, "Mr. McLoughlin kindly
invited me to a part of his house in a half-finished state. Therefore on Christmas Day all my little things were removed to my
new dwelling." [23]

The two scientists had come too soon to partake of the luxu-
rious hospitality for which Vancouver was, within a few years,
to become famous from California to Russian America. Nevertheless, what their gracious host failed to give them in the way
of comfortable quarters, he more than balanced by his sympathetic and intelligent coöperation.

Often, during that first year, Doctor John's thoughts turned to Margaret and the children back in Canada. He longed to have them with him in this garden spot for the retention of which he had waged such a stubborn battle with the governor. Writing years later, at a time when his memories could scarcely have been pleasant, he recorded his first impressions of Oregon as follows: "In 1825, from what I had seen of the country, I formed the conclusion, from the mildness and salubrity of the climate, that this was the finest portion of North America that I had seen for the residence of civilized man." [24]

Chambers of Commerce may have waxed more eloquent in subsequent outbursts but seldom more sincere.

CHAPTER VII

COMPETITION

I

For many years, as Doctor John well knew, Spokane House had served first the North West and later the Hudson's Bay Company as an interior headquarters. From the lips of old-timers he had heard its romantic story. With its fine buildings, stockade, and solid bastions, its ballroom, its racetrack and fine horses, Spokane House had once been an exceedingly gay rendezvous! But the old fort had seen its best days.[1]

Governor Simpson, visiting Spokane House with the doctor in 1824, was impressed not only by its inaccessibility but also by its lack of agricultural facilities. He kept the matter in mind and, during the winter at Fort George, discussed it at length with his new chief factor. The governor, influenced in part by his own observations but mainly by the advice of Tom McKay and others who had been longer in Oregon, suggested a more northerly location for the new inland depot. Kettle Falls on the Columbia was the spot selected. So situated as to afford ample room for agricultural expansion, the depot gave every promise of becoming self-supporting—always an important consideration with the practical-minded George Simpson.

At first Doctor John failed to share his chief's ardor because the proposed site lay on the south bank of the Columbia. With an eye to the future, the cautious chief factor realized the possibility of losing the post to the Americans in the event that the river should be chosen as the boundary line. That, of course, had been the principal consideration involved in locating Vancouver on the north shore. But the governor's word was law, and so, with more than a little reluctance, the doctor, toward the middle of 1825, undertook the task of building the new fort. Because of his manifold duties at Vancouver, however, he selected, as the man best qualified to carry out the company's program, a clerk most appropriately named John Work.

Work was a jovial Irish giant—a man of almost unlimited physical strength who lived up to his name in no uncertain manner.[2] Already he had established himself securely in the fur trade of the far West, having come out to Fort George in 1823 with Peter Skene Ogden, a whole year ahead of Doctor John. No doubt the Hibernian half of the doctor warmed to this jolly trader who was described by one of his contemporaries as "a tender hearted, generous Irishman who often amused his associates by his murder of the French tongue."[3] But if Vancouver's chief factor had not recognized the marked organizing talents that lay beneath John Work's amiable and easy-going exterior, he would never have entrusted to him a mission so vital to the company's progress.

Charged with the responsibility of dismantling Spokane House and building the new post at Kettle Falls coincidently, John Work started operations immediately upon receiving his orders in the summer of 1825; but the inland winter was so severe and the attitude of the natives so uncertain that he was not able to show much progress until well into the spring of 1826. At length, however, the new settlement was completed and ready to take its place as one of the links in the growing chain of Hudson's Bay forts.

In accordance with specific instructions left by Governor Simpson, the Kettle Falls depot was christened Fort Colville in honor of Andrew Colville, then the London governor of the Hudson's Bay Company. Colville had once befriended George Simpson by relieving the fur-trading end of the business in America of certain unreasonable charges which the London Council had been levying against it, and no doubt the selection of Colville's name settled an old debt of gratitude.[4] At all events, the completion of the fort was a mighty step forward in the company's ambitious program as, henceforth, accounts of the surrounding posts could be centered there, thus saving a trip to Vancouver for settlement.[5]

2

During the month of May, 1826, Doctor John visited the new fort in order to inspect the improvements which had been made and to leave his instructions for trading with the Indians.[6] Forgetting completely his initial prejudices against the location, he expressed himself as highly pleased with the new depot. John Work had won his spurs early in the McLoughlin régime, and the doctor, always quick to recognize ability in the men under him, congratulated the big Irishman with unstinted warmth. Solely responsible for the company's future profits in his district, he had every reason to rejoice over the successful culmination of the project.

At Fort Colville, the chief factor had the pleasure, once again, of visiting with David Douglas, who had journeyed up from the junction of the Spokane River to gather specimens. Because of his pleasant manner and sincerity of purpose, the young Scotch botanist had become the idol of the Hudson's Bay Company officers. He refers, in his journal, to John Work as one "to whom I was known and from whom I had [received] many good offices."[7] Even the businesslike Governor Simpson, in writing to John Work, displayed a sense of humor few had suspected him of possessing, and the cause was David Douglas. In a letter which contained a lengthy recital of routine instructions, he concluded as follows: "Do me the favour to collect all the seeds plants Birds and quadrupids & mice & rats you can and let them be forwarded by ship of next season to H [Gosmy] Esqur, care of Wm. Smith Esqur. Secty H. B. Cmy., London." [8] Such hearty coöperation in the wilds of western America must have been thankfully received by a grateful if puzzled naturalist.

It was to Doctor John, however, that Douglas turned for his closest and most lasting friendship. During his sojourn at Kettle Falls, the young scientist fell into the habit of wandering far afield in his collecting expeditions, and the doctor, desirous of protecting him from the Indians, resorted to an ingenious device. He led the natives to believe that Douglas was the "grass man" and, as such, "possessed great powers over flowers and shrubs." [9] This was enough to make the modest Scottish botanist an awesome figure among the natives, and, though he may not have suspected the cause of his sudden deification, he traveled everywhere without molestation. Doctor John knew his Indians. No one else could have invented so effective a ruse, and we can imagine him enjoying hugely the humorous aspects of his own strategy.

On another occasion the ubiquitous Douglas completely eluded the watchful eye of his protector, and, thanks again to the journal, we can turn to his own words for a description of what occurred. "I started at daylight for a trip to the hills south of Kettle Falls," wrote the botanist on May 26, 1826. "The weather was warm, the thermometer 86°, and sitting down to rest a while . . . I fell asleep and never woke until late in the afternoon, when being twenty miles from home, I would have gladly taken up my quarters there for the night, but that I feared Mr. McLoughlin, who expected me back, would be uneasy. I therefore returned with all speed over a mountainous and rugged way, and arrived near midnight, and found him on the point of sending two Indians to seek for me; his anxiety however lest any accident should have befallen me was changed into hearty laughter when he heard of the manner in which I had been spending my time." [10]

From this and similar accounts which abound in the Douglas journal, it is evident that an unusually strong affection had grown up between these two. Indeed the kindly and thorough manner in which Doctor John and John Work saw to Douglas's security in the rough interior country enabled him to add materially to his growing collection of specimens.

Later in the year, after the chief factor had returned to Vancouver, a messenger came to him one day from John Work with the startling information that a party of Americans had been seen trading with the Flathead Indians not far from Fort Colville. Competition was not to be tolerated! Promptly and vigorously the doctor rose to the occasion. If he had ever questioned the ability of his company to hold the new post against the aggressive Yankees, certainly there was no trace of timidity in the instructions he issued to cover the situation.

"In case the Americans come to the Flat Head Country," he wrote to John Work in a letter dated August 10, 1826, "they must be opposed as much as we can, but without a waste of property because the right to remain there will be decided between the two governments. As an opinion, I think from discovery & occupancy we will have that part of the country, therefore it is not our interest to spoil the Indians, however, we must do so if necessary and treat them as liberally as the Americans . . . the Americans have no right to assume any authority, or claim this country as part of their Territory and I feel confident that the Company will abandon none of their Establishments until they are informed our government has given up its claims to the Sovereignty of the Country on which they are situated." [11]

Had the good doctor been able to gaze into the future, into the time when he himself would join forces with the Yankees, he might have softened his message. For the moment, however, he was a loyal Britisher, and his words were bold ones for a man who had been none too sure of his ground a few months earlier. The White-Headed Eagle was fast learning how to use his power.

3

Who were these Americans who dared to cross swords with the strongly intrenched Hudson's Bay men in their own baili-wick? We can only guess. William Ashley, of the North American Fur Company, had been gathering peltries for some time on the eastern slope of the Rocky Mountains.[12] He had built a fort on a small body of water near Great Salt Lake which he had modestly named Lake Ashley. In due time this had become the headquarters of his flourishing enterprise. Early in 1826, however, Ashley had sold his interests in the North American Fur Company to Jedediah Smith, William Sublette, and David Jackson, who, in turn, had organized the Rocky Mountain Fur Company.[13] These three men were certainly among those who had had the hardihood to cross the mountains to the north and invade the precincts of the Hudson's Bay Company.

It was in the Snake Country, in 1826, that American trappers and traders first clashed with their British rivals and thus encountered the initial stumbling block in their determined advance upon Oregon.[14] Whoever they were, their presence was not desired. As visitors, possibly; as rivals in trade, never—on that score the chief factor's mind was clear.

When it came time for Doctor John to send his ringing message to John Work regarding the company's future policy in dealing with the Americans, he knew vastly more about what these meddlesome Yankees had been up to than Work's brief report had taught him. Less than a month earlier, Peter Skene Ogden had returned from his second Snake expedition, and, before the doctor's fireside at Vancouver, he had given a detailed account of his experiences with the invaders.

Ogden's trip had been a dismal failure. The cutthroat practices of his rivals had made his returns small, and, worse, forty-eight of his original seventy-five men had deserted, twenty-three of them to the Americans.[15] One authority suggests that between 1826 and 1829 there were as many as six hundred American trappers working in and about the Rocky Mountains.[16] While this seems incredible, it is nevertheless certain that Yankee trappers, either organized or independent, were present in such numbers as to cause the doctor genuine alarm. Here was the first serious challenge to his authority, and it is little wonder that he was thoroughly aroused.

Ogden kept a journal of his various Snake expeditions which, for detail, was rivaled only by the efforts of the meticulous George Simpson. No matter how discouraging the day, no matter how exhausted in mind and body the evening had found him, this intrepid chief trader put on paper the significant incidents of his wanderings. From his diary we can glean some notion of the distressing story he related to Doctor John.

From the very first it had been a heartbreaking experience. On Tuesday, December 27, 1825, Ogden wrote as follows: "Weather very cold. On collecting horses, we found one third limping and many of them could not stand. . . . Some of the trappers started trenches, the rest visited the traps, returned at night with no success, their traps fast in ice, and no beaver from the trenches. . . . The hunters came in with 5 small deer. If this cold does not soon pass my situation with so many men will not be pleasant, but last year I met with so many reverses, men grumbling and discontented, that I am in a manner prepared, but can afford them no relief. If we can escape starvation it will depend on the hunters. God preserve us. Today 4 beaver." [17] But Ogden had only started.

"About 30 Indians paid us a visit," wrote the chief trader on March 20, 1826. "They report that a party of Americans and Iroquois are not three days' march from us, near the spot one of my party was killed last spring. If this be the case, I have no doubts our hunts are damned, and we may prepare to return empty handed. With my discontented party I dread meeting the Americans. That some will attempt desertion I have not the least doubt, after the sufferings they have endured." [18]

Already the harassed Ogden had begun to fear the wholesale desertions which were soon to follow. Shortly after this, on March 24, he "saw another Snake camp of 200 who wintered with the Americans and carry an American flag. They had 60 guns and ammunition not scarce." [19] Apparently the Yankees had been "spoiling" these red men with a vengeance!

A ray of hope enters the sinister story on April 10, when the tireless chronicler observed that "our deserters are already tired of their new masters and from their manner will soon return to us." In view of his very next comment, however, we suspect that Ogden was merely whistling in the dark to keep up his courage. "I cannot imagine," he continued wistfully, "how these Americans can afford to sell their beaver to reap a profit when they pay $3 per pound for coarse or fine, but such is the case." [20]

But even the Americans had Ogden's sympathy when they suffered serious reverses. "Had a visit from the Snakes," runs an entry dated June 8. "Within the last 10 months they have plundered 180 traps from the Americans and guns, knives and other articles. This, with 13 men murdered in 1825, is sufficient to make them independent of trade. The Americans swear to make an example of them; I do hope from my soul they may." [21] Peter Skene Ogden, like the White-Headed Eagle, could not abide an outlaw.

Safe back at Fort Vancouver, having taken leave of his trusted lieutenants, Finan McDonald, Tom McKay, and Thomas Dears, who were to proceed to Nez Percés to gather in the few furs the expedition had netted, Ogden made this final entry on July 17. "Thus ends my second trip and I am thankful for the many dangers I have escaped with all my party in safety. Had we not been obliged to kill our horses for food, the success of our expedition would have yielded profits. As it is, fortunately no loss will be sustained." [22]

With set features and furrowed brow, Doctor John heard the story out. These Snake Indians needed some of his own brand of discipline and, as for the Yankees—he'd take care of them in due season. With Ogden's disquieting narrative surging through his mind, the doctor penned his bold message to John Work. It was war, and he knew how to fight!

4

On the fifth day of July, 1826, almost a fortnight prior to Peter Skene Ogden's return to Vancouver, Doctor John, having finished his midday meal, walked slowly down to the boat landing with several men who, for some days past, had been his guests. It was a red-letter day at the headquarters post, for, at one o'clock, the interior brigade was scheduled to leave for Fort Colville, Thompson's River, Nez Percés, New Caledonia, and York Factory. In the manner of a field marshal inspecting an army about to go into action, the doctor ran his eye over the nine boats lying at the wharf, laden to the gunwales—all of them—with merchandise for the interior posts.

For a few moments he chatted with William Connolly, the visiting chief factor from the New Caledonia district and the brigade's commanding officer, and then, passing on to the others, he exchanged a friendly word of farewell with each. Numbered among them was James Douglas [23]—the same Douglas, incidentally, who had been the doctor's protégé at Fort William seven years earlier. The young man had come along splendidly in the company's service and had been serving under his father-in-law, William Connolly, in New Caledonia. In the long interval, Doctor John had not forgotten his promising pupil, and it was with unrestrained enthusiasm that he had welcomed Douglas to Vancouver. Perhaps the idea had already taken root in his mind that this energetic and gifted clerk would make an ideal assistant for him on the Columbia, though it is doubtful if either of them, on that July afternoon, had even an inkling of the close association that was eventually to be theirs.

Shortly, the doctor left this congenial gathering of Hudson's Bay traders from the north to spend the little time remaining before the departure of the brigade with another group. Standing near by, with a bright shawl wrapped over her shoulders, was a dark-skinned woman surrounded by her brood. The chief factor approached them tenderly. For a long time he had anticipated the pleasure of having his family gathered around him on such an occasion, and now, at last, they were there—Margaret and the children.

How and when the chief factor's family had reached Fort Vancouver remains a mystery. The answer, if it is anywhere, lies buried in the old records of the Hudson's Bay Company in London and, until these are made public, we can only speculate upon probabilities. It is true that in the brief manuscript biography of her father which she wrote many years later, Eloisa McLoughlin Harvey made certain statements which, on the face of things, would seem to settle the matter. "Then he [Doctor John]," she wrote, "came to Fort George—Astoria. The whole family came. . . . We came over the mountains and down the river in boats." [24] In fact, she even mentioned the winter spent at Fort George and the removal, in the spring to Vancouver.

It must be remembered that Eloisa was a little girl of six when all this took place. Her biographical sketch of the doctor did not appear until 1878, and, in attempting to recapture the crowded events of more than half a century, she doubtless found it necessary to fall back upon hearsay. The true explanation, we suspect, is not so simple.

For one thing, the conditions of that memorable dash overland—especially the relentless pace set by Governor Simpson— were far from ideal for the transporting of a family. Furthermore, it seems obvious that if Margaret and her children had been members of the expedition, the governor, with his never failing fondness for minutiæ, would have mentioned them; yet there is not a single reference to the McLoughlin family in his journal, nor is there any allusion to his kinsfolk in the doctor's own letters of the period. But perhaps the most conclusive bit of evidence against Eloisa's statement is the patent fact that Governor Simpson, when he reached the forks of the Spokane River in 1824, found only three boats waiting to transport his party to Fort George—scarcely sufficient accommodation for his own extensive equipage. Certainly there was no room for a mother and her brood of small children.

Nevertheless, there they stood at the boat landing with Doctor John on July 5, 1826. John Work, in his diary comment for that day, mentions that among those ready to depart with the brigade were "9 children viz—Dr. McLoughlin's family, Mr. F. McDonald's family and 2 children of Tom McKay." [25] The mystery deepens. They could not have arrived at the fort that year since the annual express from York Factory did not reach the Columbia until October or November. Indeed they must have journeyed west with the express of 1825, in which case they would have been with the doctor since the preceding fall.

Vancouver, with its rude buildings, only partially completed, must have seemed to Margaret a dreary haven in which to raise a family. But even the chilly winter rains of Oregon could not dampen the ardor of a woman who had longed, through many weary months, to be with her husband. Her John had already become a great man—a power in the fur trade. She was proud and happy.

The chief factor, it appears, had arranged to send one of his children with the brigade to be educated east of the Rockies— which child, no one can say. We know that Joseph, the eldest son, received no education at all,[26] and it seems unlikely that Margaret would have allowed either the eight-year-old Eloisa or the five-year-old David to leave her. Eliza had not come west with the others,[27] and hence, by the process of elimination, it would appear that John, Jr., was the only one who could have made the trip. Where he went is equally obscure. Fort St. James, the leading settlement of New Caledonia, may have boasted a school, but it is much easier of belief that the doctor's son traveled as far east as the Red River Colony, where educational facilities of a type were available.

At last the hour for departure arrived. The White-Headed Eagle assisted his son into one of the boats, wished him Godspeed, and then stepped back on the low wharf where Margaret stood with her brown arms wrapped around her two youngest. James Douglas, grateful for the many kindnesses he had received, promised to keep watch over the boy as far as Fort St. James, his destination.

There was a general bustle as the men scrambled into their places, and then, one after another, the nine boats swung out into midstream, east bound. As soon as their oars touched the water, the French Canadian voyageurs struck up their familiar boat song. It was a spectacle that never failed to thrill the doctor. As he stood there beside Margaret, leaning on his huge cane, his features relaxed, and a broad smile stole over his countenance. Instinctively his massive head began to wag from side to side in time with the swinging rhythm of the boat song. For a little while he looked on, fascinated by the color and animation of the vanishing flotilla, and then, with a rush, the thought came home to him that his second son had grown up—grown old enough to embark alone upon a long and perilous pilgrimage. In that moment the regality of the King of Old Oregon gave way to the human emotions of a father. Margaret slipped her arm through his, and together they listened and watched—listened until the voyageurs' song could be heard no longer, and watched until the brigade had disappeared from view.

It was soon over. Straightening up to his full height, Doctor John turned and walked majestically back to the fort, Margaret behind him. The King had returned to character. The day was but half spent, and there was still work to be done.

5

Throughout the remainder of 1826 he worked diligently to improve the living quarters at the fort and to extend his agricultural development. He watched over the few head of cattle which he had brought up from Fort George in a large, flat-bottomed craft built especially for the purpose.[28]

By the 20th of March, 1827, he was able to send Governor Simpson the news that "our cattle thrives well, we lost no Pigs by poison since last year, but the Wolves have destroyed several of them." Then, in his very next statement, he takes the governor to task. "It is a pity," his letter continues, "that the Pumpkin seed I requested was not sent, potatoes and Turnips in this warm climate are subject to fail; if we could raise a sufficiency of Pumpkins it would enable us to feed our Pigs, in house all Winter they would thrive better and none would be devoured by the Wolves." [29]

Discussing his agricultural achievements in this same letter, the doctor observes that "Our Potato Crop failed, from two hundred barrels which we planted we got six hundred barrels—one hundred and fourteen bushels of pease from nine and a half, twelve bushels wheat from two, twenty-seven bushels barley from Two, and Six of Oats from one, and one and a half bushel of Indian Corn from the Seed you sent, which was at first very bad and with the Wheat and Oats got greatly injured in bringing here." On the whole, he had not done badly with his farming enterprise.

What concerned the chief factor most keenly, however, was the growing activity of the Americans in his department. Following closely on the heels of Peter Skene Ogden, other Hudson's Bay traders had returned to Vancouver with similar rumors of Yankee aggressiveness. No doubt many of them were gross exaggerations, but the immediate result of these reports was to arouse the doctor to a full realization of a new set of problems. It had been the established custom of the company to use merchandise of various kinds as a medium of exchange for furs. For the purpose of trading with the natives, these goods were marked up about seventy per cent above cost, and Doctor John, facing stubborn if unorganized competition, complained to the governor of what he considered an excessively high margin.

"I beg to observe," he wrote, "that the advance of 70 pc on the prime cost put on the goods in this department seems to me too high. The additional requisition for Outfit 1826, and the requisition for Outfit 1827 which you took from this amount to £5874.12.8ᵈ, the advance on this at 70 pc is £4812.4.10¼. . . . What may be real costs of bringing goods here I cannot say but certainly the present rate of advance is too high." Then, with prophetic vision, he concluded on a modern note by remarking that "Whatever may be the decision you may depend if we have to compete for the trade the cheapest shop will carry the day." [30]

Ultimately the White-Headed Eagle's view was to prevail. By 1831 he was able to write, with a touch of swagger, "I broke up the American party in the Snake Country and I did this simply by underselling them and showing them we could afford to sell the trappers at European servants' prices . . . and clear handsomely by them." [31]

There were, however, many obstacles to surmount before he could make this boast, and the years between 1827 and 1831 were devoted mainly to the arduous task of rendering the Hudson's Bay Company's monopoly secure.

CHAPTER VIII

SUMMARY JUSTICE

I

HARASSED by the aggressiveness of the independent American fur traders operating in the Columbia department, Doctor John had reason, by the end of 1826, to be even more deeply concerned over the proposed Oregon policy of his own company. A lengthy document, forwarded by Governor Simpson along with a bundle of dispatches, had given him cause to fear for the very future of the company's western interests. When it came time for the spring express to leave Vancouver in the month of March, 1827, the doctor had a vigorous note of protest, addressed to the governor, ready to accompany it.

In order to understand the chief factor's anxiety, it is necessary to go back a little and catch up the thread of George Simpson's activities since leaving the West. In 1825, after his return to York Factory, he had made a journey to London for the purpose of consulting with the chiefs of the Hudson's Bay Company regarding affairs west of the Rockies. He had impressed upon the new London governor of the vast enterprise, Sir John Pelly, the necessity of settling a permanent boundary between Great Britain and the United States before the expiration of the Ten-year Covenant in 1828.

On the 9th of December, 1825, no doubt with the energetic Simpson at his elbow, Governor Pelly had penned an elaborate communication to the Honourable George Canning, Secretary

of State for Foreign Affairs, urging him to consider the boundary question seriously. In this letter he had pointed out the
undeniable fact that although the Oregon country had been
open, in theory at least, to both governments, only Britishers had
established permanent trading posts there. The Americans, he
had argued truthfully, had not availed themselves of this privilege.

Pelly, in the hope of acquiring all the territory possible for
Great Britain without pressing claims that would seem unreasonable, had suggested that "starting from Lat. 49 at the Rocky
Mountains the Line ought to be continued Southward along the
height of the Land to the Place where Lewis and Clarke crossed
the Mountains, said to be in Lat. 46°42 then Westerly along the
Lewis's River, until it falls into the Columbia, and thence to the
Sea, leaving the navigation of both these Rivers free to the Subjects of both nations. This line," the communication had continued, "would leave to America the Trade and Possession of
an extensive and valuable Country, and would furnish fewer
opportunities of collision between the Traders of the two Nations
than any other Line that could be suggested." [1]

When Doctor John read the Pelly recommendations, he could
scarcely believe his eyes. To him, the practical man in the field,
it seemed as if the company was proposing a short cut to suicide.
What did Pelly know about Oregon? What were they thinking
of over in London? Perhaps they knew international policy, but,
most assuredly, they didn't know the fur trade. Worse still, had
George Simpson, for political reasons, been forced into an agreement against his own better judgment, or had he so soon forgotten the lay of the land out in this far-away department?
Puzzled and gravely concerned, the White-Headed Eagle lost
no time in sending the governor his reasons for opposing the
suggested plan.

Writing on March 20, 1827, in the forthright style so characteristically his own, he "begs to observe by the Boundary demanded in Governor Pelly's letter the Americans will have in their power to intercept the Flathead trade, as these Indians hunt principally on the head waters of the Missourie and toward Henry's fork, and if we are prevented sending to Indians and sending trappers on the South side of the Columbia, we shall be deprived of the whole of the Snake trade, nine-tenths of the Walla Walla, Willameth and a fourth of that of Spokan, in short will leave us only the Kootonais trade, three-fourths of that of Spokan and the trade of this place [Vancouver], which in the event of an American opposition being here and the post of Frasers River cutting off our trade from the North will reduce the trade of this place to a mere trifle."

Having delivered this bombshell, the doctor, defending his empire with the zeal of a tigress watching over its young, continued with the pertinent observation that "it is mortifying to be obliged to abandon a business after such pains have been taken and such expenses incurred to organize and establish it, yet it is preferable to do so than to carry on a losing concern."

Then, satisfied that he had given his superior officer considerable material for thought, he concluded somewhat naïvely. "I beg to state," he wrote, "that I would wish to know if an opposition establish themselves here whether it is wished we should oppose them to the utmost by underselling them or if you would approve of our making an arrangement not to spoil the trade . . . your directions on the subject if their Honours [the London Governor and Committee] have not already given theirs will relieve us from a deal of anxiety and enable us to conform to what is wished."[2] In the vernacular of a later century, George Simpson was indeed "on the spot."

This letter stands out as a flawless example of mental fencing. Well did Doctor John know the vulnerable spot in George Simpson's armor—the gnawing fear of losing the gains already made on the Columbia. Sparring with fine technique, he had delivered a bold thrust at the proper moment and then had edged nimbly away with a parry designed to force a decision from his opponent.

Whether or not the chief factor had in mind an alternative boundary line is not clear, though it is evident that he believed Great Britain deserving of more territory than Pelly's recommendation would have allowed her. The question is purely academic, for this intra-company controversy came to naught when the Anglo-American negotiations of 1826–27 for a partition of the Oregon country broke down. Instead of settling upon a permanent boundary, the assembled delegates merely postponed the evil day by adopting the Convention of 1827 which extended the old agreement of joint occupation for an indefinite period.[3] While the matter was decided upon issues entirely foreign to those Doctor John had raised, and he had no part whatsoever in the ensuing deliberations, still the practical result was a triumph for his point of view.

Communication was so slow in those early days of Oregon that the doctor was not to learn of the new agreement until some time had elapsed. Living on tenterhooks meanwhile, he continued to fight his battle, striving to avoid "spoiling the trade" when possible but not hesitating to undersell his competitors when necessary. When the news of the Convention of 1827 finally reached him, the White-Headed Eagle began immediately to develop the trade in his department with renewed vigor, assured as he was of reasonable security for the future.

At an early date, Doctor John had been accorded a measure of independence unprecedented among the company's chief factors. The London Governor and Committee had made this quite clear to George Simpson in a letter dated February 23, 1826. "The great distance from the seat of Council," had run the communication, "renders it necessary that the gentleman in charge of the Department [Doctor John] should be invested with discretionary powers in respect to its management, it is therefore our wish that such arrangements as he may direct may be carried into effect." Then, for fear they had granted the doctor too much latitude, the London dignitaries had added a safeguard to the effect that "in these arrangements he will of course be regulated by such instructions as he may from time to time receive from you in Council."[4]

As a practical matter, Governor Simpson knew that his chief factor had been given carte blanche, and, for a time at least, he accepted the situation in good grace. In the original instance it had been the isolation of the West rather than any special faith in the doctor that had necessitated this arrangement, though the London leaders must have been aware of the hazards involved. Clearly, had such unprecedented power been granted to an officer less capable, the result could only have spelled disaster. So completely did Doctor John justify the trust that had been placed in him that in time he came to be responsible only to London.[5]

2

On March 20, 1827, the busy chief factor left Fort Vancouver with the annual express en route for the Kettle Falls post where he planned to investigate the further progress of the trade and where, no doubt, he hoped to discuss the boundary question with the two men stationed there, John Work and John W. Dease. Troubled in mind as he must certainly have been on that journey up the Columbia, the White-Headed Eagle consoled himself with the knowledge that, tucked away with the outgoing mail in his boat, was the strong message he had penned to Governor Simpson. His ultimatum had been started on its way—he could only await results.

He apparently made the river trip in good company for, numbered among the passengers traveling with the express, were

François Annance, John McLeod, and Pierre C. Pambrun, bound for the interior, as well as Edward Ermatinger and David Douglas, the botanist, en route to Hudson Bay.[6] It was, in consequence, a notable group of Hudson's Bay men who found themselves gathered at Fort Colville on April 16, 1827. By mutual consent, the evening meal around the mess-hall table resolved itself into a spirited farewell party in honor of young Douglas, who was to start the following morning on the first leg of his long journey to England. Utterly unlike the rank and file of the fur traders with whom he had been associating for the better part of two years, the visiting scientist was, none the less, as loath to part with his hosts as they were to let him go.

The party evidently broke up early. "At nine o'clock that night," wrote Douglas on April 16, "I was conveyed to my camp, about a mile above the establishment, where we pitched in order that no time would be lost in starting in the morning. . . . Having now just bid farewell to my Columbia friends, I cannot in justice to my own feeling refrain from acknowledging the kindness shown me during my stay among them, a grateful remembrance of which I shall ever cherish."[7]

It is not likely that any of the Hudson's Bay men regretted Douglas's departure more keenly than did Doctor John himself. He had become genuinely attached to the brilliant young Scot whose presence in the Northwest had brought back to him a fleeting taste of the civilized world he had once known. To the doctor, Douglas's visit had seemed a pleasant interlude in a stern battle with realities.

3

But the White-Headed Eagle, ever the busy executive, had little time for reminiscing. Immediately after he had attended to certain routine business at Fort Colville, he embarked once more for Vancouver, where the Hudson's Bay schooner *Cadboro* was already overdue from London. With the arrival of this vessel, another of the doctor's hopes would be realized—direct water communication with the old country. News from London brought by English gentlemen seemed a highly pleasing prospect, and meeting them would perhaps compensate for the loss of Douglas. As the chief factor sped down the turbulent Columbia, lulled by the song of his voyageurs, he leaned back to dream his dreams of empire. He reveled in these jaunts because they gave him brief snatches of leisure in which to lay plans for the future.

At length the *Cadboro* reached Fort Vancouver, where the first to greet her master, John Pearson Sawn, was Doctor John himself.[8] In fancy we can see him standing at the boat landing, his white hair flowing in the breeze, his black cloak hanging majestically from his broad shoulders, and his huge gold-headed cane raised high in welcome to the sea-weary captain and his thirty-eight men. While the *Cadboro,* a trim little vessel of seventy-two tons burden, was casting anchor in the stream, Indians put out in their swift canoes to bring her officers and men ashore. In all likelihood the friendly behavior of the natives astonished these visitors from abroad, who were prepared, from all they had heard, for a very different type of reception. Indeed there had been no opportunity for tidings of the miracle Doctor John had wrought among his red-skinned subjects to reach England. Straightway Captain Sawn and his officers were conducted to the fort, where the chief factor, in the gayest of holiday moods, ordered refreshments from his closely guarded cellar and, while the wine went the rounds, listened with enthusiasm to the story of their voyage.

Soon after the ship's arrival, Captain Sawn relinquished his command to one of his officers, Aemelius Simpson, an English naval lieutenant and an exceedingly colorful figure. A born gentleman and an able leader of men, Simpson nevertheless had

certain peculiarities which caused no end of merriment at the
fort. Doctor John roared with lusty Irish mirth when he learned
that the *Cadboro's* new captain would not issue an order aboard
ship unless his hands were encased in kid gloves! And worse—
if the situation with which he had to cope chanced to be a
particularly important one, white gloves were required.[9]

No doubt the doctor was relieved that Peter Skene Ogden
was not at Vancouver just then, for surely, with his penchant
for playing practical jokes, the canny Scot would have bartered
the captain's gloves for at least a dozen prime beaver! The
chief factor was not sure how great a strain the captain's sense of
humor would stand, for he was, as it happened, a cousin to Governor George Simpson.[10]

During his sojourn at Vancouver, the immaculately clad
Simpson unwittingly contributed in no small degree toward the
agricultural progress of the community. While dining one evening with the doctor, he was reminded by one of his men of a
promise he had made to a certain young lady back in London.
It appears that during the dessert course of a farewell banquet
given in his honor, this young lady had extracted the seeds from
an apple and had laughingly presented them to Simpson with
the request that he plant them when he reached his destination
in the Northwest wilderness. The incident had been forgotten
until that moment, but when the captain's attention was called
to it by his aide, he reached into his coat pocket and there,
reposing under his kid gloves, he found the little packet of seeds.
A ripple of laughter ran around the table as he handed them
over to his host.

Doctor John was not the man to underrate such a gift. The
very next day he entrusted the apple seeds to Robert Bruce, the
venerable Scotch gardener of the fort, who planted them with
great care under glass. "By and by," wrote the doctor's daughter,
Eloisa, "my father came to me and said, 'Now we are going to

THE OLD APPLE TREE

Planted in 1826 from seeds brought to Vancouver by Captain Simpson.

have some apples.' The little things were just coming out." Soon the seedlings were taken out and planted in the ground. "My father," recalled Eloisa at a later date, "used to watch the garden so that no one would touch the tree. At first there was only one apple on it and that everyone must taste . . . but the second year we had plenty."[11] Thus, in the spirit of jest, the redoubtable white-gloved Aemelius made possible the first Oregon apple. Countless legends have sprung up around that now famous tree which soon became the pride of the chief factor's modest garden.

4

The chief factor had not forgotten Governor Simpson's ambition to establish, on the Fraser River, a post which could command the lands and waters of that rich northern fur-bearing territory. Indeed he had been waiting only for a ship large enough to carry northward an adequate supply of materials, and now, with the *Cadboro* available, he was free to push the long delayed project forward to completion. Secure in the knowledge that Vancouver had been accepted as the logical headquarters for the Hudson's Bay Company interests west of the Rockies, the White-Headed Eagle threw his whole soul into the undertaking. No longer was his first love—his precious Vancouver—in jeopardy.

In casting about for the right man to head this important expedition, he selected James McMillan, the able chief trader whom George Simpson had sent to the Fraser River in 1824. One wonders whether the doctor may not have taken a bit of sardonic pleasure in the hope that McMillan, who had failed under the governor's banner, would succeed under his own. Chosen to accompany the chief trader were the three clerks, Donald Manson, François Annance, and George Barnston as well as a score of French Canadian servants of the Company.

Carrying with them Doctor John's explicit instructions, the party embarked in small boats, leaving Vancouver on June 27, 1827. They proceeded northward to Puget Sound and thence to Port Orchard, where, by arrangement, they were to have met the *Cadboro* laden with provisions, building materials, horses, and carts. Through some misunderstanding, Captain Simpson's ship missed connections and did not pick up McMillan and his men until they had penetrated as far north as Protection Island in the Straits of Juan de Fuca. From this point the *Cadboro,* with the entire expedition, sailed through Rosario Strait into the Gulf of Georgia in search of the elusive entrance to the Fraser River.

At last, after numerous disappointments and several narrow escapes, Captain Simpson entered the river on July 24 and continued upstream for a distance of thirty miles, where the *Cadboro* was brought to anchor. James McMillan selected a likely-looking spot on the south shore as the best possible location for the new fort. Construction was begun immediately, and by the 8th of September a rectangle forty by forty-five feet had been enclosed.[12] Such was the humble beginning of Fort Langley, a post which was soon to assume significant proportions in the British fur trade, and which was to bring great credit both to McMillan and to his chief factor. The doctor was highly pleased when he learned, some weeks later, of the expedition's success. It was a distinct feather in his cap to have succeeded where Governor Simpson had failed, but his brief businesslike report of the achievement reveals no trace of braggadocio. To him it was just another routine job out of the way.

McMillan and his men struggled on into the winter with the building of the fort, battling both the elements and the neighboring Indians, who were anything but neighborly. On November 26, some days after the *Cadboro* had departed for Vancouver, the Union Jack was raised and Fort Langley was officially dedicated to the service of the Hudson's Bay Company. The routine work of trapping began immediately, and the men remained exiles until late in December, when, to their surprise and joy, Alexander McKenzie with four men arrived from Vancouver bearing the first tidings from the outside in six months as well as a congratulatory message from the chief factor. These five visitors remained at the fort over the holidays and celebrated the advent of 1828 by getting themselves royally drunk. It is to be hoped that these poor fellows enjoyed their New Year's orgy for it was destined to be their last. On their return to Vancouver, they were suddenly attacked by the Clallam Indians of Lumni Island, and all five were brutally murdered.[13]

News of the massacre was carried immediately by runners to Doctor John, who was torn between sympathy for the victims and determination to wreak vengeance upon their murderers. His decision was made promptly—these natives had broken the unwritten laws of his empire, and they must pay the price. Frank Ermatinger, a chief trader who happened to be at Vancouver just then, noted that "a muster was made of all effective men upon the ground . . . and they were told by Chief Factor McLoughlin of the necessity of going off in search of the murderous tribe . . . to make a salutary example of them, that the honour of the whites was at stake, and that if we did not succeed in the undertaking it would be dangerous to be seen by the natives any distance from the fort hereafter."[14] In our mind's eye we can see the irate doctor, storming up and down before his impromptu army, firing them with a desire for vengeance and employing, with consummate tact, the urge for self-preservation as his most effective argument.

Ever cautious, the chief factor took pains to guarantee the loyalty of his men by making the matter of service purely voluntary. "Mr. McLoughlin," wrote Ermatinger in this connection, "appears delicate in requesting anyone to go, lest an unwillingness should be shown." Apparently there was no unwillingness to serve, for the doctor succeeded in mustering a party of sixty men under the command of Chief Trader Alexander R. McLeod, and, not satisfied to leave matters solely in the hands of this sizable land force, he ordered Captain Simpson, kid gloves and all, to proceed northward with the *Cadboro*.[15] The White-Headed Eagle was taking no chances—with his "army" and "navy" in action, he felt confident of victory.

Events moved swiftly. Simpson and McLeod joined forces in the vicinity of New Dungeness on Puget Sound and started at once to track down the luckless Clallams. They succeeded, eventually, in locating the native village, and, upon demanding the murderers, they were greeted only by shouts of defiance. Instantly, McLeod's men opened fire. As a result, twenty-five of the Clallams paid with their lives for the depravity of a few members of the tribe.[16]

Though Alexander McLeod was the man directly in charge of the punitive expedition, Doctor John accepted full accountability for the massacre and incurred no end of criticism as a consequence. While he may have been overzealous in his determination to avenge the murder of McKenzie's party, he had at least one champion in C. O. Ermatinger, a nephew of Frank Ermatinger, who wrote, many years after the event, that "it would be unjust to charge Dr. McLoughlin with the responsibility for the entire proceedings of this merciless expedition. What his instructions to McLeod were that gentleman kept pretty much to himself. Unfortunately the latter showed vacillation and timidity at the moments when firmness and promptness were required, disputed and quarrelled with Captain Simpson on board his own vessel, assumed too much authority at one time, too little at another, with the result that indiscriminate slaughter and destruction of property seems to have taken the place of just and merited punishment."[17] But, having made an unfortunate choice, the White-Headed Eagle stood by him even at the risk of undermining his own standing.

He simply followed his own counsel in facing a situation that required prompt and vigorous action. Had the amateur jurist, Peter Skene Ogden, been available for consultation, he would doubtless have ruled that his "lex non scripta" justified reprisals. The massacre, of course, was unfortunate, and we can easily believe that if the doctor had been present in person, it would never have taken place. At all events, future travelers were to journey through the Clallam country without molestation.

5

But the natives in another part of the chief factor's empire were far from subdued. Some months after the Clallam affair, the doctor was roused, in the dead of the night, by a great commotion at the gates of the fort. Slipping his feet into Indian moccasins and throwing a shawl over his shoulders, he hurried downstairs and sent a servant out to discover the cause of the disturbance. Grasping a tall candelabrum and standing majestically in the open doorway of his house, he peered out into the summer night, his disengaged hand shading his eyes. In a few moments the gates were flung open and a bedraggled trapper, utterly exhausted, was escorted into the doctor's living room.

The chief factor ordered one of his French Canadians to throw some logs on the dying fire while he set about making the stranger comfortable. Drawing up a chair, he studied the poor fellow's gaunt features and tattered clothing. Not a voyageur, he mused, and not a Britisher. Perhaps an American! In a little while the man was able to speak.

Black was his name, and, as Doctor John had surmised, he was an American. He explained that he had been a member of a party of Yankee trappers headed by Jedediah S. Smith. The chief factor raised his bushy eyebrows. Jed Smith! How often he had heard Ogden, Work, and others speak of this daring adventurer!

Revived by a gulp or two of the doctor's carefully guarded whisky, Black raised himself on one elbow and went on with his tale. It was a gruesome one, and the chief factor listened with growing sympathy. Smith and his men, it developed, had been returning to their headquarters at Salt Lake. Having traveled up the Sacramento valley without finding a pass through the mountains to the eastward, they had made for the coast with their cargo of beaver skins. Hostile Indians had stolen their only axe —an implement sorely needed for making rafts—while they were encamped on the beach near the mouth of the Umpqua River. Later that same day, they had succeeded in recovering the axe and in making a prisoner of the thief. Pausing in his recital, Black asked for another drink, and the doctor obligingly passed over the forbidden decanter.

Refreshed, the American continued. On the morning following the axe episode, Smith and two of his men had started out on a reconnoitering expedition, after having issued strict orders against allowing any Indians in camp. Black himself had remained with the main party. No sooner had Smith left than several Indian women appeared on the beach, making overtures to the men. Disregarding the orders of their leader, the trappers invited the women into their camp, and, while their attention was distracted, a group of braves, creeping stealthily from behind, fell upon the whites, killing them to a man and quickly making away with their furs. Black alone had escaped by swimming the Umpqua after a desperate hand-to-hand encounter with three red men. He held out scant hope for the safety of Smith and his two followers in spite of the fact that they had not returned before the massacre.

With folded arms, Doctor John heard the story out. Making

no comment, he rose and paced slowly before the fire, his brow furrowed. Once again the redskins had broken his laws, and once again they must be punished. To him it made no difference that their victims had been his bitterest rivals in trade—justice must be done, and promptly. Without uttering a word, the chief factor crossed the room, climbed the stairs and threw himself on his bed. Vancouver settled back into the drowsy stillness of the August night while the doctor tossed about, unable to sleep. Smith must be found, dead or alive, and his property recovered! Not until he had worked out his plan of attack did he drop off.

He was up early the next morning. His first act was to send Indian runners with tobacco to the Willamette chiefs, ordering them to go out in search of Smith and his companions. The chiefs were given to understand that if any harm came to the Americans, provided they were found alive, the red men themselves would suffer. On the other hand, a handsome reward would be paid for their safe return to Vancouver. The discerning White-Headed Eagle knew how to handle his subjects.

Later in the day, having assembled a party of forty well armed men, Doctor John was on the point of sending them packing after the Willamettes as an extra precaution when, to his utter amazement, Smith and his two men came wandering into the fort. With outstretched hands, the chief factor greeted this tall Yankee and bade him welcome to Fort Vancouver. In his soul he thanked God for the safe deliverance of this intrepid rival whom, no doubt, the Hudson's Bay Company would have been happy to see out of the way. In that moment, Jed Smith was no enemy to the doctor, whatever he may have been to the company. He was simply an unfortunate human being standing in the need of friendly assistance.

The gaunt visitor, on his part, was deeply moved by his host's kindly reception. A character as colorful as any the West had yet produced, Jed Smith was indeed a strange mixture. A loyal American and a rough Indian trader, he was, at the same time, an ardent Methodist who engaged in daily prayer and invoked divine favor at his meals.[18] As a partner of Sublette and Jackson, he had already distinguished himself in the growing fur trade of the Missouri valley. The chief factor, whose impressions of men were as quick as they were accurate, took Jed Smith's measure at a glance and concluded that he liked him.[19]

6

In his handling of the expedition to retrieve Smith's property, Doctor John again revealed his uncanny insight into Indian character. To the commanding officer of his scouting party, John McLeod, he gave sealed instructions which were to be opened only upon the expedition's arrival at the Umpqua. A puzzled look came over the officer's face, but the doctor, with a smile and a shrug of his broad shoulders, explained that if the men knew in advance what was expected of them, the information might leak out to their Indian wives and eventually find its way to the ears of the hostile red men.

If John McLeod succumbed to the human temptation to peek at the forbidden paper under his coat, he at least kept the secret, for the doctor's plan worked well. When the Indians were discovered, they were invited to trade just as if nothing out of the ordinary had happened. Of the furs acquired in trade, many bore the distinguishing mark of Smith's company. For these the Hudson's Bay men, acting under the chief factor's orders, refused payment on the ground that they had been stolen from the Americans. With wounded dignity the Indians disclaimed any knowledge of either the theft or the murders but admitted that they had bought the furs in good faith from another tribe. McLeod refused to part with Smith's property, suggesting to the Indians that payment be extracted from the murderers.

Again the White-Headed Eagle had triumphed. The immediate result was that hostilities broke out between the rival tribes and the offenders were doubtless punished more severely than they would have been had the Hudson's Bay men intervened. Jed Smith's furs, valued at $3,200, were restored to him, and the Indians in still another quarter of the West were grimly reminded that they had a master capable of ruling them.[20]

Doctor John, prompted only by his conception of Christian duty, had performed the first of his many unselfish acts of kindness toward an American citizen.

CHAPTER IX

PLAGUE, PILLAGE, AND PROPAGANDA

I

JEDEDIAH SMITH found himself marooned at Fort Vancouver for the winter. With numerous commercial interests clamoring for his presence elsewhere, we can well believe that he was none too happy over his forced exile, but there was no chance to leave until the departure of the spring express the following March. He could only remain as the doctor's guest.

Between Vancouver's chief factor and the visiting Yankee, there soon developed a strong and lasting friendship. They were men of the same general stamp—able, courageous, and unreservedly loyal to their respective interests—and these very similarities of character led quite naturally to a mutual attitude of congenial rivalry. Each in his own way set out to learn what he could of the other's affairs. Smith, of course, had the advantage since he was on the ground and hence in a strategic position to observe the Hudson's Bay Company methods in operation. No one could have guarded trade secrets from this alert Yankee.

So observant was Jed Smith, in fact, that when he finally left Vancouver, he was able to send to his government in Washington an amazingly accurate account of the progress Doctor John had been making on the Columbia. "The crop of 1828," he penned in his comprehensive report, "was 700 bu. of wheat. The grain full and plump and making good flour; fourteen acres of corn, the same number of acres of peas, 8 acres of oats, 4 or 5 acres of barley and a fine garden. Some small apple trees and grape vines. The ensuing spring 80 bu. of seed wheat were sown and they had about 200 head of cattle, 52 horses and breeding mares, 300 head of hogs, 14 goats, the usual domestic fowls. They have mechanics, viz: coopers, blacksmiths, gunsmiths, carpenters, tinners and bakers, a good saw mill on the bank of the river 5 miles above, a grist mill worked by hand, but intended to work by water. Their influence on the Indians is now decisive. Of this the Americans have constant and striking proofs, in the preference which they give to the British in every particular." [1]

Had Smith been a reporter sent out to cover the Northwest, he could scarcely have written a more enticing description of the country or a more convincing account of Doctor John as an empire builder. Of the various reports destined to arouse a quickening interest in Oregon, his, if not the first, was at all events the most alluring. Among the earliest to be inspired by his words were Nathaniel J. Wyeth, the Yankee skipper, and Hall J. Kelley, the Boston schoolmaster. Within a few years the doctor was to greet them both at Vancouver.

But the chief factor, during this time, was not asleep. He seized every opportunity to talk with his Yankee boarder and to obtain from him opinions regarding the future settlement of the Columbia River country by Americans. For that matter, Jed Smith had nothing to hide. While he was shrewd enough to observe that the Hudson's Bay Company meant to protect its interests at any cost, he was well aware of the treaty of joint occupation, and he knew that if his countrymen could not successfully compete in fur trading, they could at least attempt to colonize the country. That they would do so seemed to him a foregone conclusion, and he saw no reason to avoid a frank discussion of the inevitable. However that may be, Doctor John, from 1828 onward, anticipated Yankee settlement and prepared for it.[2] The wonder of it is that so long a time elapsed before the first covered wagon came lumbering over the old Oregon Trail.

2

On October 25, 1828, during Jed Smith's sojourn at the fort, Governor Simpson arrived on his second tour of inspection. As he had traveled toward Vancouver, this time by the northern route, he had been favorably impressed by the various posts of Doctor John's western empire. If the doctor could have seen the communication his chief penned shortly after his arrival, he would have been pleased though perhaps a bit puzzled.

"The Honble Co^y's affairs at the different places I visited," wrote George Simpson on November 17, "were in a prosperous state, and the Natives on this side of the Mountains are I am happy to say more quiet and orderly than heretofore, this favorable change in their conduct toward us, arises more from the fear of punishment should they continue their outrages, than good will or improved disposition as their whole character is marked by crime of the Blackest Dye." [3]

Granted that the governor had passed through some of the Columbia department's most hostile territory, his sweeping condemnation of the red man's character seems difficult to reconcile with his former high opinion of certain native leaders. Even more surprising is his utter disregard of the progress Doctor John had made toward civilizing the western tribes through a humane and enlightened rule. No doubt Simpson had already been advised of the Clallam and Umpqua affairs, and he may, therefore, have assumed such lawlessness to be universal. At least he recognized the results of his chief factor's work, however little he may have understood the methods employed to bring them about. Gradually we are drawn to the conclusion that George Simpson never really knew John McLoughlin.

By this time, the governor had abandoned once and for all

his dream of locating the principal western depot on the Fraser River. Not only had he been told that his company would make no effort to encroach upon the exclusive rights of the East India Company with a view toward securing the Canton trade, but he had himself visited the river on his journey to the Pacific. Apparently his disillusionment had been complete.

"Frasers and Thompsons Rivers which were never passed until this season by my Canoes," he wrote in this same letter of November 17, "are found exceedingly dangerous even to perfectly light Craft under the most skilful management, & in the most favorable state of the water, & cannot under any circumstances be attempted by loaded Craft."[4] At last the Fraser River site had given way to Vancouver, and Doctor John's will had prevailed.

Coincident with the final decision to make the Columbia River post the company's permanent western headquarters came the resolve to move it to a location nearer the water's edge.

Undoubtedly this matter was finally settled between the governor and his chief factor in the fall of 1828, and, though the work of building the new stockade and houses may have been commenced immediately, it is not likely that the project was completed until well into 1829, after both Governor Simpson and Jed Smith had departed. It is singular that the letters of neither make any mention of the transfer—certainly one of the major events of their visit.

Shortly after his arrival at the post, George Simpson concerned himself with the lot of furs Doctor John had retrieved from the Indians for Jed Smith. The doctor, in performing this service, had been prompted solely by motives of altruism. His only thought had been to lend a helping hand to an unfortunate fellow human being—the same treatment he would have expected had the circumstances been reversed. The governor, however, was too much the efficient executive to overlook the business aspects involved, and though he had his way, we can imagine that Doctor John, chagrined and embarrassed, argued eloquently against it.

However that may be, the close-figuring governor, in a letter addressed to Jed Smith and dated December 26, 1828, reviewed the whole matter, emphasizing particularly the hazards assumed in recovering the property, the time lost, and the expense entailed. He then proceeded to remind Smith that his company had asked no fee for its services though "either in Law or Equity we should be fully entitled to Salvage." Gradually building his case, he took occasion to let the American know that Doctor John's officer in charge, John McLeod, had "learnt that the Melancholy catastrophe was occasioned by some harsh treatment on the part of your people toward the Indians who visited your Camp some of whom they said had been beaten, and one of them bound hands & feet for some very slight offense." Apparently the governor, for business reasons, found it convenient to exempt these treacherous Umpquas from his "Blackest Dye" pronouncement of a few months earlier.

It remained only for him to observe, with reference to Smith's property, that "Your Beaver . . . is of very bad quality the worst indeed I ever saw, having in the first instance been very badly dressed & since then exposed to every storm of Rain that has fallen between the Month of April & the 22nd Inst." The stage was now set for a magnanimous offer. "I am willing," wrote the governor, "to take [the beaver] off your hands at 3 Dollars p Skin payable by Bill at 30% sight on Canada, which I conceive to be their full value at this place, and your Horses I will take at £2 St^g p Head payable in like manner." And then, in a final burst of sportsmanship, he concluded with what must have struck the Yankee as a particularly empty alternative. "But if these terms are not satisfactory to you," wound up the lengthy communication, "the Furs may be left here until you have an opportunity of removing them & the Horses are at your disposal where you left them."[5] For the disappointed Smith, it was Hobson's choice.

The question of whether or not the Yankee trader was treated unfairly seems unimportant compared with the contrast between the final settlement he was forced to take and the one he might have received had Doctor John been permitted to deal with him single-handed. In the light of the chief factor's subsequent acts of charity, it involves no tax upon the imagination to picture him sending Smith off over the mountains with his furs and horses and perhaps with a Hudson's Bay escort! That much would to him have seemed a moral obligation. It might have been poor business, according to George Simpson's view, but it would most assuredly have been good diplomacy. Smith, after all, was an American, and the White-Headed Eagle was looking far ahead to the time when Yankee good will would mean something.

3

During the month of February, 1829, the chief factor received word that the American brig *Owyhee,* commanded by Captain John Dominis, had entered the river and had begun a vigorous trade with the Clatsops and Chinooks.[6] As this was the first Yankee vessel to crash the gates of his empire since he had assumed charge, he was naturally concerned and lost no time in paying the captain a visit, ostensibly to extend a welcome but actually, we suspect, to ascertain how great a threat to the company's trade the intruder might prove.

Captain Dominis, a swarthy giant of Italian origin, was a man of consequence. Though this was his first visit to the Columbia in some years, he had been trading spasmodically in Northwest waters since 1820. His ship was the property of Josiah Marshall of Boston, and Dominis had worked up from the forecastle to a master's commission in the service of his chief. A typical sailor, he had "wives" in many ports, but the favorite of his far-flung harem resided in Hawaii. In fact his son by her, John C. Dominis, was later to become the Beau Brummell of the Islands and the husband of Queen Liliuokalani.[7]

The conference aboard the *Owyhee* came to naught. No sooner had the formalities of introduction been completed than Doctor John offered to buy Dominis out, suggesting that payment be made in lumber which the mill at Vancouver had already begun to produce. But the Yankee skipper was something of a diplomat on his own account. Charged by his Boston superiors to "make a stand" in the river at any cost, he thought it wiser to discuss the doctor's proposal at some length but to substitute terms which he knew would not be acceptable to the Hudson's Bay Company. Accordingly, he offered to sell out provided payment could be made either in furs or in sterling exchange. It is not surprising that the negotiations resulted in nothing more tangible than pleasant conversation.[8]

Nevertheless, the visit with Captain Dominis was not entirely wasted for, during the course of their parley, Doctor John picked up two useful bits of information. One was that the *Convoy,* Josiah Marshall's other ship, commanded by Captain D. W. Thompson, was due within the month, and the other was that an extremely wealthy fur-bearing area lay to the northward in Russian America along the banks of the Stikine River. Doubtless this hint, invaluable to a competitor, was inadvertently dropped by Dominis, but the doctor, quick to follow up any advantage, promptly relayed the news to Governor Simpson.[9] It is quite possible that the initial urge to extend the Hudson's Bay Company activities into Alaskan waters sprang from this impulsive remark of the captain's.

A short time later the *Owyhee* sailed up the Columbia only to run aground at Deer Island, some thirty miles below Vancouver. Doctor John, hearing of Dominis's plight, not only dispatched a party of half-breeds to help pull the vessel off but also sent, with his compliments, some potatoes and a quarter of beef. Immediately, F. A. Lemont, one of the *Owyhee*'s crew, not to be outdone in hospitality, presented the chief factor with three young peach trees he had brought from San Juan Fernandez.[10] These were planted by the conscientious Bruce and proved a welcome reinforcement to Vancouver's orchard.

In due course the *Convoy* arrived in the river, and the two American navigators, following a lucrative trade with the natives, departed early in the summer on voyages up the coast. Doctor John hoped he had seen the last of them, but the *Owyhee* returned in the autumn of 1829 to winter near Deer Island while the *Convoy* proceeded to the Hawaiian Islands.[11] Although Captain Dominis, during his sojourn of nine months in Oregon, succeeded in gathering a cargo of furs and salmon valued at $96,000, he was forced by his British competitors to pay dearly. "On our arrival here," wrote Captain Thompson of the *Convoy* to his chief in Boston, "the English were getting six large Beavers for one Blanket and twenty for a musket, but opposition has reduced it to ¼ of the former price. Our cargo, the most of it, is suitable for the market—Blankets, Muskets, Powder, Shot, Blue Cloth &c are the leading articles."[12] To the whites this warfare was ruinous, but to the Indians it must have seemed as if the millennium had at last arrived. They, in truth, were the sole beneficiaries.

During this troubled period, the doctor fought the Americans at every turn, and, greatly as he deplored the attendant demoralization of the trade, he managed to hold his share of the business. Indeed he showed the Yankees that two could play at the game of "spoiling the Indians." So zealous was he, in his determination to guard the company's interests, that he was accused of resorting to unethical methods. Comcomly and Casseno, influenced by the British, had taught their people that only Hudson's Bay Company vessels were permitted to trade in the river and, while many of the natives were tempted by the attractive prices Dominis quoted, others were actually afraid to offer their skins for sale except at Fort George or Vancouver. We can readily believe the doctor guilty of keeping this notion alive, but it seems unlike him—as one writer intimates[13]—to have planted the thought in the minds of the red men that the great plague of 1829–32 was traceable directly to the visit of the Boston ships. Nevertheless, when the principal chief of the Willamette tribe, firm in his conviction that such action would be pleasing to the Hudson's Bay men, proposed to cut off the *Owyhee,* the White-Headed Eagle rebuked him severely.

When the *Owyhee* finally sailed for Boston on March 29, 1830, "after giving us," as Doctor John expressed it, "an immensity of trouble," [14] she took leave of a sadder but wiser chief factor. Beyond any doubt the Yankees had played havoc with the trade. In a letter addressed to the "Governor & Committee" and dated October 11, 1830, the doctor mournfully observes that "we can never bring the Indians to the old prices of five Beaver for one Blanket, and I do not know if ever we will be able to increase the present price of one Large Beaver for a Blanket" and later in the same communication, he laments the condition prevailing since the *Owyhee*'s departure. "We have no opposition," runs the dispatch, "but we have been obliged to keep our parties running to Indians as much as ever to prevent their having any number of skins in the event of another coaster coming here." [15] He had learned his lesson in the hard school of experience, and never again was a Yankee skipper to catch him unprepared.

Captain Dominis's voyage had one interesting result with regard to the international situation. When he arrived in Boston, many months later, the United States customs officials of that port attempted to assess a duty on his cargo of salmon. Josiah Marshall made a vigorous protest, but President Jackson's comptroller of the treasury ruled that since the fish had been caught by natives in a section of the Columbia which "was not claimed as a part of the territory of the United States, they must be regarded as foreign-caught fish." [16] We can only guess what encouragement this letter would have given the Hudson's Bay leaders could they have seen it!

4

In the spring of 1829, while the *Owyhee* was lying at anchor near Deer Island, an epidemic of fever and ague broke out with sudden and devastating virulence. Because it originated among the Indians camped near the American vessel, a story soon spread from tribe to tribe to the effect that the Yankee sailors had emptied "a vial of bad medicine" into the river with the avowed design of destroying the native population. [17] The Americans naturally suspected the British of having invented this fiction. While it is quite possible that some of the Hudson's Bay employees, aroused by the advent of vigorous competition, may have allowed the hoax to circulate freely, it is difficult to conceive of savages so dull as to believe it, especially since they realized only too well how completely Captain Dominis and his crew depended upon them for furs and salmon. Nevertheless, absurd as it was, the story gained headway as the plague spread, and it would no doubt have gone hard with the Boston visitors had not Doctor John interceded on their behalf.

But some of the Indians were led to believe that all of their trouble could be chalked up against the British themselves. It so happened that the outbreak of the plague coincided not only with the arrival of the *Owyhee* but also with the first extensive upturning of the soil near Vancouver for cultivation. Out of this development grew the highly fantastic notion that the epidemic was directly traceable to the liberating of malevolent forces long held securely within the earth.[18] Here, beyond a doubt, was a Heaven-sent opportunity for the hard-pressed Yankees to divert the native mind from the "vial of medicine" fable, and they doubtless made the most of it. We can only assume that such a battle of propaganda took place between the opposing white forces on the Columbia, but, if it did, the British came out on top. Up and down the river, their prestige remained impregnable.

Throughout the remainder of 1829 and during the three years following, the plague continued with increasing fury. Whole villages were wiped out, and the loss of native life was enormous. Simon Plomondon, an old Hudson's Bay employee, reported to James Douglas that "in 1830 . . . the living sufficed not to bury their dead, but fled in terror to the sea-coast, abandoning the dead and dying to the birds and beasts of prey. Every village presented a scene harrowing to the feelings; the canoes were there drawn up upon the beach, the nets extended on the willow-boughs to dry, the very dogs appeared, as ever, watchful, but there was not the cheerful sound of the human voice." [19]

It was a dismal prospect for the overworked chief factor, who wrote, on October 11, 1830, to the "Governor & Committee" that "the Intermitting Fever (for the first time since the trade of this Department was established) has appeared at this place and carried off three-fourths of the Indian population in our vicinity." The malady, however, was not confined to the natives, for "at present," we read further in the doctor's letter, "there are fifty-two of our people on the sick list, in which number is Mr. Ogden, but thanks be to God for his great goodness all our people are on the convalescent list." [20] With all respect to the religious fervor of Doctor John, it appears that the Almighty had less to do with the sparing of British life than the immunity built up by these hardy fur traders against disease. Lacking such defensive armor, the Indians were mowed down relentlessly.

On the doctor himself fell the heavy burden of caring for the company's employees on the sick roll as well as for the many natives who, in desperation, flocked to the fort. George T. Allan, the young clerk whom his chief had educated in the rudiments of medicine, noted that "at one time we had over forty men laid up . . . and a great number of Indian applicants for 'la médecine'; and as there was then no physician at the fort, Dr. McLoughlin himself had to officiate in that capacity, although he disliked it, as it greatly interfered with his other important duties, until he was himself attacked with the fever, when he appointed me his deputy; and I well remember my tramps through the men's houses with my pockets lined with vials of quinine, and making my reports of the state of the patients to the doctor." [21]

Allan, however, did not make this observation until 1832, after the plague had been raging through the country for three long years. Prior to that time, according to his reminiscences, there had been no quinine at Vancouver, and the doctor, resourceful as always, had been forced to employ the roots of the dogwood tree as a substitute.[22] Indeed we marvel that the White-Headed Eagle, driven to such extremities, was able to save any of his cases at the fort; but his letters mention no deaths among the whites.

With the natives, however, things went from bad to worse until the harassed doctor, torn between his sympathy for them and his natural concern over sanitary conditions, was compelled to send them away from the vicinity of the fort. "The Indians," he wrote on November 24, 1830, "who were frightened at the mortality amongst them came in numbers to camp alongside of us, giving as a reason that if they died they knew we would bury them.

Most reluctantly on our part we were obliged to drive them away." [23]

It must have caused the chief factor intense mental torture to issue this order. He had made heroic efforts to save his subjects—in truth, no man could have done more—but their own peculiar notions of how to cure the disease had persisted. From the very beginning of the epidemic, these poor natives, terror-stricken and crazed with fever, had fallen into the habit of plunging headlong into the river to cool their burning bodies, and few were able to survive the colds which inevitably followed.[24] The White-Headed Eagle was powerless to change their ways, and all the dogwood root and quinine in Christendom would have availed nothing after those icy immersions in the Columbia.

During the plague years from 1829 to 1832, nine-tenths of the Indians residing on the river below Celilo were swept away.[25] Most men would, at the first opportunity, have quitted a scene so depressing, but the doctor was not of that stamp.

5

Toward the end of March, 1829—before either the plague or the ruinous Yankee competition had commenced in earnest—Governor Simpson and Jedediah Smith departed from Vancouver with the annual express. Whatever Smith's feelings toward the governor may have been, he was so grateful to Doctor John for the hospitality extended him at the fort and especially for the prompt recovery of his furs in the original instance, that he ordered his own company, Jackson, Sublette, and Smith, to confine its trapping and trading activities to the territory east of the Rockies in the future. That the doctor may have anticipated such a result when he sent John McLeod after Smith's property does not detract from the Christian charity of his act, however much it enhances our opinion of his business judgment. He had formed a high opinion of Jed Smith, and no one could have felt more sincerely grieved when the daring Yankee trader was killed by the Comanches on the Cimarron in 1831.[26]

Even before Governor Simpson had reached Vancouver on his second tour of inspection where he was to meet Jed Smith so unexpectedly, he had received a mandate from his superiors in London to investigate the possibilities of settlement south of the Columbia. "The Country on the West of the Mountains remaining common to the Americans and us for an indefinite period," the "Governor & Committee" had written him in 1828, ". . . it becomes an important object to acquire as ample an occupation of the Country and Trade as possible, on the South as well as on the North side of the Columbia River, looking always to the Northern side falling to our Share on a division, and to secure this, it may be as well to have something to give up on the South when the final arrangement comes to be made." [27]

With this bit of company policy to guide them, George Simpson and Doctor John probed Jed Smith for information regarding the future intentions of his countrymen. Smith evidently convinced them that nothing could stop a substantial American migration to Oregon for, in his final instructions to the doctor before leaving Vancouver, Governor Simpson, after urging further development of the timber trade, suggested that "the Saw Mill will require Eight men and should be kept constantly at Work, as I expect that fully as much advantage will be derived from the Timber as from the Coasting Fur Trade and if you find that in its present situation it cannot produce the quantity required, it will be well to remove it to the Falls of the Willhamet (south of the Columbia) where the same Establishment of people can attend to the Mill, watch the Fur & Salmon Trade, and take care of a Stock of Cattle, indeed the sooner you remove it to the Willhamet I think the better." [28]

The real motive of the Hudson's Bay Company appears to have been the securing to itself of the water-power privileges at Willamette Falls, and the conscientious governor had hit upon the sawmill project as perhaps the least objectionable means of carrying out the wishes of his superiors. Having passed the suggestion along to his chief factor, George Simpson could quit Vancouver satisfied that he had followed instructions. Doctor John, however, could not embark lightly upon this undertaking. Well did he know that it signified a complete reversal of his company's previous policy, and he must have realized, even then, the complications certain to arise with the advent of American settlers. Indeed it appealed to him—the one man upon whose shoulders the ultimate responsibility for such an act would fall—as a matter deserving of sober consideration.

Through the summer and autumn he hesitated, perhaps hoping that the annual express might bring a revocation of the order, but if such was his motive in delaying, he was doomed to disappointment. Finally, in December, he took possession of a tract of land strategically located at the picturesque falls of the Willamette, and, from Vancouver, he dispatched a party of men who built three log houses and cut timber for the mill. The work progressed slowly, and, at every turn, the Hudson's Bay employees encountered stubborn opposition from the Indians, who resented bitterly what they construed as an unwarranted invasion of their domain. So hostile did they become that, during the second winter, they burned both the log houses and the cut timber. In spite of these setbacks, potatoes were planted in the spring of 1830, and a mill race was blasted from the head of the island in 1832.[29]

Because it served to identify Doctor John personally with what was eventually to become American territory, the staking of this claim in the name of the Hudson's Bay Company was to prove, in future years, one of the most unfortunate acts of his career. Long after he had become an American citizen, it was to embarrass and embitter him and, beyond a doubt, to shorten his life.

CHAPTER X

WARRIOR AND DIPLOMAT

I

IN his parting letter of instructions to Vancouver's chief factor —the same letter in which he had urged the establishment of a sawmill on the Willamette—Governor Simpson had gone out of his way to praise the doctor's efforts. "Your whole administration," ran the opening paragraph of this important bit of correspondence, "is marked by its close adherence to the spirit of the Govr & Committees wishes and intentions and it is conspicuous for a talent in planning and for an activity & perseverance in execution which reflect the highest credit on your judgment and habits of business."

We can picture the good doctor peering incredulously through his gold-rimmed spectacles at the folded sheet and wondering if perhaps the chief had sent the wrong letter. To say the least, it was not what he had expected; and, as he read on, his astonishment mounted, for the governor had concluded his opening remarks in an even more generous vein. "I do no more than my duty," he had written, as if apologizing for his laudatory mood, "to you, to the concern at large, and to myself."[1]

No one knew better than Doctor John himself how unlike the chief it was to scatter praise indiscriminately, and hence these observations must have been deeply appreciated. It would seem that the old differences between the two company leaders had, for the moment, been forgotten. At perhaps no other period in their long association were their personal relations more cordial. Save for the governor's treatment of Jed Smith and for the doctor's reluctance to settle in the country south of the Columbia, there had been little to foment discord between them since the fate of Vancouver had been settled. On the other hand, George Simpson could scarcely have been other than well pleased with what he had seen in the Columbia department, and we can readily believe that his outspoken approval of the doctor's work had been penned in all sincerity.

In the chief factor's house at Fort Vancouver, during the winter of 1828–29, Doctor John had worked out, in collaboration with his chief, extensive plans for the future, and the results of these deliberations are clearly set forth in this same lengthy communication. Nothing that offered any hope of strengthening the British position in Oregon had been overlooked. The men in the field, for instance, were instructed to meet American competition everywhere and especially "to have on hand a larger stock of luxuries than usual to meet the demands of the American trappers, with such little necessaries as they are likely to be deficient in"—an ingenious scheme designed to secure a good share of the American furs.

Also from this letter we learn that Peter Skene Ogden's illness had forced John Work to relieve him as commander of the Snake Expedition. "Mr. Work," according to the general orders, "should endeavor to draw off any of the late deserters found attached to American camps—also if any respectable American trappers wish to join the Expedition there can be no objection if they deposit skins to cover the supplies they receive." No doubt the intrepid Ogden, recalling the numbers he had lost to the Yankees in 1826, derived some satisfaction from this new policy even though he was forced to lie idly by and watch his colleague put it into execution.

Further development of the agricultural project is urged, and a goal of "8000 bushels of grain p Annum" is set. The doctor is cautioned—quite needlessly—against killing any cattle until "our stock . . . amounts to 600 head and our Piggery enables us to cure 10,000 lb. of Pork p^r Annum." Doctor John himself probably requested that this admonition be put down in writing, for Governor Simpson notes that "I am aware that some little dissatisfaction has been occasioned by your refusing to Slaughter Cattle for the Shipping from England," but he hastens to add that "both you and I can say that so anxious have we been to increase our Stock, that neither of us has ever indulged ourselves by tasting either Beef or Veal." Only on rare occasions does the governor, in his voluminous correspondence, condescend to link his name with the doctor's in so human a fashion.

Then, after suggesting that the chief factor construct two vessels of 200 tons each for the lumber trade, the ambitious chief executive brings his long list of recommendations to a close by directing that "the 'Cadboro' or 'William & Anne,' whichever arrives in the Columbia first is to be sent at once for the returns of Frazers River, touching, within the Gulf of Georgia, wherever skins are likely to be, so as to anticipate the *Owyhee,* Capt. Dominies, now lying at the mouth of the Columbia." [2]

There can be no gainsaying that much of this long communication represented the doctor's own seasoned thoughts upon the affairs of his department, and it could scarcely have been other than galling to read them set down in such a manner as to indicate that George Simpson's mind had conceived them in their entirety. But, fortunately for both himself and the company, he was not inclined, at that time, to harbor personal grievances or to indulge in petty jealousies. His one ambition was to build a trade in the West that would do credit to the Hudson's Bay Company, and, in the mandate before him, he saw the path to this goal clearly charted. The authorship of the document was of small importance; the attainment of its objectives was paramount. Such was the White-Headed Eagle's frame of mind when Governor Simpson, for the second time, left him to work out the destinies of the Columbia department alone.

2

But if he had hoped to bask serenely for a little while in the afterglow of the governor's pleasant comments, his desire was stillborn. Scarcely had the ubiquitous Simpson started on his eastward journey, in the latter part of March, when one of Donald Manson's men arrived at Vancouver with the sinister news that the Hudson's Bay Company's bark, the *William and Anne*, had been wrecked in attempting to cross the bar of the Columbia.[3] It was a real blow to the doctor, who had been counting heavily on this vessel to help the *Cadboro*, also due in the river, make things difficult for the Yankee skipper, John Dominis. Manson's scout brought no details—merely the bare fact of the disaster.

Immediately the chief factor organized a party to investigate the wreck; but before it was ready to start down the river, the ship *Convoy* arrived with a more complete account of what had happened. Captain Thompson and his officers explained that they had crossed into the river just behind the *William and Anne*. Through the mist of the late afternoon they had seen her strike a sand spit and list dangerously while the heavy surf pounded against her sides. Then, having safely negotiated the bar themselves, they had sent back a boat with the hope of rescuing the unfortunate souls aboard the stranded vessel but, in the face of ugly weather and oncoming darkness, the boat party had been forced to turn back. By the following morning it had become apparent that the entire crew of the British bark had perished.[4]

When the doctor reached Fort George with his expedition, he found that Donald Manson had already gathered further particulars regarding the wreck from Chowa, a princess of the Chinook tribe. This loyal Indian woman, a daughter of old Comcomly and the former wife of McKenzie, one of the Astor partners, had hurried to Fort George with the news that the Clatsop Indians had seized the entire cargo of the ill-fated British bark.[5] Manson had verified the princess's story, but, very wisely, he had awaited his chief's arrival before taking action.

Doctor John soon became convinced that the Clatsops, whom he knew to be treacherous and hostile, had not only commandeered the goods from the wrecked vessel but wantonly murdered her crew. Whether Princess Chowa reported the alleged tragedy or whether it was simply a surmise born of the moment, we cannot say. At all events, the explanation offered at the time—and the one the doctor believed to his dying day—was that the crew had landed safely at Clatsop Point with wet firearms and that, in this defenceless condition, they had been brutally massacred by the Indians, who wanted no interference in the work of salvaging the cargo.[6]

His quick Irish temper aroused, the chief factor was in no mood to proceed cautiously. At the head of his small scouting party, he went immediately to the camp of the Clatsops and demanded restoration of the stolen property. The red men who came out to meet him were insolent and not only refused to part with their spoil but insisted that, according to Indian law, they were entitled to whatever the ocean washed up on the beach. Here was defiance of a type certain to set the White-Headed Eagle on fire. Rising to his full height and brandishing his huge cane menacingly, he reminded the Clatsop leaders that he, not they, made the laws in British Oregon, whereupon one of the younger chiefs tossed over an old tin dipper with the boast that nothing more would be forthcoming.[7]

The doctor calmed down a bit, however, when he realized how little avail his small force would prove against the scores of hostile Clatsops. So, after warning the savages that they would be punished if the stolen goods were not restored promptly, he returned to Vancouver to await a more favorable chance for administering justice. During their sojourn at Clatsop Point, the doctor's men found one of the *William and Anne's* boats lying on the beach with its own oars intact—convincing evidence that the crew had reached shore in safety. Although the chief factor did not openly accuse them of murder, the Clatsops, divining his suspicions, insisted repeatedly that the ship's boat was washed ashore.[8] Their very manner suggested guilt, and we can scarcely blame the doctor for suspecting them.

During the spring and summer of 1829, Doctor John fretted over the Clatsop affair. Devoutly he hoped that the red men would spare him the necessity of chastising them by returning the stolen goods to Fort George, but, as the weeks passed, it became apparent that they had no intention of doing so. Once again the White-Headed Eagle's authority was at stake. Such a situation he could not long abide. Circumstances, however, forced him to delay his administration of justice for, though the *Cadboro* had reached Vancouver on schedule, the brigade from the interior was not expected until June.[9] Without substantial reinforcements, he could not hope to make a sufficiently impressive stand against the natives.

At length all was in readiness. Immediately upon the arrival of the brigade, the doctor dispatched the *Cadboro*, still commanded by the white-gloved Simpson, and an expedition nearly a hundred strong under James Connolly, down to recover the company's stolen goods. We can only imagine how bitterly he must have resented the fever epidemic which held him chained to his medical duties at the fort.

Nevertheless, Captain Simpson and James Connolly did good work without their chief. The schooner was proudly brought to anchor in front of the Clatsop village, and, under cover of her guns, a boat party was landed. The natives, still defiant, opened fire, but luckily the Hudson's Bay men succeeded in making their way back to the ship in safety. That night a council of war was held aboard the *Cadboro,* and in the morning, at a given signal, Captain Simpson began to bombard the village. Protected by this barrage, the boat party made another landing, and this time the Indians fled to the woods in terror. A few of them were killed in the skirmish, but the whites came through the ordeal without casualties. Connolly then ordered his men to search the deserted village, where they found a part of the *William and Anne's* cargo.[10]

Although the Clatsops received rather light punishment for the crime they were supposed to have committed, especially in view of the insolent manner they had assumed, the lesson was not lost. Indeed, when the British ship *Isabella* was wrecked on Clatsop Point the following year, her crew was not molested.[11] The White-Headed Eagle was still the undisputed chief of all the tribes under him.

3

The thoughtful boy of Rivière du Loup had traveled far from the little farmhouse on the shore of the St. Lawrence, but he had never forgotten his own people. Difficult as it had been to maintain contact with his mother, he had written to her by each annual express, and, through her, he had kept in touch with his Canadian kinsfolk. Years before, in 1817, he had deeded his share of his father's estate—three modest tracts of land in Rivière du Loup—to each of his three younger sisters.[12] One of these, Julie, had married a farmer, Jean-Marie Michaud, of St. André, the parish nearest Rivière du Loup. It appears that the young couple had given the doctor a mortgage on their farm at St. André and this he had held until Michaud's untimely death. Then, in 1829, while so many difficulties were raising their heads to torment him, he took occasion to remember both his mother and his widowed sister in a manner eminently befitting his nature. To his agent in St. André, M. Pierre Canac Marquis, he wrote on March 20, 1829, as follows:

Dear Sir:

I Beg to inform you that I make over all claims rights and pretensions to the Mortgage I have of one hundred pounds Halifax currency on the land or farm of the Deceased Jean-Marie Michaud with whatever on the same may be due by you to my Mother Mistress Angélique McLoughlin with whom or her agent you will be pleased to settle all accounts relating to it—as it is to her that it belongs.

I am Sir,

Yours truly,

JOHN McLOUGHLIN [13]

So it was that the doctor severed the last physical tie connecting him with the scenes of his boyhood. Though he may have heaved a nostalgic sigh as he affixed his name to the letter, we can believe that the performance of so generous an act on behalf of his own brought him real pleasure. At the very least it afforded him a welcome though momentary relief from the drab routine of chastising rebellious Indians and of thwarting the plans of marauding Yankees.

4

Few were the events of those crowded and turbulent years that Doctor John could recall with any degree of gratification, but to this rule there was one notable exception. It was the arrival, early in 1830, of James Douglas, who came this time not as a visitor but as a permanent member of the staff. His coming marked the beginning of a close association that was to last as long as the doctor remained in charge at Vancouver.

The way for Douglas had been opened by the resignation of Edward Ermatinger, who had for some time been in charge of the company's accounts at the Columbia River post.[14] After the departure of Ermatinger in the fall of 1829, Doctor John gave serious consideration to the problem of finding a successor. It was no simple task. The position itself was an important one, and, as the chief factor reviewed in his own mind the talents of each of the thirty-two men under him, he realized that none had just the proper balance of qualifications. None of them, for that matter, could be spared from the work they were then doing. It was but natural, in the circumstances, for the doctor to turn to Douglas, whose career he had been following with a fatherly interest ever since the old days at Fort William. Indeed, from the time the promising young clerk first visited the Columbia in 1826, it had been one of Doctor John's secret desires to lure him away from New Caledonia.

Though Douglas's orders to leave Stuart Lake, where he had been serving under his father-in-law, Chief Factor William Connolly, had come direct from the company's eastern headquarters, it is quite probable that Doctor John had prevailed upon Governor Simpson to make the change during the chief's sojourn at Vancouver. In this instance we can be sure that the governor and the chief factor, so often at loggerheads, saw eye to eye though it is also apparent that they were prompted by widely divergent motives. With the doctor, who had introduced Douglas to the fur trade, it was largely a matter of sentiment, however keenly he may have appreciated the young man's ability. With the governor, business was the sole consideration.

Always a little jealous of Doctor John, the chief executive had, since his last visit, developed a certain distrust of him—not of his basic loyalty to the company but rather of his willingness to carry out the governor's own ideas. Already it had become apparent that the doctor wanted to establish additional trading posts in the interior and along the coast—a policy frowned upon by Simpson.[15] The matter had, in fact, been openly discussed between them. That being so, the artful governor may have considered it excellent strategy to send young Douglas, who owed him much, to Vancouver, where he might prove useful in fighting for the Simpsonian policies or, at the very least, check the doctor's ambitions along contrary lines. But if such was his purpose, he had woefully misread both men. Indeed the debt Douglas owed to his old friend and benefactor transcended any obligations to the governor, and, as for Doctor John, he was the last man on earth to be swerved from his honest convictions. Years later he was to resign his post rather than submit to orders he could not conscientiously carry out. We can be quite certain that, in accepting his new appointment, the clerk from Stuart Lake knew he would be compelled to carry water on both shoulders. Fortunately, his shoulders were broad.

When James Douglas reached Vancouver in the early spring of 1830, he was just twenty-seven. Tall and slender, he was a fine specimen of young manhood. His coal-black hair soon earned him the sobriquet "Black Douglas,"[16] and indeed he possessed many of the qualities of the great Scottish chieftain. In manner, the newcomer was cool, deliberate, and methodical— a pronounced contrast to his chief, who was always bubbling over with enthusiasm.

Something of a stickler for form, Douglas had carried with him into the wild western country not only the manners of a gentleman but also the desire (not always realized) to dress accordingly. "I have often smiled," wrote George B. Roberts, a young naval apprentice who had arrived on the Columbia in 1831, "at Douglas's behavior to people, honest perhaps, but rough, who had not been accustomed to show much outward respect to anyone; his excessive politeness would extort a little, in that way, from them."[17] But for all his grand airs, Douglas was an honest, able and conscientious worker—a man bound to make his mark in the service. Immediately upon his arrival, he was given charge of the books of the post, and, from the very first, he found ways of making himself indispensable. As early as February, 1831, Archibald McDonald found occasion to write to Edward Ermatinger that his successor "James Douglas . . . is rising fast in favor." [18] Though Doctor John may have found his former pupil a bit out of tune with the general mode of life at the fort, the presence of a man of culture and refinement brought him no little consolation. Theirs was to prove an ideal friendship.

Douglas had his own reasons for welcoming a change of scenery. Never particularly adept in handling the Stuart Lake natives, he had emerged with scant glory from two encounters with them; and, on one of these occasions, he had come near losing his life. [19] It so happened that Governor Simpson, on his second trip to the coast, had visited the Stuart Lake post shortly after one of these unfortunate affairs, and it is quite probable that his first-hand knowledge of the incident had suggested the wisdom of transferring Douglas. [20] Happily, the youthful clerk's troubles were soon to be over. At Vancouver, where Doctor John's original methods had long since reduced the irksome business of managing the Indians to a routine, he could dismiss the redskins from his mind and turn his full attention to the keeping of accounts—a branch of the fur trade in which he was vastly more at home.

Two years before his transfer, Douglas had married Amelia, the attractive half-breed daughter of William Connolly. Mrs. Douglas soon became a great favorite at the fort, where Margaret, the doctor's lady, showered upon her every sort of kindness. Since most of the British traders and trappers had married full-blooded Indians, these two women—only half-breeds—were held in great respect by the natives and whites alike. During the early years at Vancouver, the officers' families lived lives so isolated as to suggest Oriental seclusion. They never dined with the men, nor were they even permitted to meet the infrequent visitors who called at the post. "Gentlemen who came to the Fort," wrote Doctor John's daughter, "never saw the family. We never saw anybody." [21] It was not until the arrival of the American missionaries some years later that this condition was modified. But to Margaret, the coming of Amelia Douglas brought companionship and a measure of release from a life so lonely that at times it must have seemed unbearable.

5

With James Douglas at his side, eager and qualified to assist in the routine management of affairs at the post, Doctor John felt free to devote more time to other matters sorely demanding his undivided attention. Already the plague had begun to assume alarming proportions, and the ruthless Yankee sea captains, gone but not forgotten, had left chaos in their wake. Then, as if these misfortunes were not enough, another problem of a very different kind had suddenly presented itself. It involved a matter of company policy, and it required the doctor, isolated by the breadth of a continent from the councils of his superiors, to establish a precedent which would inevitably become the recognized custom in his department. For a time he evaded the issue, but he was not long in summoning the courage to make a decision—a decision that could be squared both with the dictates of his own conscience and, as he hoped, with the designs of his company.

Long had the chief factor feared complications in connection with land settlement, and now, at last, a test case had arisen. As early as 1828, Louis Labonte, an industrious French Canadian who had completed his six-year term of service with the company, had applied to Doctor John for permission to start a small farming enterprise in the Willamette valley. He was forced to refuse on the ground that to grant it would violate a rigid regulation of the Hudson's Bay Company. Under this rule, company servants, upon the expiration of their terms of service, could be discharged only at the points where they had originally enlisted.

But Louis Labonte was a determined fellow. He dared, in fact, to argue the matter with Doctor John—in itself sufficient evidence of his courage—contending that since he had joined the Hudson's Bay forces in Oregon, he should be entitled to receive his discharge at Vancouver.[22] The chief factor knew that back of the company's strict regulation lay certain fixed motives. Some time previously, Governor Simpson had interpreted this decree as merely a wise precaution against the danger certain to ensue if undesirable whites were turned loose in the Indian country, where, if they were so inclined, they could incite the natives to rebellion.[23] It was the truth but not the whole truth. Doctor John had been too long in the service and was himself too high in the councils of the company not to know that perhaps the main purpose of the order was to prevent permanent settlement in Oregon, especially in the country south of the Columbia.[24] Though he knew in his soul that Labonte would cause no trouble among the Indians, the doctor could not afford to take the risk of violating this regulation. So, with deep reluctance, he informed the disappointed Labonte that he would have to make the long journey overland to Montreal in order to secure his discharge. For the moment, the White-Headed Eagle was checkmated.

Like a good soldier, Labonte obeyed orders—he made the trip East with the annual express, secured the papers certifying to the termination of his service, and returned to Vancouver, arriving in the fall of 1830.[25] A free man at last, he settled on a fertile tract of land in the Willamette valley some fifty miles south of the Columbia which, because of the predominating nationality of its earliest pioneers, became known as French Prairie.

Not long after Labonte had first raised the question of land settlement with Doctor John, Étienne Lucier, another French Canadian, confronted him with a similar request. Lucier, who had traveled overland with Wilson Price Hunt in 1812 to join the Astor enterprise, and who had later become a Hudson's Bay trapper, was a man of no little consequence in early Oregon. He had married a princess of the Chinook tribe, and his eldest daughter, Félicité, had become the bride of Donald Manson.[26] This close tie with an officer of the company had greatly enhanced his position, and to refuse such a man would have been especially distasteful to the doctor, who was always eager to please his ex-employees.

Fortunately, by the time Lucier got around to present his case, the chief factor had found a way to circumvent the embarrassing regulation. "If he went to Canada," wrote the doctor with reference to Lucier, "and unfortunately died before his children could provide for themselves, they would become objects of pity and a burden to others—for these reasons I would assist him."[27] His handling of the situation was masterful. In order to grant Lucier's request and still conform to the company's order, he decided to retain the ex-employee's name on the post roll. At the same time he agreed to loan him seed to sow and wheat with which to sustain his family, with the understanding that payment was to be made in produce from the farm. Lucier was also permitted to purchase implements from the company's store at Vancouver at fifty per cent on prime cost.

This adroit solution permitted Lucier as well as other former employees to settle in French Prairie and remain, at the same time, under the protecting wing of the Hudson's Bay Company. If the sagacious chief factor had violated the spirit of the regulation, what did it matter? His humanitarian instincts had triumphed, and he had made possible the beginning of private farming in Oregon. Other ex-servants of the company were quick to avail themselves of his generosity, and, before long, French Prairie was to become a promising settlement.

Some of these French Canadians hesitated to establish farms south of the Columbia for fear that the country would eventually become ˙American territory, and that, because of their former affiliations, they might not enjoy the same privileges as American citizens. In answering them, Doctor John could only say that "the American Government and people know only two classes of persons, rogues and honest men; that they punished the first and protected the last, and it depended only upon themselves to what class they would belong." [28] Seldom has sounder advice been given to prospective American citizens by a foreigner. In the years ahead, the United States government was to experience very little difficulty in assimilating these sturdy French Canadians.

Is it possible that, even then, Doctor John was playing with the idea of some day turning Yankee? He was, at least, leaving the door open.

CHAPTER XI

THE EMPIRE GROWS

I

EARLY in the thirties, thanks to the unremitting efforts and unique organizing ability of her chief factor, Fort Vancouver had become a secure and comfortable post—a sanctuary of civilization in the heart of the savage western country. To John Dunn, one of the naval apprentices who reached the Columbia on the bark *Ganymede* in 1831, we are indebted for perhaps the finest contemporary account of life at the Hudson's Bay Company western depot.[1] Though it is not likely that the fort had, by that time, attained the cosmopolitan air which Dunn ascribes to it, most of its basic characteristics must already have been apparent.

Through the eyes of this observant British lad, we are permitted an amazingly vivid glimpse of the community the doctor had labored so assiduously to build. The fort itself, according to Dunn's account, was an enclosed parallelogram measuring roughly 250 yards in depth by 150 in width. The walls were constructed of closely fitted pickets, sunk securely into the ground and supported from within by stout buttresses. Placed at each corner was a bastion mounting two 12-pounders, while in the center, against the front wall, were several 18-pounders. For all their impressiveness, these guns were little more than scenery —grim reminders that the White-Headed Eagle's authority was not to be taken lightly. Evidently they served their purpose well, for there is no record that they were ever used in defense of the post against the natives.

Dunn describes in detail the forty-odd single-story buildings which lay inside the enclosure—offices, warehouses for furs, English goods, and other commodities, as well as workshops for mechanics, carpenters, blacksmiths, coopers, wheelwrights, and tinners. In the center, dominating the whole scene, stood the chief factor's two-story residence, and close by it were two more important structures, the dining hall and the public sitting room. Such signal evidence of progress must have been highly gratifying to the man who, in so short a span, had made it possible.

It became the custom, quite early in the history of Vancouver, for the officers of the post to dine together in the great hall, comfortable in their masculine exclusiveness though perhaps secretly resentful of the social distinctions which separated them from their families at meal time. Though this had been the established custom in Hudson's Bay posts for years, the doctor, always a law unto himself, could have changed it had he chosen to do so. Indeed his strict adherence to the old tradition throws an interesting sidelight on his character. Devoted as he was to his family, he could not forgo the exultation it brought him to preside over a dignified company of gentlemen. It was one of the few remaining links with the life he had long since forsaken.

"The dinner," wrote Dunn, describing Vancouver's midday meal, "is of the most substantial kind, consisting of several courses. Wine is frequently allowed; but no spirituous liquors. After grace has been said, the company break up. Then most of the party retire to the public sitting room, called 'Bachelors' Hall,' or the smoking room; to amuse themselves as they please, either in smoking, reading, or telling and listening to stories of their own, and others' curious adventures. Sometimes there is a great influx of company, consisting of the chief traders from the outposts, who arrive at the fort on business; and the commanders of vessels. These are gala times after dinner; and there is a great deal of amusement, but always kept under strict discipline, and regulated by the strictest propriety. . . . The voyageur and the trapper, who have traversed thousands of miles through wild and unfrequented regions; and the mariner, who has circumnavigated the globe, may be found grouped together, smoking, joking, singing, and story telling; and in every way banishing dull care, till the period of their again setting out for their respective destinations arrives." [2] All in all, the Vancouver that Dunn presents to the imagination is more suggestive of old world civilization than frontier life in the wilderness of North America.

But such unreserved optimism regarding affairs at the western headquarters post was not universal—at least not as early as 1831. "I am sorry to inform you," wrote J. E. Harriott, a clerk then stationed at Vancouver, in a letter to his friend John McLeod, "that the Columbia has again been prolific in misfortunes, in fact more so than ever." Then, after narrating a distressing series of calamities, including the plague, the ruinous effects of the Yankee trading activities on the river, and the wreck of the *Isabella,* the disillusioned Harriott refers to the anticipated departure of several prominent officers by the spring express. "This makes a great hole in our complement of gentlemen," runs the doleful communication, "and a number of recruits will be wanted but really I do not see where they will come from. There are now very few who have not tasted the sweets of the Columbia and New Caledonia and it would certainly be considered hard to send those back who have already passed three or four years and have had the satisfaction of getting safe out of it." [3]

Apparently Doctor John made no attempt to censor outgoing mail. Otherwise, he would scarcely have permitted such a sweeping indictment of his régime to go out. Though Harriott's reaction was by no means typical, it is obvious that similar expressions of dissatisfaction found their way East and even across the Atlantic. Years later, the doctor was to complain bitterly of the opinions some of his officers expressed in their letters. At all events, the council in London saw fit to transfer Chief Factor Duncan Finlayson, a diminutive Scotchman, from the Red River Settlement to the Columbia so that if the doctor should avail himself of a furlough due him in 1833, he would have an officer of his own rank on the ground to take his place.[4] Such, at least, was the reason advanced, but Doctor John, always adept in divining hidden motives, fancied he knew better. Indeed he had grounds for suspecting that the new chief factor had been sent out to investigate the inroads upon the company's trade which the enterprising Yankees had been making on land and sea.

By the time Finlayson reached Vancouver, in the fall of 1831, the doctor, forewarned by intuition, if nothing more substantial, had planned his campaign with military precision. He would take no furlough two years hence—certainly not if Finlayson was still around. He would accord the newcomer every courtesy, but he would guard his own trade secrets closely. He would count on Douglas to help him. The spy from the East, if such he was, would find little enough to report to the council.

For that matter, there was nothing in the doctor's stewardship that could have caused him any embarrassment; but realizing how easily facts could be distorted, he wisely resolved to divulge none. It would have required the services of a very shrewd man to oust him from his empire, and if we can believe that he referred to Finlayson in a letter penned to Edward Ermatinger some years later, we can be certain that the Scot from Red River was not such a person. "You have one great satisfaction," wrote Doctor John, "you act for yourself. . . . While you know that in this Country you would be working for others and people who Know Nothing of the Business—have the power of deciding on the Merits of your conduct—and who would place a Runt of a fellow that Knows Nothing—can do Nothing—as your Colleague—Merely because they want to reward—a Creature." [5] Notwithstanding the bitterness of this letter, the "Runt of a fellow"—if indeed he was Finlayson—became a loyal supporter of Doctor John and a valuable worker in the Columbia department.

2

Ever since the day, back in 1829, when Captain Dominis of the *Owyhee* had unintentionally dropped a hint regarding the rich fur-bearing country to be found northward along the coast of Russian America, the chief factor had had it in mind to extend his operations in that direction. He had hoped, in fact, to get an expedition under way in 1830, but too many of his men had been ill with the intermittent fever.[6] Now, in 1831, with the men fully recovered, with the Columbia trade slipping, and with Duncan Finlayson on hand to learn what he could learn, it was high time to conquer new fields.

The doctor's decision to enter and occupy this new territory marks a turning point in his career because it signifies his intention to break openly with the fixed policies of Governor Simpson. The governor, as Doctor John well knew, did not favor the establishment of additional posts, however much he may have desired an increase in the trade of the Columbia department. But Vancouver's chief factor had long since convinced himself that he could not compete advantageously with the Yankees and Russians along the northern coast unless he planted permanent settlements to serve as bases. With all his independence of spirit, he doubtless hesitated to take a step which would amount to open defiance of his chief's firmly intrenched views; but he finally came to regard the proposed project, after long

deliberation, as the lesser of two evils. Indeed the now determined doctor concluded that the London council, sitting in
isolated ignorance of practical affairs on the Pacific, would be
so pleased to welcome additional profits that its members would
not cavil over the exact means employed to obtain them.
Deliberately, he placed all his eggs in one basket. If the campaign proved successful, George Simpson could not consistently
oppose it; but if, for any reason, it were to fail, Doctor John
might suddenly find himself holding down a less important
post. The stakes were high, but the game was well worth the
candle.

Fortunately, the groundwork for the doctor's plan had already been laid through diplomatic negotiations. As early as
1825, a treaty had been concluded between Great Britain and
Russia according to the terms of which subjects of either nation
were allowed to navigate the Pacific freely and to trade with
the natives of any shore already occupied by Europeans. It was
stipulated, however, that an Englishman could not land in a
Russian settlement except for protection or repairs without first
receiving permission to do so from the resident governor, and
this rule, of course, was intended to apply both ways. The
boundary line between the two governments was to start on
the Pacific at latitude 54° 40′ and to continue in a general
northeasterly direction as far as longitude 141°, along which
meridian it was to run due northward to the Arctic Ocean.[7]
Doctor John, from his knowledge of the country and from his
study of contemporary charts, knew that he could locate, on
British territory, posts strategically situated to tap this rich
northern area. Indeed Fort Langley, the first link in the chain,
had already been operating some four years.

In 1830, the doctor had dispatched the *Cadboro,* still commanded by Captain Aemelius Simpson, northward to explore
the coast line and, in particular, to investigate the Nass River

with a view toward finding there a desirable site for a fort. "With respect to its [Nass] proving a favorable trading post," Simpson had written his chief on September 30, 1830, "it certainly appears a Country abounding in Beavers (& those of a good quality) tho' the trade owing to the frequent visits of the American Coasters will be at a high Rate, could parties be sent up the River to trade I imagine they could be procured at a much cheaper rate."

We can readily picture what encouragement this enthusiastic report must have given the chief factor, eager as he was to begin trading operations in earnest. Nor was he in the least dismayed when the captain noted further that "the unexpected length of our voyage in consequence of a succession of contrary winds prevented our visiting ports for the purpose of trading which I regret as a favourable impression might have been made by visiting a few places tho' I must state the Americans appear to have goods more in demand on this part of the coast than us. Arms & Ammunition they sell without limits & ardent spirits in great abundance & these articles with the exception of Blankets I found in greatest demand at Nass. Of the first of these articles I sold none, as for the last, half stock'd green I had on board, they offered only one Beaver Skin. I regretted being under the necessity of selling a quantity of the latter as I found it impossible to trade without it nor do I see how it can well be avoided till opposition is done off the Coast." [8]

Captain Simpson had taken north with him a second vessel called the *Vancouver,* a craft which had been built on the Columbia in 1829 under the doctor's supervision.[9] On his return voyage, the captain, observing an American coaster trading in the Straits of Juan de Fuca, had wisely left the *Vancouver* behind to oppose her.[10]

Early in 1831, the doctor's plan of campaign was ready for execution. To insure its success, he needed ships, men, and supplies, and luckily, he had a sufficiency of each. So important was the project, in his program of trade revival, that he placed two of his most trusted men, Peter Skene Ogden and Donald Manson, in charge of the expedition.

Sailing northward on the *Cadboro,* the party reached the Nass River, by way of the Portland Inlet, and penetrated upstream to a distance of six miles. At this point, on the north bank of the river, Ogden selected what he considered a suitable location for the new post, and, with high hope, the men began the construction of Fort Simpson. Even before its completion, however, the project was abandoned in favor of a site nearer open water; but the name persisted and Fort Simpson, christened in honor of the governor, soon became a fur-trading establishment of some consequence. The one major tragedy of the expedition was the untimely death of Captain Aemelius Simpson of the white gloves. He was engaged in building a ship at the first Fort Simpson when he contracted pneumonia, late in 1831, and quickly succumbed.[11] A willing worker and a brave officer, he was sorely missed by his chief.

3

Doctor John, still weighed down by manifold routine duties he could not delegate to others, managed nevertheless to make definite progress in rehabilitating the fur trade of his vast department during 1832. Douglas had proved of great assistance in his own field of accounting, but as yet, with the exception of George T. Allan, there was no one to help the doctor care for the sick; and, among the natives at least, the plague had shown no appreciable signs of abating.[12] Still the chief factor was encouraged by the results of the first year's efforts at Fort Simpson, though the actual returns had fallen far below his expectations. We gather some idea of his optimistic frame of mind from a letter he sent to his old friend, John McLeod, who had returned to Norway House from a vacation spent in Scotland.

"As to us here," runs the message, "we go on in the old way. Ogden is at Nass. Last year though [we had] three vessels only two could go on the coast and one was only fifteen days and the other was only three months still the coasting trade will clear itself; and this year [1832] when we have nothing to interrupt our proceedings we intend to give it the first fair trial it has had and from what has been done this year we have every reason to expect it will do well."

In this same letter, the doctor offers impressive evidence as to the progress his farming enterprise had enjoyed, stating that "our farm yielded: 1800 bushels wheat; 1200 bushels barley; 600 bushels pease; 400 bushels Indian corn, and 6000 bushels potatoes."

In high exultation, he suggests that "the last article would be enough for all the King's posts." He then goes on to reveal himself as something of a propagandist for his own cause. "I hope," he wrote with no little naïvety, "if an opportunity offered that you produced my letters to you on the subject," [13] and he refers, of course, to some extended reports of progress on the Columbia which he had sent McLeod in the hope that they might be displayed in London, where they would be expected to count most heavily in his favor. With Duncan Finlayson at his heels, he apparently realized the desirability of tooting his own horn.

In spite of the chief factor's sanguine outlook, Americans again threatened his empire in 1832, and one of them had the audacity to play havoc with the trade at his very doorstep. Dominis and Thompson had taught him to be wary of Yankee skippers, and when word reached him, toward the middle of 1832, that Captain William McNeill of the Boston brig *Llama* had entered the river, he was greatly perturbed.

Working his way up the Columbia, Captain McNeill paid

the doctor a brief visit in the hope of learning some additional "tricks of the trade" from the Hudson's Bay men. As a matter of fact, he could have taught the Britishers a good many, as events were soon to disclose. At Vancouver he was received politely but without enthusiasm, and he was quick to notice how suspiciously the chief factor eyed his generous stock of American-made gimcracks, which included wooden soldiers, tiny wagons, jumping-jacks, whistles, and brightly colored toys of every description. If McNeill entertained any doubts regarding the acceptability of his wares among the natives, Doctor John did not. Indeed he knew at a glance that the shrewd Bostonian had brought along just the right selection of trumpery to entice furs away from the Indians at rock-bottom prices.[14] Here was a fellow who would bear careful watching!

While the doctor awaited results with genuine concern, the Yankee skipper started down the river to try his luck; and reports soon began to drift in which bore ample witness to the lucrative trade he was enjoying. Though the Hudson's Bay men had been making strenuous efforts to keep the Indians' stocks of furs at a low ebb, William McNeill encountered no scarcity of them on his triumphant cruise down the Columbia. For once it appeared that the White-Headed Eagle's subjects had outsmarted him, having kept, as their ace in the hole, a reserve supply of skins which the British never dreamed existed. To the childish mind of the savage, staple English goods seemed drab compared with the captain's worthless stock of trinkets from New England.[15]

For a while the doctor hesitated, uncertain what course to follow, but eventually, acting upon the advice of none other than Duncan Finlayson, he bought out the American sea captain—ship, cargo and all.[16] He must have regarded the situation as desperate for, some years earlier, he had written to Governor Simpson that "I am aware that I am not authorized to buy up opposition & that buying up induces others to follow." [17] Nevertheless, this was a crisis that called for action, and the chief factor, secure in the growing independence of his position, wisely concluded that his judgment would not be questioned. Then, too, it was perhaps politic, in the circumstances, to follow a suggestion offered by Finlayson.

William McNeill, whom the doctor with his rare talent for judging men had recognized as an unusually resourceful trader, joined the Hudson's Bay forces and began a brilliant career in the ranks of his erstwhile opponents. Doctor John had good reason to feel proud of this conversion, for seldom, in early Oregon, did an American go over to the opposite camp.

4

Though McNeill was the only American to offer the doctor any real opposition on the water during 1832, two other Yankees invaded his inland empire. One was the swashbuckling roisterer, Captain Bonneville, and the other was the gentlemanly Bostonian, Nathaniel J. Wyeth. Neither was to prove a serious adversary and one, at least, was to become a lifelong friend.

Notwithstanding his faults and failures, Captain Benjamin Louis Eulalie de Bonneville was one of the most picturesque characters of the early West. A Frenchman by birth and instinct and a United States Army officer by profession, he decided, having read much about Oregon and having taken a furlough for the purpose, to lead a party of a hundred men over the mountains into the trapping grounds of the Pacific Northwest.[18] According to the captain's friendly press agent, Washington Irving, he was the first man ever to bring a caravan of wagons safely over the summit of the Cascade Mountains.[19] It appears, however, that his prowess as an adventurer transcended his ability as a fur trader, for, though he spent more than two years hunting and trapping in various parts of the West, he realized no profits for his trouble and was forced, in the end, to return East.[20] In the vast country west of the Rockies, he left, besides a colorful tradition, nothing more significant than a string of broken-hearted native belles and, no doubt, a goodly number of nameless dark-skinned papooses. Whenever he crossed swords with the doctor's well organized forces he came out second best, and the wise old chief factor at Vancouver could scarcely have lost much sleep over the activities of this opéra bouffe soldier, masquerading as a fur trader.

Of a very different stripe was Nathaniel J. Wyeth. In the Boston of his day there had grown up, largely through the inspiring words of the visionary school teacher, Hall J. Kelley, a conviction that Oregon should be saved for the United States by colonization. Of all American cities, this was the most logical to nurture such beliefs. It was, of course, a Bostonian who had discovered the Columbia in the first place, and, in the years following, many a Yankee sea captain had made a fortune by trading with the Indians of the Pacific coast. So completely had this New England city of culture and clipper ships dominated the coastal trade that the natives, in Doctor John's time, knew Americans only as "Boston men." Having grown up in such an environment, Wyeth was ripe to fall under the spell of Kelley's glowing speeches, and, before he was thirty, he had decided to cast his lot with the schoolmaster's Boston Colonization Society.

"I cannot divest myself," he wrote at the time, "of the opinion that I shall compete better with my fellow men in new and untried paths than in those to pursue which requires only patience and attention." [21] It was his avowed purpose to plant a colony in Oregon while there was still time; but, from his overconfident manner, it is evident that he had no real notion of the impregnability of the Hudson's Bay Company along the Columbia. Though Horace Greeley had not as yet uttered his celebrated advice to young men, this young man already felt the urge to go West.

But as time drifted on, Wyeth became dissatisfied with Kelley's inactivity and resolved to organize his own expedition, which, with his ample means, he could do with comparative ease. Early in the year he dispatched the ship *Sultana* with a cargo of provisions and goods for trade, confident that she would be waiting for him in the Columbia upon his own arrival. Then, a little later, he started westward himself at the head of a well organized party, and, traveling some of the way on foot and the rest by rail and steamboat, he reached Independence, Missouri, in June. There, by a stroke of good fortune, he fell in with the experienced American trader, William L. Sublette, and from that point, the two parties journeyed over the hazardous mountains together. In his journal, the youthful Boston zealot describes the unbelievable hardships suffered by his men. At last, on October 29, 1832, with but twelve of his original group, he arrived at Vancouver only to discover that the *Sultana* had not put in an appearance. Not until several months had passed was he to learn that she had been wrecked en route.[22]

For Wyeth, it was an extremely awkward situation. Here he was, his original investment consumed, his ship long overdue and his entire party dependent upon the very man he had come so far to oppose. What another British chief factor might have done in the circumstances we can only surmise, but Doctor John, recognizing the unmistakable signs of integrity in the face of the bedraggled Yankee, took pity on him and extended lavishly the hospitality of Vancouver.

"Here I was received with the utmost kindness and Hospitality by Doct. McLauchland," wrote the disappointed Bostonian. "I find [him] a fine old gentleman truly philanthropic in his Ideas. . . . The Co. seem disposed to render me all the assistance they can." [23]

With all the patience he could muster, Wyeth waited for the ship that never came, occupying his time by making side trips into the country, apparently with the hearty consent of his genial host. On only one occasion did the hospitable doctor put his foot down, and that was when his impetuous guest asked permission to accompany a Hudson's Bay expedition southward to the Umpqua River. "The Gov. would not consent," wrote Wyeth, a bit disgruntled, "alleging they [the Indians] would conceive that I came to avenge the death of Mr. Smith's party who was cut off by the Umpqua Indians, all of which I interpreted as jealousy of my motives." [24]

One can scarcely blame Doctor John for wanting to keep Wyeth from learning too much about the country south of the Columbia, knowing, as he did, the American's real object in coming West. Nevertheless the reason he advanced for his objection was a sound one, and the young adventurer, if he stopped to consider the situation in its true light, could hardly nurse a grievance.

As the winter wore on, Doctor John learned much from his guest regarding the fiery preachments of Hall J. Kelley, and, partially as a result of these conversations, he developed a strong prejudice against the Boston school teacher whom he was to meet in person not many years hence. Such an attitude was but characteristic of the doctor's philosophy at that time—he could be friendly and helpful to those of any race who found themselves in need, but he could not look with favor upon those who sought openly to undermine his empire. Wyeth, however, was so sincere and so distinctly a gentleman that the chief factor, notwithstanding the conflict of interests that stood between them, treated him royally and even made a place for him at his own table. When it came time for the Yankee to start East in the spring, disappointed but not disillusioned, the foundations of a lasting friendship had already been laid. Though there is no hint of it in Wyeth's journal, it is more than probable that the doctor invited him to join the ranks of the Hudson's Bay Company. The enterprising Bostonian, however, had other plans.

5

At about this time, according to a story related by his daughter, Eloisa, the doctor narrowly escaped death for the fourth time in his career. Having come uncomfortably close to drowning on two occasions and only a little less close to the hangman's noose on a third, he was to miss connections with a bullet only because of sudden fear on the part of an Indian employee.

In order to add recruits to his force of laborers on the farm at Vancouver as well as to render a charitable service, the doctor had fallen into the habit of buying certain deserving slave boys from their native masters. On this particular occasion, one of these slave boys, a lad from the Rogue River country, happened to be working in the fields with three Englishmen who, for some time, had harbored a grudge against the chief factor. Not daring to take his life themselves, they had tried repeatedly to plant murder in the mind of the young Indian.

The day was very sultry, and the none too industrious native boy had forsaken his plow in favor of a nap. Unfortunately for him, the doctor came along at that very moment. Placing his gun against a tree, he walked over to the sleeping lad, aroused him with a good shaking and reminded him with considerable warmth that he was supposed to be working for the Hudson's Bay Company. Frightened half out of his wits, the luckless Indian scrambled up and hurried back to his plow. But the three plotting Britishers, watching the scene from close by, sensed at last an opportunity to inflame the boy's mind against his benefactor. With all manner of convincing arguments, they finally persuaded the lad to snatch the doctor's gun the next time he should be so careless as to place it against a tree and then, while he was scolding some other Indian employee, to shoot him in the back. But when it came time to carry out his part of the bargain, the Rogue River boy lost his nerve, and Doctor John, unmindful of the close call he had had, walked majestically back to the fort.

That very night the assassin-elect, haunted by fear and remorse, told his story to the cook, who lost no time in carrying it straight to the chief factor. The doctor was furious. Though he gave little thought to his own safety, he could not abide disloyalty in the ranks. That same evening he called the three Englishmen into his study and, in the presence of James Douglas, questioned them, with amazing coolness, about the whole affair. At first they denied the charge, but, after reposing in irons for several weeks, they thought it wise to confess. Instead of shipping the worthless fellows back to England—certainly the lightest punishment they should have received—the forgiving chief factor released them and restored them to good standing in the service. As for the Indian lad, Doctor John sent him back to his own people a free man.[25]

Up to that time, the indulgent chief factor had not thought it possible that any of his own people would attempt to take his life. Though his faith in the men under him remained unshaken, he had learned his lesson—never again was his gun to stand unguarded against a tree.

CHAPTER XII

Expansion in Three Directions

I

Numbered among the twelve men who had reached Vancouver with Wyeth on his expedition of 1832 was John Ball, a New England school teacher and lawyer. After a brief but brilliant career in his profession—a career which had brought him into contact with such eminent Americans as Aaron Burr and Andrew Jackson—Ball had met with serious reverses, and, more for the sake of adventure than because of any deep-rooted interest in colonizing Oregon, he had joined Nathaniel Wyeth's party.[1] It was but natural for a man of his broad sympathies and high intellectual attainments to be more intrigued by the nightly discussions at Bachelors' Hall than by Wyeth's strenuous excursions to the coast and into the interior. Doctor John, it appears, was quick to recognize, in the former New England lawyer, a kindred spirit.

"I soon gave him [the chief factor] and Mr. Wyeth to understand I was on my own hook," wrote Ball in his absorbing autobiography, published many years later, "and that I had no further connections with the others, than that for the making of the journey. We were received at the fort as guests without talk of pay or the like and it was acceptable, or else we should have had to hunt for sustenance."[2]

John Ball was a man with a keen sense of propriety, and it disturbed his New England conscience to accept so many favors without rendering some service in return. Shortly after his arrival, he made known his feelings to Doctor John, who, at first, would not hear of permitting one of his guests to work for a living. Indeed the very thought of such a thing was as distasteful to him as was that of idleness to the conscientious visitor. It was a clash of gentlemanly instincts. The doctor, who could be obstinate on occasion, would undoubtedly have stood his ground had Ball insisted upon performing manual labor, but when he realized how eager the New Englander was to occupy his time, he suggested to him that Vancouver needed a school for its children. Nothing could have been more pleasing to Ball.[3]

"I, of course, gladly accepted the offer," wrote Oregon's first school teacher. "So he [the doctor] sent the boys to my room to be instructed, all half-breed boys of course, for there was not then a white woman in Oregon. . . . Well, I found the boys docile and attentive and making good progress, for they are precocious and generally better boys than men. And the old doctor used to come in and see the school and seemed much pleased and well satisfied. And one time he said, 'Ball, anyway you will have the reputation of teaching the first Academy in Oregon.'"[4]

In this useful manner, John Ball passed a pleasant winter. His pupils, who numbered twenty-four, spoke in a variety of languages including Klickitat, Nez Percé, Chinook, Cree, and French. At first only one, the doctor's eleven-year-old son, David, could speak English, but eventually they all learned to converse in that language. Some of them committed parts of Murray's Grammar to memory and others even solved the mysteries of elementary arithmetic.

Apparently things were not always as rosy as the teacher pictured them, for, on one occasion, an Indian youth took issue with him as to how the school should be run. At that point

Oregon's first educational venture might have collapsed un-
ceremoniously had not Doctor John, who seemed always to turn
up at the crucial moment, come into the schoolroom. Sensing
the situation at a glance, he yanked the obstreperous youngster
from his seat and, after a short but stormy session, made him see
things from the instructor's point of view. The school flourished
under the careful supervision of John Ball until March 1, 1833,
when the pioneer teacher retired to the Willamette Valley to try
his luck at farming. The classes were then taken over by
Solomon H. Smith, another man who had come West with
Wyeth.[5]

2

Not only did the chief factor give heed to the education of
the half-breed boys of the post, but, during that same winter, he
began to devote serious thought to the religious needs of his people. The doctor himself had remained true to the faith of Grandfather Fraser, and, from his earliest days at Fort Vancouver, it
had been his custom to read a portion of the Church of England
service on Sunday morning.[6] This, no doubt, was highly pleasing
to the comparatively small number of the company's officers
who happened to be communicants of that faith, but one wonders how graciously it was received by the much larger group
of Scotch Presbyterians. The chief factor, however, was so broad
in his personal conception of religion that he expected others to
take a similar view—in his own mind it was always the spirit of
worship that counted more heavily than the rigid letter of any
one creed. No doubt he reasoned that these gentlemen, marooned
in the wilds of western America, were fortunate to be able to
attend any church service—however primitive—and we can well
believe that they found it convenient to be on hand when Vancouver's self-appointed vicar mounted his improvised pulpit in
the dining hall.

FORT VANCOUVER

From an etching made by Lieutenant Warre of the Warre-Vavasour Expedition in 1845.

The doctor's daughter Eloisa has made it possible for us to gather some notion as to how these Sunday morning rites were conducted. "My father and the clerks," she recalled, "would read the Bible and the Testament. My father used to read the Episcopal Service. James [Douglas] read the Bible and another gentleman the Testament."[7] Even in his devotions, the efficient chief factor believed in a proper division of labor.

While the chief factor may not have worried over subjecting his Presbyterian associates to the more formal ritual of the English Church, he gave more serious thought to the spiritual exigencies of his laborers and voyageurs, practically all of whom were Roman Catholics. Having himself been born and baptized a Catholic, he knew in his soul that these simple French Canadians could not be expected to attend a Protestant service. So, in order to grant their wishes as best he could, he established the custom of reading, at a separate service of their own, sermons or tracts in the French tongue.[8] For the versatile chief factor, Sunday was a very busy day.

But as time went on, he realized that he was less successful in his attempt to masquerade as a priest of the Catholic faith than he had been in his rôle of amateur Episcopal clergyman. On July 3, 1834, therefore, he addressed a petition to the Bishop of Red River, Monsignor Provencher, requesting that an ordained priest be sent out to minister to the needs of his French Canadian voyageurs. Receiving no reply, he dispatched another appeal on February 23, 1835—stronger than the first—but still there was no answer.[9] Oregon, it appeared, was too far off the beaten path.

But the determined doctor would not give up, and, a few years later, he prevailed upon Governor Simpson to intercede with the authorities of the Church. The governor's letter to the Bishop of Quebec, dated February 17, 1838, and written from London, is interesting from a religious as well as from a political point of view. From the contents of this message, it is obvious that negotiations between the Church and the company had been going on for some time. "I am requested," wrote George Simpson, "to communicate with your Lordship on the subject of sending two priests to the Columbia River for the purpose of establishing a Catholic mission in that part of the country. When the Bishop [of Juliopolis] first mentioned this subject, his view was to form the mission on the banks of the Willamette, a river falling into the Columbia from the south. To the establishing of a mission there, the Governor and Committee in London and the Council in Hudson's Bay had a decided objection, as the sovereignty of that country is still undecided; but I last summer intimated to the Bishop that if he would establish the mission on the banks of the Cowlitz River . . . falling into the Columbia from the northward, and give his assurance that the missionaries would not locate themselves on the south side of the Columbia River . . . I should recommend the Governor and the Committee to afford a passage to the priests." [10] Even the Church, it seemed, was to be enlisted by the Hudson's Bay Company as an ally in the fight to keep the meddlesome Yankees south of the Columbia, if indeed they were to come West at all.

George Simpson had succeeded where Doctor John had failed, but the White-Headed Eagle had sown the seed. Following the sending of his first petition, four long years were to elapse before the arrival of the Catholic priests. It seems a strange reversal of religious history that the Catholic missionaries, though the first of any faith to be officially invited, should have been the last to reach Oregon.

3

While these issues were being settled elsewhere, Doctor John continued, in his own way, to build up his company's trade in the Pacific Northwest. In the vast continent of North America there were few men busier than he, and yet, for all of that, he never allowed himself to neglect his growing family.

Through the years Margaret had remained a constant source of comfort to him. Barred by tradition as well as by the doctor's own strict regulations from any contact with the white men of the fort, she appears nevertheless to have exerted a profound influence over her husband. Just as in the earlier stages of their marriage, he continued to have complete confidence in her judgment. When his honest Irish temper chanced to run away with him, as it frequently would, she, with the possible exception of James Douglas, was the only one capable of calming him quickly. Angered by some stupid mistake of a subordinate, he would storm up and down before the fire while she, knitting peacefully in her corner, would listen in silence for what experience had taught her was the proper interval. Then, smiling up at him, she would offer a word or two of sound advice, and the doctor, completely disarmed, would burst into a roar of laughter, kiss her lightly on the forehead, and hurry out of the house in the best of spirits. Indeed the dark-skinned Margaret, like so many women in history who have been eclipsed by the deeds of their consorts, did much to make life bearable for Vancouver's chief factor during the early years of his stewardship.

For his children the doctor entertained a regard that transcended the customary parental affection. It was, in fact, a love so sweeping that he could balance, in his own mind, the faults and virtues of each with sufficient accuracy to permit an impartial estimate.

Joseph, the oldest, had become an expert horseman and had accompanied Tom McKay on many a hair-raising expedition into the wilds. He was brave, trustworthy, and strong but, as the doctor knew, too much the Indian. Handicapped by his lack of education,[11] Joe's rightful calling, if he could be persuaded to settle down, was that of farmer in the Willamette valley. John, Jr., promised more, but again the honest father entertained no illusions. The young man might eventually become a clerk or even a chief trader in the company's ranks, but, beyond that, he could scarcely hope to rise. He was bright enough, yes, but still too much the red man—too quick-tempered and too impatient.

The doctor worshiped his two daughters, especially the blue-eyed Eloisa who, at fourteen, had become the toast of the settlement. They, at least, presented no problems—they would marry in due course and become loyal and faithful wives of fur traders. In the case of Eloisa, exactly this was to happen. As for Eliza, we know that she eventually married an English army officer named Epps, and that, for a time, the couple resided at Quebec.[12]

But, of all his children, the doctor pinned his greatest faith on the little fellow David, named for his uncle, already a famous physician in Europe. David, precocious and none too strong, had shown considerable promise in John Ball's school, and he was the one deserving of an education abroad—the best that money could buy. The indulgent father believed that David had it in him to become his successor—to become Vancouver's ruler. So it was with confidence and boundless pride that the White-Headed Eagle sent the eaglet David over to his brother in Paris with the spring express of 1833.[13]

Had the doctor, in the years ahead, been able to maintain this sane and impartial estimate of the true worth of his sons, he would have been spared endless grief and humiliation.

4

Though the plague, by this time, had ceased to be a serious threat to the white population of Vancouver, it had continued to take a heavy toll of native life. Doctor John was deeply concerned. Even with the willing if none too competent assistance of George T. Allan, he found it next to impossible to carry on his medical work with important matters of business clamoring for his undivided attention. The wonder is that he salvaged any time at all to devote to the fur trade. At all events, realizing that his usefulness to the company was being impaired, he dispatched a letter to the London council requesting that two physicians be sent out as soon as possible.[14] The response was amazingly prompt, considering the great distance involved, for when the brig *Ganymede,* under the sponsorship of Sir William Hooker, arrived at Vancouver on May 4, 1833, she brought a pair of young Scottish medics, Doctors Gairdner and Tolmie.[15] Seldom had recruits arrived more opportunely.

Merideth Gairdner, who had studied under the celebrated Ehrenberg, was passionately devoted to the then popular science of infusoria while William Frazer Tolmie, a graduate of the University of Glasgow, had chosen botany as his hobby. Whatever their respective interests in these specialized fields may have been, they were soon to find matters of a more practical nature demanding their attention on the Columbia.

From Tolmie's absorbing journal, we gain some idea of Doctor John's joy in receiving these welcome assistants. "Knocked at the gate," wrote Tolmie in his diary for May 4, "which, after some delay, was opened by the gardener, who I at once discovered to be a Celt. Our approach being announced to Governor McLoughlin, he appeared in shirt and trousers on the staircase of the common hall and welcomed us with a cordial shake of hand. Sat down in the dining hall and, while refreshments were being prepared, communicated the political intelligence of Europe to Mr. McLoughlin who is an able politician." (Indeed he must have been to have digested the political situation of Europe in the time required to prepare refreshments!) "From what I have seen of the Gov.," continued Tolmie, "like him and think my prepossessions will be confirmed by a longer acquaintance." [16]

The two physicians from Scotland had apparently quarreled aboard ship, for Tolmie mentions that they agreed to patch up their differences when the chief factor asked them to share the same apartment.[17] It was as well that they did so, for bad blood between them, with plenty of hard work ahead, would inevitably have destroyed their usefulness. No doubt the wise old doctor, sensing a rift, conceived the plan of bunking them together as the only means of providing himself with the freedom he sorely needed.

Apparently the two recruits lost no time in getting down to business. "Visited and prescribed for my patients," runs Tolmie's entry for May 5, the day following his arrival. But the routine had scarcely gotten under way before he discovered that the chief factor intended to regulate even the practice of medicine. "Received intimation this morning at 4 of Plant's death," continues the young physician's record for the very next day, May 6. "Mr. McLoughlin did not think it advisable, when I spoke at breakfast, that the body be inspected as from the force of Canadian prejudice such a thing had never been done. Must endeavor to overcome these prejudices when I become better acquainted with their nature and extent." So, strongly tempted as he must have been to perform an autopsy, he was peremptorily restrained from doing so by Doctor John, who knew the ways of the simple people over whom he ruled.

Though he probably deplored the prejudices of these French Canadians, Dr. Tolmie could not hide, in his description of them, a certain implied admiration. "There were the Canadians," he wrote, "mostly dressed in blue capots, large glazed hats with a red military belt, and having their coal black hair dangling in profusion about their shoulders—wild, picturesque looking and their horses rougher and more shaggy than themselves."

No one has penned a more vivid sketch of these western voyageurs.

Equally favorable was the newcomer's opinion of the equipment Doctor John had collected for his improvised hospital. "There is," the journal tells us, "an excellent supply of surgical instruments for amputation, 2 trephinning, 2 eye instruments, a lithotomy, a capping case, besides 2 midwifery forceps and a multitude of catheters, sounds, bandages, probings, forceps etc." [18] Surprised indeed were the two medics to find such an adequate supply of surgical necessities at Vancouver, and, in such time as they could steal from their regular duties, Tolmie and Gairdner took pride in putting "Apothecary's Hall," as the hospital was called, in order.

5

Doctor John was at last able to devote himself whole-heartedly to his ambitious program of expansion. Throughout the years 1833 and 1834, he carried forward his cherished project, determined to stake everything on the outcome.

In addition to the founding of the two northern posts, Forts Langley and Simpson, much had already been accomplished. Late in 1832, following John McLeod's return to the West, the chief factor had dispatched that worthy officer southward to the Umpqua River for the purpose of planting a trading station. Ever since Jedediah Smith's unfortunate experience, he had been anxious to subdue the Indians of that vicinity as well as to divert their annual harvest of furs into Hudson's Bay channels. By that time the demand for beaver and seal furs had grown so heavy that it was both advisable and necessary to solicit the trade of the various coast tribes residing in the southern portion of the Columbia department.

With McLeod, Doctor John had dispatched Michel La Framboise, a colorful French Canadian trapper of proven ability.

Together these two had established the company's only permanent trading post south of the Columbia. From its very inception, the new settlement met with stubborn opposition from the natives, and, in the years immediately ahead, it was to be the scene of many a bloody struggle.[19]

Earlier in the eventful year of 1832, the chief factor had taken steps to found an agency on the Hawaiian Islands. Always keenly alive to new trade opportunities, he had been quick to realize the commercial advantages of such an undertaking, for, with many whalers and fur traders touching there, the Islands were certain to prove a ready and lucrative market for European goods and Columbia River salmon as well as for the surplus produce of Fort Vancouver.[20] Accordingly he had sent Duncan Finlayson to Hawaii on a tour of inspection, and it was during his sojourn at the islands that the "runt of a fellow" had completed negotiations for the purchase of William McNeill's ship, the *Llama*.

"I therefore sailed in July last for the Sandwich Islands," wrote Finlayson in a letter penned upon his return to Vancouver, "where I purchased a fine new copper brig of 150 tons for the sum of £1250 paid from the proceeds of the salmon and timber sent to that market."[21] The Hawaiian Islands post grew rapidly, and it was not long before Fort Vancouver was receiving coffee, sugar, molasses, and rice in return for exports of flour, fish, and lumber. So ably had Finlayson handled this expedition that, in spite of his suspicions, Doctor John found himself warming to the man. Indeed he must have been a little ashamed of his original prejudices.

Though these various undertakings, successfully accomplished, had served to launch the doctor's pretentious program, much remained to be done. The Yankees, following a lull in their activities, had renewed trading operations in northern waters with increased vigor. So, in 1833, spurred by the double necessity of building up his own trade and of thwarting competition, the chief factor turned his attention to that quarter. Finlayson had acquitted himself so well in the Sandwich Islands enterprise that the doctor now called upon him to head an expedition to Milbank Sound, which was situated on the coast southwest of Fort Simpson. The immediate objective was the establishment of another post.

The urgency of the situation was quite apparent to Finlayson, who wrote in the same letter to his friend John McLeod that "returns are still good, but the strong opposition on the North West Coast for the last outfit, rendered it absolutely necessary to take some steps for the protection of the trade at that place, or abandon it altogether. . . . I am just about starting on a cruise to the North West Coast." [22]

Never had Doctor John organized a more pretentious expedition than the one he dispatched from Fort Vancouver, with lofty expectations, in that spring of 1833. In Donald Manson and Alexander C. Anderson, Finlayson had two able lieutenants at his disposal, and in the stanch little ship, the *Dryad,* commanded by Captain Kipling, he had a vessel ideally suited to his needs. The *Dryad* cruised northward to the Nass River and thence to Fort Simpson, where the bulk of the supplies of that post were taken aboard. These were immediately removed to a strategic site on Milbank Sound, which appealed to Finlayson as the best available location for the new establishment. Very shortly, Captain William McNeill, on his first northward voyage under the Hudson's Bay banner, brought the *Llama* to anchor with an additional contingent of men. Having staked everything on his mighty program, the chief factor was determined to spare neither men nor material in the hope of making this present undertaking successful.

Protected from hostile natives by the guns of both vessels, Duncan Finlayson and his men began immediately the task of building the new post. By June the project was well under way, and by October the fort was ready for occupancy.[23] Most appropriately it was christened Fort McLoughlin.

Not long after the founding of this new post, Finlayson returned to Vancouver, leaving Manson and Anderson in charge. Anderson, however, found himself in constant trouble with the Indians—so much so that Doctor John replaced him with the young Scottish physician, William Frazer Tolmie.[24] Though affairs at Fort McLouglin did not assume proportions sufficiently alarming to warrant the change until November, it appears that the chief factor had set his mind upon it even before the Milbank Sound post had been begun. He must, therefore, have had other reasons.

At all events, Tolmie, in his journal for May 9—shortly after his arrival at Vancouver—noted that "I am to be despached northward in the Str. Vancouver which is to set out on a trading voyage in a few days along the coast. Shall probably be left with Mr. Finlayson at the new fort on Milbank Sound which is to supplant Fort Simpson. . . . I would have preferred remaining here but 'il n'import'; as we are to coast a great part of the way and touch at several stations in Puget Sound and the Gulf of Georgia, the voyage I anticipate will be agreeable."[25] This plan, for reasons unknown to us, was not carried out, and the medical recruit from Scotland did not reach Fort McLoughlin until November, 1833.

Tolmie was not a particularly happy choice to relieve Anderson. After he had endured both the rigors of the hard northern winter and the frequent uprisings of the natives as best he could, the chief factor mercifully relieved him in May of the following year. One might logically expect to find, in Tolmie's Fort McLoughlin journal, a rich and informative account of events and personalities; but the document, for all its careful composition, reads more like the doleful lamentations of an exiled bookman than like the virile outpourings of a red-blooded fur trader.[26] The learned Scottish doctor was simply not in his element at Fort McLoughlin.

6

Determined as he was to bring the fur trade of his department to a high point of efficiency, Doctor John had not lost sight of other possible sources of income. It is quite obvious that he had in mind still further expansion in agriculture and animal husbandry with a view toward exporting hides, wool, tallow, and grain to England along with timber. The farm at Vancouver had proved an excellent beginning, but the doctor was looking far ahead. In all probability his authority was limited by the London council to the fur trade alone; but, as early as 1833, he began to consider the formation of a subsidiary concern to handle sheep husbandry, grain culture, and cattle production. Chief Trader Archibald McDonald, who had been in charge of Fort Langley since 1828, is credited with having first made this suggestion to his chief.[27]

Only too well did the chief factor realize the impracticability of carrying on such a development south of the Columbia, for, in his own mind, he had long since conceded that rich country to the Americans. He clearly indicates this in a letter written to John McLeod, and, in the same communication, he makes an odd confession.

"Gervais and others," he writes, "have begun farms in the Willamette and though I have been here since 1824 still I never could find time to visit it till last year and certainly it is deserving all the praises Bestowed on it as it is the finest country I have seen & certainly a far finer country than Red River for Indian traders to retire to—and before long you may depend it will be settled as there is now a plan on foot to colonize it from Boston."[28] Sly old doctor! We recall that, five years earlier, he had, with all the eloquence of a modern realtor, recommended to Lucier, Labonte, and Gervais the glories of a country he had never seen! Between the lines, however, we surmise the chief factor's thoughts—that if the British hoped to gain a permanent foothold in the Columbia region, they had better give some heed to the development of the country north of the river.

McDonald, it appears, shared his chief's views, for, in a letter to John McLeod, he expressed grave doubts concerning the future. "You have," runs the communication, "the Quebec Mercury & Montreal Herald wet from the press the 2'd & 3'd morning after publication and of course have become brimful with Canadian politics—a most fertile field of subject of discussion these days, so much so, that if he does not look sharp His Majesty will ere long be apt to lose his valuable domains on this side of the Atlantic." [29] McDonald had evidently been listening to some potent stories of anticipated Yankee aggression! No doubt his fears caused him to conceive his plan for the organization of a subsidiary concern.

At all events, Doctor John recalled his chief trader from Fort Langley in the early spring of 1833 and discussed with him, in detail, the views which were so strongly held by both. As a direct result of this conference, he dispatched McDonald northward to the Nisqually River with orders to establish a new trading post. The site chosen was on a broad expanse of table land close to Puget Sound. It was on the direct line of overland travel between Forts Vancouver and Langley, and because it was there that boats and horses were exchanged, a settlement had long been needed.[30] Such at least was the reason advanced for the founding of Fort Nisqually; but it is obvious that Doctor John and his able lieutenant recognized in the new post an ideal spot for the further development of cattle raising and agriculture. Though the Nisqually settlement was eventually to become an important farming community, several years were to elapse before the chief factor could secure the necessary authority to organize it as a subsidiary enterprise.

Slowly but surely, the great commercial dream of the White-Headed Eagle was unfolding.

CHAPTER XIII

"NERVES"

I

IT was with mixed feelings that Doctor John hailed the new year of 1834. He had good reason to be pleased with what had been accomplished on the coast, especially at Forts Langley and McLoughlin, but he was frankly discouraged with the state of affairs in the interior. Had he not taken the bold step of invading the rich northern country, the returns from the rest of his department for the two years preceding would have been pitifully small.

In a letter to John McLeod, dated March 1, 1834, the doctor unburdened his mind. "As for us here," he wrote, "we are going on in the usual way. We have an additional post at Mill Bank Sound [modesty forbade him to use his own name] and Expect to be able to Establish another at the River in Latitude 59° and which will enable us to extend our trade into the country north of New Caledonia. But this year we have no party in the Snake Country as Work arrived so late last fall it was impossible for him to get Back this season." [1]

The chief factor could not, however, have regarded this as an unlooked-for reverse, for, a whole year earlier, in another communication to his favorite correspondent, McLeod, he had noted that "the Snake Country is ruined and there are at present 400 Americans in it and I see nothing that they can do to live but go in a body to the Pie-Gan Lands which will be a

Death blow to the Saskatchewan." Even if the doughty Irishman, John Work, had been available for an excursion into the Snake country, it seems obvious that his efforts, in the presence of so many Americans, would have been wasted.

Work, upon his return in the late spring of 1833 from a sixteen months' journey to the southward, had a distressing story to relate. In 1832, under instructions from the chief factor, he had set out with J. T. Larocque, for the so-called "Bonaventura Valley"[2] via Ogden's River with every hope of collecting a handsome haul of skins. But John McLeod and Michel La Framboise, who had preceded him, had found conditions on the southern coast unfavorable and had turned to the interior. Prior to Work's arrival, they had obtained all the beaver available. Everywhere, failure had dogged the path of the luckless Irishman, Work. Still farther south he had encountered an energetic American, Ewing Young, who had been carrying on a successful trade with the Indians.[3] This was the first contact of Vancouver's forces with the Yankee firebrand who was, a little later on, to be much in evidence on the Columbia.

Upon the completion of this futile journey, Work revealed his dejection in a newsy letter to Edward Ermatinger. "My last expedition," he wrote, "was the most unpleasant one I have yet had. It was to the Southward, to California. We had a good deal of trouble and some skirmishes with the hostile tribes of savages who are there very numerous. Some parts of the country are very rugged and difficult to pass, but what was worst of all the fever broke out among my people (near 100 in number) and spread so rapidly that in a short time more than three-fourths of the party, myself, the three little ones & their mother among the number, were attacked by it. 2 men and Indians and ten children belonging to the party died on the way."[4] With such a woeful tale to greet him, it is little wonder that Doctor John, who had been anticipating a very different outcome, was deeply concerned. Indeed the sending out of two parties so close together, with every chance that their paths might cross, indicates considerable uneasiness on his part regarding the state of the fur trade.

From the time of his first visit to the Willamette valley in 1832, it had become the doctor's habit to journey southward with each outgoing brigade for a hundred miles or more. On such occasions he would ride at the head of his suite with the dark-skinned Margaret, arrayed in brilliant colors, at his side. Having crossed the Columbia in canoes, the chief factor's regal train would mount horses which had been sent to the landing place from Tom McKay's near-by farm.[5] Though the doctor's stepson was still active in the company's service as a scout, he had settled his family on a picturesque tract of land a few miles to the westward, where he spent a portion of his time and where he took particular pride in raising fine horses.[6] He was always happy to provide mounts for the annual southbound brigade.

Doctor John, it appears, had a twofold purpose in making these periodic pilgrimages through the Willamette valley, his inherent sense of showmanship vying with his instinctive humanitarian qualities. He could appreciate the value, now and again, of impressing the natives with his power, while, at the same time, he could understand how keenly his men, who had little enough by way of diversion, would relish a ride into the country solely on pleasure. In fancy we can see him swinging along in stately fashion through the virgin woods of Oregon, his keen eyes gazing straight ahead, his white hair flowing in the breeze, and his long black cloak hanging majestically from his shoulders. He was, in truth, the king of the Columbia.

When, on the 22nd of May, 1834, John Work started southward again to try his luck in the Umpqua valley, it is not likely that the chief factor's colorful procession accompanied him for, as the Irishman recalled, there was "a very heavy rain the greater part of the day."[7] That, we may be sure, was not the sort of weather to inspire one of the doctor's holidays. This expedition, like its predecessor, proved unsuccessful, and, upon Work's return, Doctor John placed him in charge of the Hudson's Bay Company coast shipping with headquarters at Vancouver.[8] Since John Work, next to Peter Skene Ogden, was perhaps the ablest fur trader in the Columbia department, this sudden decision to remove him from the service of the interior seems but further evidence that the chief factor was, at that time, staking everything on the trade of the Northwest coast.

One cloudless afternoon, in the late summer of 1834, he stood with folded arms at the gates of Fort Vancouver, and gazed southward across the peaceful expanse of the mighty Columbia. He was, in truth, the monarch of all he surveyed, yet never again was this literally to be true. He was soon to share his sway over Oregon with a tiny band of religious crusaders—the modest vanguard of a mighty army of Yankee settlers. Little did he dream, as his thoughts ran the gamut of the years, that even he—the undisputed king of the Columbia—would one day renounce his throne to join the swelling ranks of the Americans. Momentous events were just around the corner.

2

Back as far as 1830, the Governor and Committee of the Hudson's Bay Company had informed Governor Simpson that "a clergyman is to be sent out . . . as a missionary for the West Side of the Mountains," and, though they had seen fit to add that "we desire that measures may be concerted to carry this object into effect with the least possible delay,"[9] nothing was done at the time. Indeed six years were to elapse before the company itself was to take this step. Whether the plan was discouraged by Governor Simpson in 1830 or whether it was simply lost sight of in the face of more pressing issues, we cannot say.

Had the London committee carried out its design, it seems obvious that a clergyman of the Church of England would have been sent, and such a man would not have solved the doctor's religious problem of the moment—that of providing spiritual leadership for his French Canadian servants. As we have already noted, it was finally left to the chief factor himself to take the initiative in the matter of bringing clerics to Oregon by inviting the Catholic Church of Canada to send out two priests. It hardly seems likely, however, that as early as 1834 he would have considered it advisable to import Black-Robes for the exclusive purposes of saving Indian souls. Practical man that he was, he probably felt that his own efforts to civilize the red men were more resultful, just then, than any widespread attempt to teach them formal religion could hope to be. Then too, he was enough the politician to know that a blanket appeal for missionaries would almost certainly bring American church workers into the field—an eventuality scarcely to be sought by a Hudson's Bay man, however broad his outlook.

Whatever the doctor's thoughts may have been, forces of which he had no knowledge were already conspiring to awaken interest in his empire as a fertile field for missionary endeavor. It appears that in 1831 four Indians of the Flathead tribe had made the difficult overland journey to St. Louis for the purpose of learning more about the white man's religion. From Yankee and British fur traders they had heard enough about the Bible to whet their appetite. Though two of the red men died in St. Louis that winter, the bravery and obvious sincerity of the survivors aroused the sympathetic interest of Catholics and Protestants alike.[10]

Time went by, but the visit of the Flatheads was not forgotten in the United States. At length Dr. Wilbur Fisk, president of Wesleyan University at Middletown, Connecticut, took up the cause of the Indians and induced the General Conference of the Methodist Episcopal Church to investigate the desirability of ministering to the spiritual needs of the natives west of the Rockies. As a result, Jason Lee, a young Methodist minister, was chosen as "Missionary to the Flatheads" in the late spring of 1833.[11]

Lee proved a rapid and efficient organizer, and, before the year had spent itself, he had gathered a small band of religious workers, including his nephew, the Reverend Daniel Lee, and three lay members, Cyrus Shepard, P. L. Edwards, and Courtney M. Walker. Having heard that Nathaniel J. Wyeth contemplated another expedition to Oregon, the newly appointed missionary sought him out and found him quite willing to pilot the Methodist crusaders across the continent. In addition to that, Wyeth gave Lee permission to ship his freight westward on the brig *May Dacre,* which had been chartered by the Bostonian to carry his supplies to the Columbia.[12] So much good fortune must have seemed to the devout Lee a direct answer to his prayers. Starting January 29, 1834, Jason Lee and his followers made many stops along the route for the purpose of raising funds to finance the mission. They joined forces with Wyeth at Independence, Missouri, on April 22.[13]

Jason Lee, though a man of lofty idealism, was nevertheless extremely practical in his concept of religion. He knew that, in order to make the Word of God a living reality to the Indians, he would not only have to work patiently and ceaselessly but also have to demonstrate the truth of his doctrine in his own conduct. Few missionaries have been better suited to their calling. Lee was described as "a man of light hair, blue eyes, fair complexion, spare habit, above ordinary height, a little stoop-shouldered, with strong nerve and indomitable will, yet a meek, warm-hearted and humble Christian, gaining by his affable and easy manners the esteem of all who became acquainted with him." [14] It was inevitable that Doctor John should find, in such a man, a willing ally in working out his humanitarian program among the natives. Though ever on the watch for political motives hiding behind the Church, he was always sympathetic to pure religion of any creed. It was only when Jason Lee broke away from his original purpose, some years later, that the doctor cooled toward him.

In spite of Nathaniel Wyeth's willingness to aid the "Flathead Mission," it is apparent that he became weary of waiting for Lee and his workers at Independence. In his journal for April 17, 1834, he observed, a bit testily, that "there are none of the Dignitaries with me as yet and if they 'preach' much longer in the States they will lose their passage for I will not wait a minute [longer] for them." [15] Indeed one wonders what these temperate Methodists would have thought had they been able to read an earlier entry in their pilot's log. "The bbl. of Rum at Wyeth and Norris," the Bostonian had written, "will require to be carefully examined to see it is tight." [16] Lee, however, owed everything to the Yankee trader, and without his timely help, this ardent crusader would have had a most difficult time in reaching Oregon on schedule.

It was a notable party that assembled at Independence in that spring of 1834. There, with his missionaries safely in tow, Wyeth joined forces with an old friend, Milton Sublette, and, on April 28, the expedition, with its wagons, its cattle, and its variegated assortment of human beings, began its long, lumbering journey across the plains. [17] Traveling with the party were two young men whose later work in Oregon was destined to enrich the nation's store of scientific knowledge. One was John Kirk Townsend, a Quaker ornithologist from Philadelphia, and the other Thomas Nuttall, an eminent botanist from Harvard College.

Following the same route Wyeth had traversed two years earlier, the party continued its westward trek without mishap until the Snake River was reached in July. There, in the rich bottom lands formed by the junction of the Portneuf and Snake rivers, Captain Wyeth decided to build a trading post to provide storage for a quantity of goods that had fallen unexpectedly into his hands en route. This settlement, which was christened Fort Hall, was later to become one of the most important stations on the Oregon Trail.[18]

For two weeks Lee remained with the party, and during that sojourn he conducted the first formal Protestant service ever held west of the Rocky Mountains—an achievement that thrilled his eager soul.[19] Among those assembled on that bright Sunday afternoon was none other than Doctor John's ubiquitous stepson, Tom McKay, who had met the Yankee expedition some weeks earlier with his brigade of French Canadian trappers. Seated in a little grove not far from the site of Fort Hall, these devout Catholics listened in reverence to the simple, unadorned Word of God preached by the lanky American, whose lack of vestments was soon forgotten in the sincerity of his message.

Jason Lee, however, was anxious to press on, and so, with the genial Tom McKay and his men acting as guides, the missionaries and the two scientists renewed their journey, reaching Fort Walla Walla on September 1. There, arrangements were made with Pierre C. Pambrun, the Hudson's Bay clerk in charge, for the trip down the Columbia. On September 4, Captain Wyeth and his followers having overtaken the missionaries, the reunited party started down the river on a Hudson's Bay barge bound for Vancouver, where they arrived on September 16.

3

Doctor John hurried to the boat landing as soon as he was informed that the missionaries had been sighted. To the travel-weary pilgrims he must have seemed an impressive figure as he stood proudly on the shore, towering above his suite and brandishing his trusty cane in friendly welcome.

Jason Lee, in his diary for September 16, described the scene vividly. "Arrived at Vancouver at 3 o'clock," he wrote, "found the governor and other gentlemen connected with the fort on shore awaiting our arrival, and conducted us to the fort and gave us food, which was very acceptable, as we had eaten our last for breakfast. We received every attention from these gentlemen. Our baggage was brought and put into a spacious room without consulting us and the room assigned to our use, and we had the pleasure of sleeping again within the walls of a house after a long and fatiguing journey, replete with mercies, deprivations, toil and prosperity. I have been much delighted today in viewing the improvements of the farm, etc. The dinner was as good and served in as good style as in any gentleman's house in the east." [20]

If the dinner was pleasing to the grateful Lee, the conversation at table must have been even more so, for, in his diary reflections for that same day, he observed that "Dr. McLoughlin, the governor of the fort, seems pleased that missions have come to the country and freely offers any assistance that it is in his power to render. It is his decided opinion that we should commence somewhere in this vicinity. O Lord, do thou direct us in the choice of a location." [21]

But while the zealous Methodist was praying for divine guidance, the hard-headed chief factor was plying him with practical arguments in favor of the Willamette valley as against the barren and hostile Flathead country to the eastward. Not only was the fertile valley more inviting, he contended, but the French Canadian settlers already there would afford the newcomers a measure of protection. "I observed to them," wrote the doctor, "that it was too dangerous for them to establish a mission [in the Flathead country]; that to do good to the Indians, they must establish themselves where they could collect them around them, teach them first to cultivate the ground and live more comfortably than they could do by hunting, and as they do this, teach them religion; that the Willamette afforded them a fine field, and that they ought to go there, and they would get the same assistance as the settlers." [22]

There was also a more significant reason. Sympathetic as he was with the noble aspirations of the devout Lee and anxious as he was to aid him in every way possible, he could not overlook the fact that his guest was an American and that other Americans, less concerned with matters of pure religion, would be bound to follow. If the Yankees must come, he reasoned, let them settle below the Columbia—the doctor was still a "good Hudson's Bay man."

"Is not the hand of Providence in all this?" queried Lee near the end of his recorded impressions of that same eventful day—his first at Fort Vancouver—and then he added, in deep reverence, "Would to God that I could praise him as I ought for his gracious dealings with us." [23] Indeed he had good reason to express his thanks to the Almighty, for, on that very evening, news reached the fort that Captain Wyeth's brig, the *May Dacre,* had been sighted in the river. If the earnest preacher needed proof of the efficacy of his prayers, he must have found it in such an amazing succession of fortuitous events.

Very wisely, Jason Lee decided to follow the doctor's sound advice. After a brief sojourn at the fort during which he found occasion to preach to "a mixed congregation of English, French, Scotch, Irish, Indians, Americans, half-breeds, Japanese, etc., some of whom did not understand five words of English," [24] he "began to make preparations in good earnest for our departure to the Willamette, and after dinner embarked in one of the Company's boats kindly manned for us by Dr. McLoughlin, who has treated us with the utmost politeness, attention and liberality. Arrived at the lower mouth of the Willamette where Capt. Wyeth's brig is, late in the evening." [25]

Not long after the arrival of the missionaries, the doctor sent them a substantial testimony of his good will in the form of a subscription. "I do myself the pleasure to hand you the enclosed subscription," he wrote, "which the gentlemen who have signed it request you will do them the favor to accept for the use of the Mission; and they pray our Heavenly Father, without whose assistance we can do nothing, that of his infinite mercy he will vouchsafe to bless and prosper your pious endeavors, and believe me to be, with esteem and regard, your sincere well-wisher and humble servant." [26]

The Methodists founded their mission close to the east bank of the Willamette on the southern fringe of French Prairie. There, under the watchful eye of the indulgent doctor, they began their labors. "It is but justice to these pioneers," he wrote, "to say that no men, in my opinion, could exert themselves more zealously than they did." [27] Time, unfortunately, was to change his opinion.

4

During this time the ambitious Wyeth was not idle. Though Doctor John knew well enough that the Yankee had returned for the avowed purpose of competing with him, his welcome had been just as cordial as before. Already their friendship had become sufficiently strong to withstand the personal animosity which so often goes hand in hand with commercial rivalry. Nevertheless, the situation must have been a little embarrassing, for, on the day following his arrival at Vancouver, Wyeth, with the two American scientists, hastened down the river to meet his ship.

At the mouth of the Willamette, where the *May Dacre* was

moored, the Bostonian was warmly greeted by Captain Lambert. Though the vessel had made good connections with Wyeth, she had actually lagged far behind the schedule he had planned for her. It had been his hope that the *May Dacre* would reach the Columbia in time to gather in a cargo of salmon from the river; but severe storms en route had made this impossible.[28]

After discussing future plans with his skipper, the disappointed Boston merchant set out with Townsend and Nuttall to find a suitable site upon which to build a trading station. The spot chosen was on the lower end of Sauvé Island, several miles west of Fort Vancouver.

Wyeth was evidently a fast worker, for on October 6 he was able to write: "We have built a few buildings for store houses, smiths and Cooper shops, and dwellings. We are near the mouth of the Multnomah [Willamette]. About 40 miles up this river I have begun a farm on a beautiful prairie of about 15 miles long one end touching the river a good mill stream in the center the whole surrounded with good and well assorted timber, of fine soil and mild climate, much game, in fact all that a man ought to have."[29] Ironically, at least from Doctor John's point of view, Captain Wyeth had christened his Sauvé Island post Fort William! Having dispatched the *May Dacre* to the Sandwich Islands with a cargo of timber and with orders to return in the spring with cattle, sheep, goats, and hogs for his farm, the Bostonian settled down to a winter of hard work and grandiose planning.

From Vancouver the chief factor watched the rising enterprise on Sauvé Island with growing concern. It was not the fear of fresh competition that tortured his soul—experience had taught him how to deal with that. Rather it was the realization that he must ruin his friend and drive him from the Columbia or be judged a traitor to his own company. So, while the two of them lingered over their coffee at Vancouver or Fort William, the

doctor would broach the ticklish question by making mild
overtures to buy out his competitor, whereupon Wyeth, with
equal tact, would invariably switch the conversation into other
channels. Behind all this gallantry and friendliness, each could
read the other's mind. Doctor John soon learned that more than
talk would be required to dislodge the Bostonian, and Wyeth, on
his part, was given to understand that if he remained, he must
prepare to face a bitter struggle. Richard the Lion-Hearted and
Saladin could not have waged battle on a nobler plane.

Salmon-catching could be tolerated, conceded the doctor in his
own analysis of the situation, but not fur trading—yet he knew
that success in one field would lead inevitably to vigorous aggression in the other. Circumstances left him no alternative—
Wyeth's "Columbia River Fishing and Trading Company"
must fail, and the sooner the better.

His mind made up, the chief factor lost no time in planning
his campaign. Soon after the founding of Fort William, he
used his vast influence with the lower river Indians not only to
keep them from trading with the Americans but also to nullify
such assistance as they might otherwise have given the newcomers in salmon-catching.[30] Then, too, there was the challenge
of Wyeth's Fort Hall—a challenge the watchful doctor could
not side-step. So, in the late fall of 1834, he sent the infallible
Tom McKay eastward with orders to build a rival trading post.[31]
Fort Boise, the new station, was erected on the Boise River not
far from Fort Hall, and, though it was not expected to prove
profitable on its own account, it served to checkmate Wyeth's
ambitions in the interior.

Handicapped from the start by the might and tenacity of the
Hudson's Bay Company, the plucky Boston merchant was
doomed to failure. Everywhere he met reverses. On the Columbia he found that his nets were not of the right type, and that
the Indians, upon whom he had counted so heavily, would

neither help him catch salmon nor trade with him. At Fort Hall the trade proved disappointing, and the natives hostile. Two years sufficed to ruin his venture and force him to accept the doctor's terms. Nevertheless, in the long-range appraisal of Oregon's history, Nathaniel Wyeth's labors were not wasted. He had blazed the trail which others were to follow. As for the White-Headed Eagle, it was as if he had signed the death warrant of his own brother.

5

When the company's ship *Cadboro* reached Vancouver from San Francisco Bay in the late summer of 1834, her master delivered to Doctor John a startling message from Governor Figueroa of California. A sizable party, ran the document, was headed northward, and included in its ranks were Ewing Young, the Yankee trader from Taos, New Mexico, and Hall J. Kelley, the Boston prophet. As the chief factor read on, he could scarcely believe his own eyes. At last he was to meet, face to face, the man who had inspired all these infernal Yankees to invade Oregon!

In so far as Doctor John could hate a fellow human being, he hated Kelley. Though he had never laid eyes on the man, it was sufficient that he had made disparaging remarks about the Hudson's Bay Company, and that he had preached Oregon so successfully that scores of his fellow Americans were beginning to cast covetous glances in the direction of the White-Headed Eagle's empire. The dispatch went on to state that Young and Kelley had been stealing horses in the Mexican governor's territory—then, as later, a frontier crime not to be countenanced. The chief factor was furious! These two brigands would not find the gates of his fort open to them!

Hall J. Kelley finally reached his destination on October 27, "penniless, and ill-clad," wearing "a white slouched hat, blanket capote, leather pants, with a red stripe down the seam, rather outré even for Vancouver." [32] Severe illness had caused him to lag behind Young's party, and had it not been for Michel La Framboise, who had found him in the wilds of northern California and conducted him northward with the Hudson's Bay brigade, the Oregon enthusiast might never have reached the land of his dreams alive.[33]

Bitter in the extreme was Kelley's memory of his reception. "Capt. La Framboise," he wrote, "assisted me out of the boat. With the help of his arm, I walked slowly and feebly to the fort, and entered a room at one end of the mansion-house, opening from the court. After a few minutes, the chief factor, Mr. McLoughlin, came in—made a few inquiries about my health and business, and, ordering some refreshments, retired. None of his household, none of his American guests called, nor had any of them been seen at the river, or on the way to the fort. No countrymen, though many were in the house, came to sympathize in my afflictions or to greet my coming." [34] The humble schoolmaster might as well have been a leper!

Then, training his guns directly upon the doctor, he continued in the same vein. "The prosecuting monster," he observed, "anticipating my coming to the place of his abode, was ready, with sword in hand, to cut me down; and I was treated . . . with every demonstration of inhumanity." [35] A new portrait, this, of the old chief factor!

After filling several more pages of his journal with remarks equally caustic, Kelley noted that "the first person, after the physician, to visit me in that prison-house, was Captain Ewing Young, the veteran hunter, and the conductor of my party. His call was not so much to sympathize . . . as to speak of personal abuse just received from Dr. McLoughlin. . . . He remarked, in substance, that Mr. McLoughlin had insulted him, to provoke a quarrel, and to get an excuse for hostilities; and that the company's farmers on the Wallamet had peremptory orders not to give or sell supplies nor afford quarters or relief to any of the party." [36]

Doctor John had, in truth, posted notices in the Willamette valley warning the settlers against Ewing Young, whom he had every reason to believe guilty of horse stealing; but his treatment of Kelley, even in the circumstances, seems difficult to square with his own character. In an interesting document addressed to his superiors in London, the chief factor vigorously defended his actions.

"Kelley," he wrote, "left the states with a party intending to come here by way of Mexico, but the party broke up on the way and Kelley alone reached California, and with one man overtook our California trappers on their return about two hundred miles from San Francisco, and Young, a few days after, with the rest of them; but as Gen. Fiqueroa, Governor of California, had written me that Ewing Young and Kelley had stolen horses from the settlers of that place I would have no dealings with them, and told them my reasons. Young maintained he stole no horses, but admitted the others had. I told him that might be the case, but as the charge was made I could have no dealings with him till he cleared it up. But he maintained to his countrymen and they believed it, that as he was a leader among them, I acted as I did from a desire to oppose American interests. I treated all of the party in the same manner as Young, except Kelley, who was very sick. Out of humanity I placed him in a house, attended on him and had his victuals sent him at every meal till he left in 1836, when I gave him a passage to Oahoo." [37]

As it turned out, the charge of horse stealing proved groundless, and though the doctor, once he learned the true facts, offered to trade with Young, the hot-blooded southerner refused to have any dealings with the Hudson's Bay men and settled down in isolated splendor on his fertile acres in the Chehalem valley.[38] As for Kelley, he remained a veritable outcast until his departure in 1836, but, in spite of his wounded feelings, he managed to gather a fund of useful information about the country he had so long admired from afar.[39] As long as he lived, he never forgave Vancouver's chief factor.

Notwithstanding the carefully worded disclaimer Doctor John sent to the home office, it appears obvious that he was anxious, as a loyal Hudson's Bay man, to break up American enterprise in Oregon. Even so, to have believed the meek and ailing Kelley capable of stealing horses seems but the natural desire of a harassed mind to find some measure of confirmation for its preconceived prejudices. The White-Headed Eagle suffered from a case of "nerves," induced by the presence of too many Yankees in his empire. His conduct, on this occasion, was far from admirable.

CHAPTER XIV

Too Many Missionaries

I

FOLLOWING the inrush of Americans in the latter part of 1834, Doctor John was given a breathing spell in which to recover his equilibrium. The year 1835 appears to have been a period of intensive effort to strengthen his position and to prepare for such exigencies as the advent of the Yankees might cause.

Up to that time, the doctor's sway had been so absolute that legal processes, beyond those vested in the company, had not been deemed necessary. The original grant had, of course, made provision for the governor and council to try and punish employees who committed crimes in the territories occupied by the Hudson's Bay Company. Since the charter expressly prohibited British subjects not identified with the concern from carrying on trade within the lands exploited by it, there had been little or no possibility of conflict in authority.

With the arrival of the Americans, however, Doctor John faced a new and, in many respects, a difficult problem. Obviously, the Hudson's Bay charter could not prevent these newcomers from trading in the company's territories since, under the treaty of joint occupancy, the whole area was open to citizens of both nations. Indeed, the character of the Yankees he had seen convinced the doctor that they were men likely to insist upon their legal rights, and he feared, not without reason, that their innate hatred of autocratic rule might induce them to foment discord in his own ranks. For the first time since his arrival in the Oregon country, he found himself standing in need of additional authority.

During the early months of 1835, the White-Headed Eagle discussed this situation with his favorite lieutenant, James Douglas, who was that very year to receive his chief-tradership. As a result of these conferences, the doctor made arrangements, under an act of Parliament, to have justices of the peace appointed for the various posts in his empire. These officials were authorized to impose punishment upon petty criminals and to send the more flagrant malefactors to Canada for trial. James Douglas was named Vancouver's first justice of the peace—a very happy selection.[1]

John Dunn, whom the chief factor had recalled from Fort McLoughlin in 1834, was stationed at Vancouver during this trying period. He recalled that the presence of Americans in Oregon had served to divide the Hudson's Bay men into two camps—the patriots and the liberals.[2] The patriots were, in the main, hostile to the newcomers, contending that they were a lawless lot, uncouth and ungentlemanly, and that they were bent solely upon acquiring the whole country for the United States. They even censured the doctor roundly, though perhaps not to his face, for having had any contact with such barbarians. The liberals, on the other hand, while unable to refute all of these arguments, held that the Yankees had every right to settle in Oregon though they hoped the invaders could be kept below the Columbia. Moreover, they maintained that Jason Lee and his followers were really allies of the company in so far as their efforts to civilize the Indians were concerned, and that the British government was itself to blame for having failed to send out missionaries of its own choosing.[3] Long and bitter were the debates in Bachelors' Hall, but, since the chief factor himself had espoused the liberal cause, the result was never in doubt.

It appears that he dominated the evening conversation at the fort. He was extremely fond of argument, and, whenever the discussion drifted into history, he was ready to defend Napoleon I against all comers—the natural sympathy, no doubt, of one auto-crat for another. George T. Allan recalls that on one occasion, while Wyeth was present, the doctor was dressing the injured hand of a voyageur and "in the height of the argument on the Peace of Amiens, he treated ———'s hand so roughly that ——— wished Napoleon and the Peace of Amiens in Hades."[4] Pol-itics, religion, science, and philosophy all came in for their share of debate, and a stranger within Vancouver's gates would doubt-less have marveled that such erudition existed in the wilds of North America.

Throughout this period, the chief factor continued to maintain close supervision over the former company employees who had settled as farmers in the Willamette valley. It was a relationship that possessed all the earmarks of feudalism save that Doctor John, like a wise and just lord, treated his French Canadian serfs with such liberality that they were seldom allowed to become aware of their bondage. But with all his generosity, he realized the necessity of keeping these people well in hand.

"It was," wrote Medorem Crawford, a pioneer of a later date, "a most remarkable condition. The old doctor would go down to Champoeg, and whatever he told them [the settlers] to do, they would do. If they were shiftless, he would not give them half what they wanted. If they were industrious, even if they were not successful, he would give them what they wanted. He kept himself constantly informed about these people. . . . If they went around horse-racing, he would lecture them severely, and make them afraid to do so. There were no laws or rules. If there were any disputes, he settled them arbitrarily. Just what he said was the law."[5] It is no wonder that, to these simple farmers, he seemed little less than a god.

Like the white settlers, the Indians required constant watching, and it was about this same time that the doctor, for all his vigilance, came dangerously near to falling into a trap which a certain tribe of Columbia River natives had set for him. According to the story, a deputation from this tribe came to him and, with horror written on their faces, gave him to understand that the company's post at Nisqually had been attacked, and that its inhabitants had been slaughtered to a man. Without wasting a moment, Doctor John locked up the delegation and sent a party to interview other members of the tribe who promptly verified the tale with amazing accuracy as to details. Convinced at last, he was on the point of dispatching a strong force to Fort Nisqually when, providentially, a brigade arrived from that place in time to expose the plot.[6] It was indeed a close call, for, had the red men succeeded in dividing Vancouver's meager staff, they would have been able to attack the fort with an excellent chance of victory. Exactly what punishment these conspirators received is not known, but they doubtless got what they deserved. Fortunately, attempts of this sort were rare. The tribes knew that the White-Headed Eagle would use his claws to defend his roost.

As to the fur trade, things were coming along, if not briskly, at least as well as the doctor could reasonably expect. The northern posts had continued to yield sufficient quantities of skins to offset the meager returns from the interior, and the chief factor was beginning to realize the fruits of his ambitious program. For a second time he had postponed his anticipated furlough, as he explains in a newsy letter to Edward Ermatinger, dated February 1, 1835.

"I see that you and several of my friends," runs the message, "expected me down last year—the truth is that I had given them to Understand that I would do so—But on reflection I considered that while I was in the country It was as well for me to remain a little longer so that when I went down—It might be optionable with me to remain if I was so Inclined."

The doctor may have been telling the truth; but assuredly he was not telling the whole truth, for there were more important reasons, just then, for his unwillingness to leave his empire. His very next comment, in fact, suggests one of them. "Last Summer," continues the communication, "I sent Ogden to erect a trading Establishment on a River on the Coast in Latitude 54 N. But the Russians would not allow him to ascend the River—this is contrary to the treaty between the two Governments and of course John Bull must interfere but until the affair is decided we will remain on our oars." [7]

Assuredly it was no time for the conscientious chief factor to consider deserting his responsibilities. With the Russians showing opposition to his program of expansion, with the Yankee missionaries struggling to establish themselves in the Willamette valley, with the hostile Ewing Young and the sulking Kelley on his hands, and with the energetic Wyeth waging a brave if losing battle both on the Columbia and at Fort Hall, he was sorely needed at home. Thus occupied, he doggedly pursued his course through a perplexing though uneventful year.

2

Although the historic visit of the Flatheads in St. Louis had first inspired action among the Methodists, it had also awakened the crusading zeal of other Protestant denominations. As early as 1834 the American Board of Commissioners for Foreign Missions, representing the Presbyterian, Congregational, and Dutch Reformed churches, had appointed the Reverend Samuel Parker, a Presbyterian minister, and Dr. Marcus Whitman, a physician and an elder of the same faith, to explore the Oregon country with a view toward establishing a mission there not later than 1836.[8] The American Board had been somewhat skeptical because, some years earlier, one of its members, the Reverend Jonathan S. Green, had visited the western country from his post in the Sandwich Islands and had turned in an unfavorable report concerning the prospects of missionary activity.[9]

In 1835 the two Presbyterians had traveled westward as far as the Green River rendezvous in the Nez Percé country, from which point Marcus Whitman, having satisfied himself that the natives needed saving, had returned to the States for reinforcements while Samuel Parker, escorted by friendly Indians, had continued his journey to Fort Walla Walla. There, the affable Hudson's Bay clerk in charge, Pierre C. Pambrun, had arranged for his safe conduct down the Columbia to Vancouver.[10]

On October 16, the "plug-hat missionary," as the immaculately clad Parker had been dubbed by the Hudson's Bay men, reached the boat landing at Fort Vancouver and found Doctor John waiting for him with a welcome fully as warm as the one Jason Lee had received thirteen months earlier to the day. "Here," wrote Parker in his journal, "by the kind invitation of Dr. McLoughlin, and welcomed by the other gentlemen of the Hudson's Bay Co., I took up my residence for the winter. . . . I am agreeably situated in this place. Rooms in a new house are assigned to me, well furnished, and all the attendance which I can wish, with access to as many valuable books as I have time to read; and opportunities to ride out for exercise, and see the adjoining country; and in addition to all these, the society of gentlemen enlightened, polished and sociable."

Almost immediately the visiting divine became interested in secular matters, and, thanks to his journal, we are given an accurate idea of the progress the chief factor had made with his farming enterprises. "In the year 1835," observed Parker, "at this post there were 450 head cattle, 100 horses, 200 sheep, 40 goats and 300 hogs. They had raised the same year 5,000 bu. of wheat, of the best quality I ever saw, 1,300 bushels of potatoes,

100 bu. of barley, 1,000 bu. of oats, 2,000 of peas, and a large quantity of garden vegetables." [11]

Merely the advance man of the main Presbyterian show which was not to begin until the following year, the Reverend Mr. Parker had come to Oregon to learn what he could about the country and about the spiritual needs of the natives as well as to choose mission sites for those who were to follow him. Doctor John was doubtless eager to keep the Presbyterians, as well as the Methodists, south of the Columbia, but, if he made an attempt to excite his guest over the charms of the Willamette valley, he was wasting his eloquence. Parker had already chosen the various sites for his missionary workers, and he was, from all accounts, a most determined individual.

The "plug-hat missionary" remained at the fort until April, 1836. Having proved to his own satisfaction that missionaries could venture safely into the interior, and that the natives were, in the main, friendly, he had accomplished the double purpose of his journey.[12] Just prior to his departure on the bark *Columbia,* he offered to pay his host for the many services he had received—merchandise with which to compensate his Indian guides, clothing, board, and lodging—but Doctor John "had made no bill against me, but felt a pleasure in gratuitously conferring all they had done for the benefit of the object in which I was engaged."[13] Notwithstanding the contrary opinion of Hall J. Kelley, who had departed some months earlier on the company's bark *Dryad,* the good doctor's open-handed hospitality was still in evidence.

Samuel Parker, however, was not to leave Vancouver until he had helped make history by taking a ride, as Doctor John's guest, in the first steamboat on the Columbia. In the early spring of 1836, the Hudson's Bay sailing ship *Beaver* had reached the fort from England, where she had been built the previous year. Deep in her hold she had carried round the Horn the wherewithal to convert her into a steam vessel,[14] and, under the doctor's supervision, the mechanics at Vancouver had installed her engines.

When the *Beaver* was at last ready for her maiden voyage under steam, the chief factor proudly invited all the company dignitaries within calling distance to accompany him on a gala excursion down the river. As the little steamboat, pouring out a heavy column of black smoke from her ridiculously tall funnel, paddled down to Tom McKay's farm and back, it is a question which group was the more agog—the company officials and guests standing a bit nervously on her deck or the red men gazing in open-mouthed wonder from the banks. Among those who made this memorable excursion were Doctor John, James Douglas, Archibald McKinlay, John Work, Pierre C. Pambrun, Samuel Parker, and John Kirk Townsend, the Quaker ornithologist.[15]

Governor Simpson had favored the *Beaver* because he wanted fewer posts and more extensive transportation facilities. The doctor, on the other hand, opposed the vessel, believing that her advent would tend to eliminate some of his pet stations. Nevertheless the little steamship was shortly to become an important factor in the West coast trade, and, on the day following her successful trial trip, she towed the *Columbia* to the company's sawmill to load lumber for the Hawaiian Islands. By a stroke of good luck, the Presbyterian advance man was thus enabled to carry home with him a convincing story of progress on the Columbia.

3

Among the passengers who, in August, 1836, reached Fort Vancouver on the company's bark *Nereid,* were the Reverend Herbert Beaver, a clergyman of the Church of England, his wife Jane, and the Reverend Daniel Lee, who had been recuperating from a pulmonary ailment in the Sandwich Islands.[16] The

London authorities had been six long years in making good their promise to send Doctor John a missionary, and, had it not been for the activities of the American Methodists in the Willamette valley, the delay might have been even longer.[17]

Although Peter Skene Ogden, with his ready wit, was to write the following year that "amongst the many good things their honors from Fenchurch street sent us last summer was a clergyman and with him his wife, the Reverend Mr. Beaver, a very appropriate name for the fur trade," [18] we gather that his cognomen was the only appropriate thing about him. He was a short man with a high-pitched voice, a marked penchant for oratory, an exceedingly poor delivery, and an unbounded capacity for lazy living—a most unprepossessing individual.[19] Had he lived a century later, he would have been called "cocky." Aside from his unfortunate personality, Herbert Beaver's experience as a British army chaplain had not given him the broad, tolerant outlook required by any clergyman in the fur-trading West. By comparison, the uncompromising Lees were almost free-thinkers. According to contemporary accounts, the rector from England was more inclined to roam the countryside with his dog and gun than to instruct the natives, whom he cordially despised.[20]

Immediately upon their arrival, the Beavers were shocked to discover that, from their point of view, all of the gentlemen at the fort were living in sin with their Indian and half-breed women. But in trying to set things aright, the self-righteous pair displayed so little tact that they soon became extremely unpopular with the company's officers, who, secure in their Hudson's Bay marriages, believed that the newcomers should find something more serious to denounce.

Doctor John was thoroughly disgusted with the choice of the London authorities. He wanted a man, and they had sent him a hypocritical nonentity. Indeed, from a letter he had penned

to Edward Ermatinger earlier that same year—some months prior
to Beaver's arrival—we gather some notion of the type of missionary he had been anticipating. "I wrote you last year," the
chief factor had confided, "that two Methodist Missionaries are
settled in the Willamette and I have the pleasure to say that
they are doing well. . . . Several Indians have joined them
who—while they are receiving Religious Instruction are at the
same time learning how to till the land—which will Enable them
to live as Civilized men and which is the only Rational plan to be
followed with Indians and which our Missionaries ought to
follow—instead of teaching them to Read and Write—and send
them Back to their Lands—which gives them a certain consequence in the Eyes of their Countrymen—and Enables them to
do harm—(if so disposed)—without having the power to do
Good—as it is impossible even if they were ever so well Disposed
to Receive Instruction for Natives to be Instructed and wander
about as they must necessarily do for their food. No, let those
who wish to do good to Indians teach them to get their food in
a different way than at present—in short teach them agriculture
while they are instructing them in Religion." [21] Perhaps unwittingly, the doctor had been molding his ideal missionary priest
after the pattern of Jason Lee, and great must have been his
disappointment when he gazed for the first time upon the smug,
mincing Beaver.

Meanwhile, the company's business in the vast Columbia
department had been taking a turn for the better. In spite of
Russian opposition, Ogden, Manson, and other Hudson's Bay
officers were achieving success at the various northern posts.
Archibald McDonald was building solidly at Fort Nisqually;
John Work was welding the coast shipping fleet into a strong
and serviceable force, and James Douglas was handling the
concern's accounts with enthusiasm and efficiency. Never had
Doctor John felt freer to leave vexatious details to others and to

devote himself exclusively to the general administration of affairs in his empire.

Then, too, from the company's angle, there were other encouraging signs. Though the American missionaries, beset by all manner of hardships, were gradually acquiring a foothold in the Willamette valley, they were concerning themselves solely with religious activities and were displaying no interest in political affairs. That, we may be sure, was a source of deep satisfaction to the doctor. For the moment, extensive Yankee colonization in Oregon seemed comfortably remote.

Wyeth, in the interim, had become thoroughly discouraged by the turn his fortunes had taken. Both at Fort William and at Fort Hall he had found the chief factor's opposition so well organized that his hopes of acquiring furs by trade had not materialized; and, on the river, his men had been equally unsuccessful in catching salmon. Already, before it was two years old, the Columbia River Fishing and Trading Company was doomed to failure. On June 25, 1836, the now completely disillusioned Wyeth left Fort Hall and started overland for Boston to consult with the members of his firm as to the ultimate disposition of their holdings in the West.[22] That Doctor John had been able to vanquish the plucky Bostonian without destroying or ever impairing the strong personal friendship that had sprung up between them is ample proof that Nathaniel J. Wyeth was an uncommonly chivalrous person—a truly noble character. Of Wyeth's two scientific friends, Thomas Nuttall had already left the West, and John Kirk Townsend was soon to follow. Both had profited greatly by their journeys through the Oregon country, and to each the sympathetic chief factor had extended every courtesy. In that summer of 1836, with only the presence of the Reverend Mr. Beaver to annoy him, the White-Headed Eagle had many reasons for hailing the future with confidence and optimism.

From that same letter to Edward Ermatinger—the one in which he had discoursed at length on the subject of teaching the Indians religion—we learn that Doctor John had changed his mind and had sent John, Jr., along with David, to be educated abroad. "I am sorry," he had added in a postscript, "you did not happen to meet my son David—in Montreal—he is now in France—or at Addiscome College—Qualifying himself for to go out to the East Indies—my other Son John—quarrelled with his Uncle—on account of his Extravagance—and I Believe he is now also on his way to the East Indies as Surgeon or Physician. My Brother says he is clever—but has no Economy this however may alter—by last accounts he was in Montreal." [23]

Sound judgment had, for once, given way to a father's natural inclination to distribute his blessings impartially, but the overly conscientious chief factor would have acted with greater wisdom had he clung to his first impulse. Young John was not worthy of the favors bestowed upon him. In fact the headstrong lad's quarrel with his Uncle David over money matters was but the harbinger of sinister events which, some years later, were to culminate in tragedy.

4

Toward noon on September 16, 1836, Dr. Marcus Whitman and the Reverend Henry H. Spalding, a Presbyterian missionary, arrived at Fort Vancouver with their wives and five other persons, including William H. Gray, a lay assistant, two teamsters, and two Nez Percé boys Whitman had taken East with him from Green River the year previous.[24] Doctor John and James Douglas were waiting to greet them at the boat landing. With his never failing cordiality, the doctor bade them all welcome and escorted the ladies to the dining hall, where the entire party joined the gentlemen of the fort in their midday meal.

Narcissa Whitman was a remarkable woman. Charming and

well educated, the daughter of Judge Prentiss of Prattsburg, New York, she had been married, only the preceding February, to the rough but wholly admirable Dr. Whitman. Immediately after the wedding, the enthusiastic young physician and his bride had started on their long pilgrimage to save the Indians— a novel type of honeymoon, to say the least. Mrs. Whitman and Eliza Spalding were the first white women to cross the Rocky Mountains into Oregon, and their unprecedented courage in undertaking such a hazardous journey appealed mightily to Doctor John. Their open and friendly manner toward Margaret McLoughlin, Amelia Douglas, and the other half-breed wives of the post promptly won the hearts of the Hudson's Bay officers, who had become disgusted with the rigid aloofness of Mrs. Beaver, the only white woman most of them had seen in years.

Indeed it appears that the arrival of these two cultured American ladies eased, to some extent, the stiff, unsociable domestic atmosphere then prevailing at the fort. Eloisa, the doctor's daughter, recalls that "when the Missionaries ladies came it was quite different. Then we mingled more. Of course we took the ladies to our mess room. But Dr. Whitman always took his meals with us. He brought the ladies and Dr. Spalding too. At the [men's] mess room there was such a hurry on account of business; they would sit down and get up and go. At our mess there was nothing to hurry [them], and they would sit down and enjoy themselves." [25] Narcissa Whitman and Eliza Spalding were Oregon's first advocates of woman's rights!

The incomers, Whitman, Spalding, and Gray, were men of noble purpose, and, from the moment they set foot on the river bank at Vancouver, Doctor John was quite as favorably impressed with them as he had been with the Methodists. In those early days, it required a rare combination of physical courage and religious fervor to lure men into the wild Indian country for the sole purpose of bringing the Word of God to ignorant natives. In an interesting letter written to his brothers, shortly after his arrival, Spalding bares his very soul. "I cannot realize," ran his message, "that I have crossed the Rocky Mountains since the morning I drove sorrowfully out of Pittsburgh, and am now actually on the banks of the terrible Columbus, but it is really so. I have already been paid a thousand fold by what my eyes have seen, and all America with her gold and happiness could not purchase a place for me in the states, if I must leave these poor heathen standing thick around, pleading with their own tongues, actually, for the bread of eternal life, unpitied." [26]

With such a man as Spalding supplying the religious zeal and with Marcus Whitman, less articulate but fully as devout, adding his unique organizing ability, it is not surprising that the "main Presbyterian show" was soon ready for vigorous action. When Whitman and Spalding informed the doctor that they proposed to locate their missions in the Cayuse and Walla Walla countries respectively, he promptly realized the hopelessness of dissuading such determined individuals and abandoned the effort to send them southward into the Willamette valley. He eased his conscience by pointing out the dangers he believed they would encounter but, as he anticipated, his words had no effect. The die had long since been cast.

After a few days of well earned rest, Dr. Whitman and the Reverend Mr. Spalding, leaving their wives for the time being in the pleasant atmosphere of Fort Vancouver, set out with Gray for their chosen fields of missionary activity. Whitman located his mission site at Waiilatpu, a few miles east of Fort Walla Walla, while Spalding settled in the Nez Percé country at Lapwai on the Clearwater River.[27] "The Lord directed us," wrote the ardent Spalding, "to a favorable location among the Nez Percés, 125 miles east of Walla Walla and 12 east of the Lewis River on a river putting in from the north called Koos-

koos. The Nez Percés are much rejoiced that I have found a place." [28]

Before Christmas, the two Presbyterians were domiciled with their wives at their respective stations, ready and eager to begin their work of mercy. They soon discovered that reinforcements would be needed to carry out the extensive program Samuel Parker had planned for them, and so, with that purpose in mind, they arranged to send Gray East the following spring.

On their long and difficult journey overland, the Presbyterian missionaries had practically exhausted their supplies. As soon as Doctor John realized their predicament, he willingly replenished their stocks of goods from his ample stores; in return, he asked only that they agree not to employ men at wages higher than the company's regular rates—an agreement the frugal crusaders would not have been likely to break.

5

Much as he admired the various American missionaries who had been descending upon him at regular intervals, the doctor longed for company of a more worldly type. He was not above enjoying an occasional story of a kind the single-minded churchmen would not have appreciated, and we may safely assume that the conversation in Bachelors' Hall, during their presence, was somewhat repressed. Jed Smith, David Douglas, Nathaniel Wyeth, and the two Yankee scientists—all these had come and gone—and the chief factor had reveled in their free and easy company. Talk of saving the Indians and of establishing native schools was well enough in its place, but, as a steady diet, even the conscientious doctor grew weary of it. That, no doubt, is why, a few days before Christmas, he was overjoyed to welcome Captain William A. Slacum to Vancouver notwithstanding the fact that he already knew something of this energetic Yankee's purpose in coming.

Slacum, who had served as a purser in the naval service of the United States, arrived on the Columbia River on the 22nd of December, 1836, having traveled from the Sandwich Islands in the brig *Loriot*. In order to understand the purpose of his mission, we must catch up the thread of the disgruntled Hall J. Kelley's activities following his return to the States. Safe back in Boston, that unhappy individual had published a flaming pamphlet in which he had scored Doctor John and the whole Hudson's Bay régime as ruthless, tyrannical, and inexorably inimical to American hopes of gaining a foothold in the country.[29] This pamphlet had been brought to the attention of the American Secretary of State, John Forsyth, who had forthwith dispatched Captain Slacum to "obtain some specific and authentic information in regard to the inhabitants of the country in the neighborhood of the Oregon, or Columbia river; and, generally, endeavor to obtain all such information, political, physical, statistical, and geographical as may prove useful or interesting to this government."[30] Couched in less diplomatic language, Slacum's instructions meant simply that he was to find out in how far the Hudson's Bay monopoly had served to prevent the free and unobstructed settlement of the country by Americans.

Though Captain Slacum tried to make his visit appear unofficial, Doctor John was quick to divine its true nature. "On arriving," wrote the chief factor many years later, "he [Slacum] pretended that he was a private gentleman, and that he came to meet Messrs. Murray and companions who had left the states to visit the country. But this did not deceive me, as I perceived who he was and his object, and by his report of his mission published in the proceedings of the Congress of the United States, I found my surmises were correct."[31]

In spite of the fact that the captain's report was ultimately to cause the doctor no little embarrassment—an eventuality which must surely have occurred to him at the time—he treated the

Yankee agent with every conceivable courtesy during his visit and made it possible for him to travel freely through the country. In his state of mind at the moment, the White-Headed Eagle regarded Slacum's coming as a welcome Christmas gift—an agreeable change from the sober and interminable deliberations of the missionaries.

CHAPTER XV

The Doctor Fights for His Empire

I

Captain Slacum was royally entertained at Vancouver. He remained there until the 10th of January, when he left to visit the Methodist Mission in French Prairie, "having been furnished by Dr. McLoughlin with a canoe and six men, and all the necessaries for the voyage." [1] During his sojourn at the fort he made good use of his time, as is evident from the complete picture of the organization and activities of the Hudson's Bay Company that found its way into the report he was later to submit to his government.

It is significant that the chief factor saw fit to volunteer so much information to this newcomer, especially in view of his reticence toward previous American visitors. The reason, however, seems obvious. Having guessed the true purpose of Slacum's visit, he probably concluded that it was wiser to give him the facts than to run the risk of having him depend solely upon his own conclusions, some of which might prove incorrect and hence injurious to the Hudson's Bay cause.

Unquestionably, the doctor displayed good judgment in candidly answering such questions as were put to him, though it is apparent that the American naval officer either misunderstood him on certain points or deliberately chose to draw erroneous conclusions. Particularly damaging was his charge that the Hudson's Bay Company had been willfully maintaining the institution of slavery as a matter of fur-trading economy.

"As long as the Hudson Bay Company permit their servants to hold slaves," he wrote in his report, "the institution of slavery will be perpetuated, as the price, eight to fifteen blankets, is too tempting for an Indian to resist. . . . The chief factor at Vancouver says the slaves are the property of the women with whom their workmen live, and do not belong to men in their employ although I have known cases to the contrary. We shall see how this reasoning applies. These women, who are said to be the owners of the slaves, are frequently bought themselves by the men with whom they live, when they are mere children; of course they have no means to purchase, until their husbands or their men make the purchase from the proceeds of their labor; and then these women are considered the ostensible owners, which neither lessens the traffic nor ameliorates the condition of the slave, whilst the Hudson Bay Company find it to their interest to encourage their servants to intermarry or live with the native women, as it attaches the men to the soil, and their offspring (half-breeds) become in their turn useful hunters and workmen at the different depots of the company." [2]

Nor was Captain Slacum the only one to make such charges, for the meddlesome parson, Herbert Beaver, had taken it upon himself, some time after his arrival on the Columbia, to write an extended letter to the Aborigines Protection Society of London in which he held the local Hudson's Bay officers responsible for the continuance of slavery among the natives. [3]

Although Doctor John was not to learn of these adverse and, as he sincerely believed, untruthful reports until after some years had passed, the Irish half of him rose hotly to the occasion when they were eventually brought to his notice. "It is incorrect," he wrote after reading a copy of the Slacum report in 1839, "that we encourage slavery and on the reverse we avail ourselves of every opportunity to discourage it. Tho' we cannot prevent Indians having slaves, we tell the masters it is very improper to keep their fellow beings in slavery. Moreover we have redeemed several, and sent them back to their own country this very season. . . . But strange as it may appear, there are instances in which the slaves will not return to their lands; and without laying claim to doing more than our duty we can say that our influence has vastly ameliorated the situation of the slaves in every part of this country in which we have been. If the plan we adopt is followed, they will before long emancipate themselves."

The indignant doctor then went on to explain a situation which the American had obviously misconstrued. "You know," he continued in this same communication, "Your Honors have sent us Instructions positively to prohibit any of the Company's servants having slaves, and prior to the receipt of your instructions my predecessors had opposed it, and one of them, J. Dugald Cameron, Esq. had emancipated the slaves of the wives of the servants and sent them from the place. But though he did this to ameliorate their situation it proved the reverse, as the servants wives made a present of them to their Indian relations, who forced them to become their slaves, by whom they were treated worse than they could have been if they had been with their former mistresses at the Fort. As for me, seeing what had occurred, I did not make the servants wives send their slaves away, but availed myself of every opportunity to make them work and pay them as other Indians. . . . We disapprove of anyone having slaves, and consider every one about the Establishment as free." [4]

During the doctor's absence from Fort Vancouver, in the latter part of 1838, James Douglas, temporarily in charge, sent a strong letter to the Governor and Committee which substantiated the views of his chief. "The plan I now follow," he wrote, "of considering every person without distinction, residing on our premises as free British subjects, who may at any time under the Company's protection, assert the exercise of their absolute

AN INDIAN TOMB

From an etching made by Lieutenant Warre of the Warre-Vavasour Expedition in 1845.

and legal rights, will greatly mitigate the evils of slavery, by operating as a security against abuse, and making affection the only bond that supports the immoral system." [5]

Captain Slacum also charged the doctor with influencing retiring employees of the company to settle in the Cowlitz valley, several miles above Vancouver, in order to render more secure the British claims to the country north of the Columbia— a course entirely logical, it would seem, in territory still held under joint occupancy. In retaliation, he urged his government to hold out for the 49th parallel as its northern boundary so as to include the rich Puget Sound country.[6] With an amazing lack of graciousness—inexcusable even when allowance is made for the political nature of his mission—the captain failed to include so much as one line regarding the many courtesies he had received from the chief factor. But in spite of its many lapses and inaccuracies, the report was, on the whole, a creditable piece of work. It served to awaken a new interest in Oregon on the part of the American government.

2

Quite by chance, the Yankee naval officer's brief stay in Oregon coincided with a sudden flare-up on the part of his countryman, Ewing Young—a flare-up which caused both Doctor John and the Methodist missionaries no little concern. Fortunately, the affair was amicably settled before Captain Slacum left Vancouver for the Willamette valley, and, in view of what the headstrong Young proposed to do, it is not unlikely that the resourceful chief factor deliberately detained his guest until things were smoothed over.

Ever since his altercation with the doctor concerning the charges which had been brought against him by the Mexican governor of California, Ewing Young had remained a bitter enemy of the Hudson's Bay Company. He had claimed, in fact, that the doctor's refusal to trade with him or even to advance him supplies on the same basis that he had assisted other settlers, had left him stranded in the country without any means of making a living. Smarting under this humiliation, he had settled temporarily at Fort William, long since abandoned, and had taken possession of a huge caldron which Wyeth's men had once used in pickling salmon. With a boastful display of arrogance, he had threatened to start a distillery in partnership with Lawrence Carmichael, one of the men who had followed him to Oregon. Fully aware of the chief factor's strong opposition to the liquor traffic among the Indians, the sharp-sighted Yankee knew that he was aiming a solar plexus blow at the most vulnerable point in the armor of the White-Headed Eagle.[7]

Doctor John, however, had long since learned to accept defeat gracefully. As soon as the first warning of this project reached him, he offered Young and Carmichael the necessary financial aid to establish themselves in some honorable enterprise, but the hot-blooded southerner's bluff was not to be called so easily. He flatly refused to discuss the matter either at Vancouver or at Fort William.

It was fortunate that the doctor had stanch allies in the Methodist missionaries, who were quick to sense the potential dangers of Young's plan. They knew him well and suspected that he was not given to the making of idle threats. As a measure of protection, Jason Lee and his workers organized the Oregon Temperance Society and, in nervous haste, addressed a petition to Young and Carmichael urging them to abandon their project and offering to advance money and merchandise as an inducement.[8] Doctor John, delighted that the Methodists were willing to make a strong issue of the affair, and convinced that the Yankee firebrand would be more likely to listen to his own countrymen, gladly lent these allies what assistance he

could. It was a new experience to find people eager to pull
his chestnuts out of the fire. "Dr. McLoughlin," wrote the grateful Reverend Daniel Lee, "seconded the efforts of the missionaries and the friends of temperance and the course he has taken
in regard to spirituous liquors has done much to preserve the
general order and harmony of the mixed community of which
the settlement is composed." [9]

While the irrepressible Ewing Young was being subjected
to strong pressure from two camps, Captain Slacum was peacefully gathering data on the horrors of Indian slavery, diligently
versing himself in the intricacies of the Hudson's Bay organization, and making side trips down the Columbia with James
Douglas. The wise old doctor knew what he was about. He
saw to it that the issue was all but settled before he sent the
American agent on his way up the Willamette.

Satisfied that he had won his point, Young capitulated, but,
in the reply he sent to the Methodist missionaries on January 13, 1837, he indicated clearly his deep-rooted resentment
against the chief factor. "We therefore do agree," ran the message which ended the hopes of the thirsty French Canadian
settlers, "to stop our proceedings for the present. But, gentlemen, the reasons for our first beginning such an undertaking
were the innumerable difficulties and tyrannizing oppression of
the Hudson's Bay Company here, under the absolute authority
of Dr. John McLoughlin, who has treated us with more disdain
than any American citizen of feeling can support." [10] To his
credit, he refused the Methodists' offer of money and goods,
but his very refusal indicated that his real motive had not been
to gain material assistance so much as to humble his chosen
enemy, the doctor. That individual, we may safely assume,
was not greatly disturbed by the Yankee's hostility once the
distillery project had been quashed. It is singular, in view of
all the facts, that Captain Slacum was later to claim that he

had been the dominating factor in staying Ewing Young's hand! [11]

3

The energetic American agent, however, rendered the Willamette valley settlers, and incidentally Ewing Young, at least one outstanding service during his mission to Oregon. One of the first things he learned, upon his arrival in French Prairie, was that the settlers, French Canadians and Americans alike, were most desirous of obtaining cattle of their own. Though Doctor John had been extremely generous in loaning live stock to these people, he had not been given authority to sell any of the company's property outright. Indeed it appeared that their only prospect of acquiring animals of their own lay in the somewhat remote possibility of importing them from the Spanish missions of California. [12]

Slacum, once he understood the predicament of the Willamette valley people, promptly offered to aid them, and, addressing a mass meeting at "Camp Maud du Sable," he "proposed to give to as many of the settlers as chose to embark in the *Loriot,* a free passage to California, where they might procure cattle at $3 per head. The advantage of being landed in California or Bodega [a Russian settlement near San Francisco] free of expense, and the risk of the road, was very great." [13] Accordingly, the Willamette Cattle Company was formed, the settlers contributing $1,600 and Captain Slacum $500.

In another of these lapses which occur in his report so frequently as to seem deliberate, the American naval officer neglected to mention that Doctor John, on behalf of the Hudson's Bay Company, made a substantial contribution to the enterprise. The fact that he did this in order to acquire additional live stock for his own posts does not detract from the great service he rendered to the settlers. Without his timely and friendly help it seems unlikely that the company could have been organized at all.

In his reminiscences, penned many years later, the doctor noted that "in 1836 [14] we found the means of forming a company to go to California for cattle. I took half the stock for the Hudson's Bay Company, so that by purchasing a larger number (as the expense of driving 500 or 1,000 was the same) it would make the cattle cheaper. Those of the settlers who had means put it in the stock; those who had none engaged as drivers at one dollar a day, to be paid in cattle at actual cost. Mr. Slacum, who came here in a chartered vessel, gave them a gratis passage from this place to San Francisco. . . . They bought, I think, about seven hundred head of cattle, which cost eight dollars per head rendered. In the Willamette the settlers kept the tame and broken-in oxen that had belonged to the Hudson's Bay Company and gave their California wild cattle in the place; so they found themselves stocked with tame cattle that cost but eight dollars per head; and the Hudson's Bay Company, to favor the settlers, took calves in place of the grown-up cattle, because the Hudson's Bay Company wanted them for beef. These calves would grow up before they were required." [15]

No more impressive evidence of the doctor's friendly interest in the welfare of the Willamette valley settlers could be found than his own lucid explanation of the part he played in the cattle project. Indeed, as we read his own words, we begin to understand Slacum's omission, for if it was the American agent's avowed purpose to present the Hudson's Bay Company as a heartless monopoly and the chief factor as an uncompromising tyrant, the complete story would most assuredly have destroyed the illusion. Silence, apparently, was his only alternative.

The first change in Ewing Young's luck came with the arrival in the Willamette valley of Captain Slacum, who magnanimously offered to put the Yankee firebrand on a better basis of understanding both with his own countrymen and with the Hudson's Bay Company. "I proposed to loan him $150," wrote the captain in his report, "get him a supply of decent clothing from the fort, in my name, and give himself and his partner, Carmichael, a passage to California as he informed me he was exceedingly anxious to go thither to clear himself of the calumny that General Figaroa, had through Dr. McLoughlin, circulated against him, producing in effect the most unjustifiable persecution. Mr. Young seemed deeply sensible to my offer: said a cloud hung over him so long, through Dr. McLoughlin's influence, that he was almost maddened by the harsh treatment he had received from that gentleman." [16]

Young had apparently misread the doctor, for otherwise— even with Slacum's backing—he would not have been tolerated as a member of the California cattle expedition; yet not only was he included but, to his own amazement, he was named its leader. The fact, too, that Doctor John was willing to take stock in a company headed by Young indicated that he had already become more than half convinced of the southerner's innocence though it is not without significance that P. L. Edwards, one of the Methodists, was sent along as treasurer. If, in the minds of some, there was still a lurking suspicion of the hot-blooded Yankee, these fears were quieted in the knowledge that honest Phil Edwards would have charge of the funds. [17]

At last, on February 10, 1837, Captain Slacum and the ten cattle-seeking settlers, headed by a happier Ewing Young, took their departure from Vancouver in the *Loriot.* Doctor John, standing on the river bank, heaved a mighty sigh of relief when the tall masts of the brig finally disappeared from view.

4

Following the departure of the *Loriot,* the chief factor became more deeply concerned than ever about the future of his empire. Up to then, the undisputed dominance of his company had been sufficient to justify him in the belief that the entire territory north of the river would eventually belong to the British. Recent developments, however, had made him uneasy. The organization of the Willamette Cattle Company, the encouragement Captain Slacum had given the enterprise, the patriotic sentiments he had inspired in the hearts of the missionaries, the covetous glances he had cast upon the Puget Sound country— all of these developments had conspired to disquiet the mind of the doctor.

He was doubly thankful, during those early months of 1837, that he had had the foresight to lend his support to the cattle venture for, now that he felt called upon to contemplate land settlement in earnest, he could use additional live stock to good advantage. To the chief factor it had become obvious that he must make some effort to place retired company employees on the land north of Vancouver if England expected to hold her own when it came time to decide upon a boundary. It was with this thought in mind that he induced Simon Plomondon, a man who had seen sixteen years of Hudson's Bay service, to locate a small farm on the lower end of the Cowlitz prairie. Doctor John loaned him animals, authorized him to take up land, and promised him protection from the natives. Plomondon was the first ex-Hudson's Bay servant to settle in this vicinity, but he was soon followed by others.[18]

All this involved, as the doctor realized, a radical departure from the traditional policy of his company. Thus far he had been primarily a law unto himself, but so bold a move required real courage. Of that he had plenty. Apparently, though, he already had the backing of Governor Simpson, who, in a long letter to Governor J. H. Pelly of the Hudson's Bay Company, had written, as early as February, 1837, that "the possession of that country [the territory north of the Columbia] to Great Britain

may become an object of very great importance, and we are
strengthening that claim to it [independent of the claims of
prior discovery and occupation for the purpose of Indian trade]
by forming the nucleus of a colony through the establishment
of farms, and the settlement of some of our retiring officers and
servants as agriculturists." [19]

Since George Simpson had not visited Vancouver since 1829,
he could only have secured information on this vital point
from Doctor John or some of his men. It would appear, therefore, that the chief factor had been quietly working to this end
for some time, and that Slacum's suspicions may have been
well founded. Throughout the remainder of 1837, this project
was uppermost in the doctor's mind, and he took occasion to
discuss it frequently with Archibald McDonald, the man who
had first suggested the idea to him. William Frazer Tolmie,
the young Scottish physician, and George B. Roberts were two
other Hudson's Bay officers who early became interested in the
plan which was later to blossom forth as the Puget Sound
Agricultural Company.[20]

Meanwhile, the Presbyterian missionaries at Waiilatpu and
Lapwai, carrying on their work as best they could, were awaiting the return of William H. Gray with sorely needed reinforcements. The Methodists, on the other hand, fared better.
On May 18, scarcely more than three months after the departure
of Captain Slacum, the brig *Diana* reached Fort Vancouver
with a sizable party of workers and a generous cargo of goods
for the Willamette valley mission. Among those who came
were Dr. Elijah White and Alanson Beers, with their wives and
families, Dr. William H. Willson, the Misses Susan Downing
and Elvira Johnson and Anna Maria Pittman, who was shortly
to become the bride of Jason Lee.[21] The novelty of their arrival
had hardly worn away when, on September 7, another party
of missionaries, even larger than the first, reached the Columbia

on the ship *Sumatra*. With the advent of these substantial reinforcements, Jason Lee's mission attained a population of sixty white persons.[22]

Whatever his private thoughts may have been, Doctor John received these newcomers with every mark of courtesy and respect. Notwithstanding the increase in its personnel, the mission encountered difficulties during the fall and winter. Serious illnesses attacked various of its members, and, to complicate matters still further, the natives became lukewarm to the somber and primarily intellectual Methodist teachings. On more than one occasion, Vancouver's chief factor was called upon to render medical service and to impart timely advice. Eager and ready to supply both, he nevertheless became convinced, as the year wore on, that the mission was gradually breaking away from its purely religious character and was becoming the rallying point for further political interest in Oregon on the part of the United States. Captain Slacum had sown the seeds of Yankee patriotism, and Jason Lee, doubtful of his status in a country theoretically American but practically British, was quick to comprehend the importance of arousing the none too sympathetic government in Washington. Lee felt more isolated than ever because, earlier in the year, Nathaniel J. Wyeth had made his third and last trip to Oregon for the purpose of selling out his holdings to Doctor John.

In the midst of their efforts to teach and convert the Indians, the Methodist leaders were gradually assembling and clarifying the thoughts which, a year later, were to find formal expression in a vigorous memorial addressed to the Congress of the United States. "First," ran the opening paragraph of this historic document, "we need a guaranty from our government that the possession of the land we take up, and the improvements we make upon it, will be assured to us. These settlements will greatly increase the value of the government domain in that country, should the Indian title ever be extinguished. And we cannot but expect therefore that those who have been pioneers in this arduous work will be liberally dealt with in this matter." [23]

Though the missionaries had not, by 1837, crystallized their sentiments into a unified program, there was, even then, an abundance of loose talk going the rounds of the valley, and much of it reached the anxious ears of the doctor. It was high time, he concluded, to start rebuilding his own fences to the northward!

5

At Fort Vancouver the mighty Beavers were making themselves increasingly unpopular. Though James Douglas, in February, 1937, had availed himself of the English clergyman's presence to be formally united to his wife in accordance with the forms prescribed in the Book of Common Prayer, Doctor John had rebelled at the very thought of having the smug Mr. Beaver perform a similar service for himself.[24] A little later, however, he and Margaret were officially married by the faithful Douglas, who, in his new rôle of justice of the peace, could legally tie the knot.[25]

Though it relieved the delicate sensibilities of the visiting rector to have the doctor's union regularized, if only by a civil marriage, relations between them grew steadily worse and finally reached a climax early in 1838. As a part of his routine work, Mr. Beaver was expected to send periodic reports to the London Council, but, in these letters, he appears to have discussed secular matters almost exclusively. Indeed his pet subject was the tyranny and inhumanity of the resident chief factor! The doctor, of course, reserved the right to read these dispatches before they left the fort, and, for a time, he seemed content to let them go without comment, firm in his belief that the London heads would pay no attention to them. But there came a day when he could contain his pent-up wrath no longer. Meeting the officious divine in the fort yard one afternoon, he held aloft the chaplain's latest report and, in a voice that could be heard from one end of the settlement to the other, demanded an explanation.

"Sir," replied the reverend gentleman, "if you wish to know why a cow's tail grows downward, I cannot tell you; I can only cite the fact."

Instantly the doctor was in a towering rage. Up went his trusty cane, and, almost before he realized what he was about, he had inflicted several sound blows upon the shoulders of the impertinent divine. Months of stored-up anger found release in that caning!

The very next day an auction sale of the effects of a certain Captain Home, who had been drowned in the Columbia, was held in the public square at Vancouver. "Mr. Beaver," spoke up the chief factor as soon as the crowd had assembled, "I make this public apology for the indignity I laid upon you yesterday." "Sir," exclaimed the outraged clergyman, "I will not accept your apology!"

From that time forward it was open warfare, and, before the year had run its course, Mr. Beaver and his wife took occasion to forsake the wild Columbia for England, where, as they believed, genteel people could be better appreciated.[26] Whatever justification the doctor may have had for his act—and he had considerable—the affair reveals him in a most unfavorable light. Strong-tempered as he was, there were few men capable of rousing him to such uncontrolled fury. Beaver had goaded him to the furthest limits of human endurance.

During the early months of 1838, Doctor John and his devoted wife had the pleasure of witnessing the marriage of their daughter, Eloisa, to William Glen Rae, one of the company's of-

ficers. Rae, who was a native of the Orkney Islands, and who had
been educated in Scotland, had served in various of the doctor's
northern posts until 1837, when he had returned to Vancouver to
assume the duties of head clerk.[27] A large, handsome man, he
made a fitting groom for the charming Eloisa. Whether or not
Mr. Beaver performed the ceremony, we cannot say, though, in
view of the strained relations existing at the time, it does not
seem likely.

6

By the spring of 1838 it had become apparent that, as far as
work among the Indians was concerned, the Methodist mission
was a failure. To the intensely patriotic Jason Lee, the establishment of civilization, with religion and good government, had become the paramount issue. His memorial had at last been completed, and he was eager to place it before the members of the
American Congress in person. Accordingly, in the month of
March, he set out, with P. L. Edwards and several others,
on the long overland journey to Washington.[28] Prior to his departure, Lee had received word that Doctor John contemplated
making his long delayed trip to England, and, eager to travel with
the Hudson's Bay Company's annual express, he had applied to
the chief factor for permission to join him.

"The Dr. could not grant my request," noted Lee in his
journal en route, "and expressed himself 'doubly mortified because he could not do me the favour and should also be deprived
of my company.'"[29] No doubt the chief factor had reasons of
his own for refusing this request. It may have been that, knowing the missionary's errand and realizing the inevitability of
trouble between Great Britain and the United States over the
possession of Oregon, he merely sought to avoid embarrassment.
Or, after four long years, he may have had more than his fill of
missionary conversation.

For Jason Lee, the trip was destined to be a sad one. Upon his arrival at the Shawnee Indian Mission in western Missouri, he was overtaken by a messenger who brought the tragic news that his wife and two-day-old son had died. The message had been sent out, and relayed from post to post, through the thoughtfulness of Doctor John's men at Fort Vancouver.[30] Poor Lee could not turn back. Stricken with grief, he was forced to continue on his lonely way.

As for the chief factor, he had himself left the Columbia even before Jason Lee started. Bound at last for London, he was determined to carry his case to headquarters. The White-Headed Eagle was not going to lose his empire without a fight!

CHAPTER XVI

FENCHURCH STREET REVISITED

I

THE passage of time, apparently, had not robbed the doctor of his independence of spirit, for, in electing to travel overland, he had disregarded his chief's orders to "proceed to England via Cape Horn."[1] His decision reveals how completely he had divorced himself from George Simpson's sway, for company discipline was rigid and few indeed were the officers who dared hazard flexible interpretations of the governor's instructions. Doctor John had come to occupy a unique position.

Though it may have given the White-Headed Eagle a certain personal satisfaction to defy the orders of the Council, he had, as it happened, far worthier motives for spurning the water route. His mother, then seventy-nine years of age, was still residing at Rivière du Loup; his favorite sister, Marie Louise, was completing her sixth year as Mother Superior of the Ursuline Convent; and his daughter, Mrs. Epps, was living on the heights of Abraham above the city of Quebec. It would have been quite natural for the doctor to visit all of them on his first trip home in fourteen years, though we can only assume that he did so.

But there were other reasons for this dash across the mountains. Through the years—isolated in his Columbia department—he had followed the vicissitudes of eastern politics with

242

keen interest, and now he wanted to learn, at first hand, something of the temper of his fellow Canadians. In the previous year, 1837, the Canadian patriot, Louis Joseph Papineau, inspired by the American Revolution, had attempted a similar coup in his own country.[2] Premature and in many respects ill advised, the uprising had been quelled by the constituted authorities, but Papineau had succeeded in attracting many thoughtful Canadians to his cause.

An instinctive lover of liberty, Doctor John displayed more valor than discretion by punctuating his trip through Canada with laudatory tributes to the fallen hero, Papineau. Such remarks were extremely embarrassing to Governor Simpson and the Montreal tycoons and it was fortunate for the western chief factor that he had long since made himself indispensable to the company. On that jaunt through Rupert's Land he was as popular in orthodox Hudson's Bay circles as Napoleon would have been at Wellington's dinner table. Nevertheless he was one of the strong men of the concern—a fact which even his bitterest opponents were forced to admit.

To some, however, the doctor's freely expressed opinions were amusing rather than offensive, and John Tod, a Hudson's Bay officer whom he met at Lake Winnipeg, observed in a letter to Edward Ermatinger that "the Doctor, who has at length descended from his roost, I met in Lake Winnipeg—we breakfasted together, and talked incessantly all the while of the late events in Canada—he was strenuous in support of that arch rebel Pappeneau and his party. I took the liberty to say in a jocund way that it was fortunate for him, he had not been with me last winter, otherwise, I should have most probably been now carrying an account of his trial, for the gratification of his friends."[3] If Tod, in a friendly way, was trying to warn his guest against the dangers of loose conversation, the warning was not heeded.

2

So once again to London, after an absence of eighteen years, journeyed the chief factor from the Far West. Time had wrought sweeping changes in his status. On that previous occasion—so very long ago it seemed—he had come as a struggling wintering partner of the doomed North West Company, uncertain of his own future and worried over the fate of his colleagues. Now he came in triumph as the absolute ruler of a rich province, both to render an account of his stewardship and to propose further developments. He had come to counsel as well as to be counseled.

However sure of himself he may have felt in the presence of George Simpson, the big doctor was prepared to walk circumspectly in the august councils of his ultimate superiors. His zeal for Papineau, his readiness to place retired company employees in the Willamette valley, his unselfish treatment of the Yankee missionaries—all of these enthusiasms were, we can believe, conveniently cast aside for the duration of the London interlude. Well did he realize how widely his own views on certain vital matters differed from those of Governor Simpson! Not only that but, to the alert ears of the doctor, had come vague rumors of the governor's dissatisfaction with him—sly intimations that it would not be displeasing to the Canadian chief if their Honors were to appoint a new head for the Columbia department. Fortunately he had come forewarned, and, again fortunately, he had brought with him a concrete program for approval. Their Honors could scarcely adopt his proposals, he thought, and deliberately send another man back to put them into practice. The White-Headed Eagle had a big job of selling to do. Once again he played for high stakes, and once again he triumphed.

Upon his arrival, he was cheered to learn that the government had just extended the Hudson's Bay Company's exclusive trading license for a period of twenty-one years,[4] but that had been expected. More specific problems were awaiting solution. There was, for example, the Russian business to settle, and no one knew the issues involved as intimately as did the doctor. He had not forgotten the rebuff his good friend Peter Skene Ogden had received back in 1834 when he attempted, in keeping with the terms of treaty between the two nations, to enter the Stikine River. Old Baron Wrangel, the Russian American governor, had politely but firmly refused Ogden permission to trade with the natives. When news of this challenge to his authority had reached Doctor John, he had raged the length and breadth of Fort Vancouver and had determined to take his case not to George Simpson but direct to his superiors across the Atlantic.

In the interim, news of the affair had reached London, where Lord Palmerston and Count Nesselrode, the Chancellor of the Russian Empire, had been searching in vain for a solution through the channels of diplomacy.[5] Later still, the doctor had exchanged views with Lieutenant Etholine, the Russian deputy-governor at Sitka, and both had agreed that the battle had better be fought across a table in London than between armed forces in Russian America.[6]

Thus it came about that when, in February, 1839, representatives of the Russian American Fur Company and the Hudson's Bay Company met in the British capital to work out an agreement, Doctor John took a prominent part in the deliberations. It was settled that the Hudson's Bay Company was to lease, for a ten-year period, from the Russian American Company "for commercial purposes, the coast (exclusive of the islands) and the interior country belonging to his Majesty the Emperor of Russia," from Cape Spencer to the southern boundary of Russian America in 54° 40' North latitude. That was one of the earliest official references to this historic parallel which was soon to enliven an American political campaign with the familiar cry of "Fifty-four forty or fight."

Another provision of the agreement permitted the British to occupy the Russian post at the mouth of the once disputed Stikine River—how Ogden would have reveled in that!—and to erect other posts in the leased territory. To compensate the Muscovites, the Hudson's Bay Company was to pay "as annual rent 2,000 seasoned Land Otter Skins (excluding Cub and damaged skins) taken and hunted on the west side of the Rocky Mountains during the said term of ten years; the first payment of the said rent to be by the delivery of the said 2,000 Otter Skins on or before the 1st June, 1841, to the agents of the Russian American Company on the North-West Coast."[7]

So far, so good. The doctor was highly pleased with the terms of the covenant, but, from his point of view, there still remained an important detail to be arranged. For years he had been hoping to develop a market in Russian America for Vancouver's surplus cattle and farm products, and so, when it became apparent that his northern neighbors wanted still further concessions in the matter of rent, he suggested that the Hudson's Bay Company supply them with Columbia River wheat, flour, peas, grits and hulled pot barley, salted beef, butter, and pork hams. This was duly written into the agreement as was also a provision for the sale of otter skins to the Russians at fixed prices.[8] It is little wonder that their Honors, impressed by the doctor's statesmanlike qualities, were little inclined to heed George Simpson's protests against him. The chief factor, it seems, had sold himself as well as his program.

3

But he had not yet completed his work in London. Indeed one of the main reasons for his trip had been to obtain official sanction of the plan Archibald McDonald had first broached to him some six years earlier—the formation of a concern, independent in theory, at least, of the Hudson's Bay Company, which could devote itself exclusively to agricultural activities. Again, through the energy and resourcefulness of Vancouver's chief factor, the way was paved for the Puget Sound Agricultural Company, and the regulations governing its subsequent organization were set forth in detail. He saw to that, for he was not one to go home empty-handed—not while his old friends on the Columbia were counting on him to open their path to what seemed a profitable investment. It was stipulated in London that the Hudson's Bay Company was to make over to the proposed Puget Sound Agricultural Company all its horses, live stock, and farm implements, and further, that it was to discontinue its various farming projects in Oregon. The agricultural enterprise, on the other hand, was expressly forbidden to engage in the fur trade. The initial farms were to be located between the headwaters of the Cowlitz River and Puget Sound.[9] Thus was the ground work laid—the details of organization could be deferred until the chief factor's return. Here was another feather in his ambitious cap; but still he was not ready to return.

He had yet to accomplish an errand of mercy on behalf of Lucier, Labonte, and the rest of the French Canadian ex-employees of the company who had settled in the valley of the Willamette largely, if not entirely, at his own suggestion. Long had these old friends waited for a priest to come and dwell among them, and Doctor John realized how inadequately Jason Lee and his fellow Methodists had filled this need. Though he knew that the Catholic Church of Canada had finally arranged to send out missionaries—that they were, in fact, already in Oregon—he also knew that the London heads of the Hudson's Bay Company had been resolutely opposed to the establishment of Catholic missions south of the Columbia.[10] Let the settlers

move northward into what seemed certain to become British
territory if they wanted their priests—so the governor and Committee had contended.

Here indeed was a poser for the doctor. He could not stress
to their Honors the necessity for Catholic missions in the Willamette without, at the same time, calling to their attention the
growth and importance of the French Canadian settlements
there. In view of their convictions, this was scarcely the ideal
method of assuring himself of their continued confidence. To
remain discreetly silent on this issue, however, was to break
faith with his old friends back home. That was out of the
question.

To conclude that he did not appreciate the hazards involved
in choosing the nobler course would be to underrate his grasp
of company policy though he may have felt, not without reason,
that his prestige was then sufficiently intrenched to see him
through unscathed. At all events, he plunged whole-heartedly
into the fight and emerged victorious. Their Honors agreed
that, in the future, priests might establish themselves on either
side of the Columbia.[11] Although the doctor won the day, his
triumph carried within itself the seeds of his own downfall.
Henceforth his superiors were to be more watchful of his good
offices toward those who had elected to settle in "Yankee" territory and more inclined to entertain George Simpson's criti-
cisms. But, for the moment, the White-Headed Eagle was
sailing before the wind. His star had reached its zenith.

4

His London business concluded, we find the doctor, relieved
and immeasurably elated by the turn of events in Fenchurch
Street, turning his whole attention to the youngest son, David,
who had been studying at the Addiscombe Military School.[12]
With mingled pride and incredulity, he looked upon this tall

lad, resplendent in his scarlet uniform, and recognized in him
the none too robust youth who had crossed the mountains
with Duncan Finlayson six years earlier. Upon his graduation
from the military academy, David had earned his ensign's commission as well as a chance to serve his country at Fort William
in Calcutta.

But the fifty-four-year-old chief factor had other plans—vi-
sions that some day, perhaps soon, David might succeed to the
distant throne of the Columbia. The young ensign, however, had
a mind of his own. The Indian color mounted in his cheeks as
he found words to express his preference for the life of a junior
officer in John Bull's army. He was convinced that no great
future awaited him in Oregon—that George Simpson would
choose his own leaders; and, true son of his father, he spoke
his mind. The White-Headed Eagle colored at the lad's insinu-
ations but held his temper. Calmly and with infinite confidence,
he pointed out that he still ruled the roost on the Columbia. Had
he not wrought miracles in London? Had he not selected his
own subordinates on numerous occasions? Had he not, only two
years before, secured the appointment of David's brother John
as a clerk and surgeon in his own department? [13] What he had
done for others, he could do for his favorite son. Unimpressed,
David listened, and there, for a time, the matter rested.

While this discussion was in progress, Dr. David McLoughlin
crossed over from Paris with his charming wife, the former
Lady Jane Capel, a sister of the Count of Essex and a niece of
the Viceroy of Ireland, to whom he had been married since 1833. [14]
In the course of the visit, Doctor David, who had formed a good
opinion of his strong-willed nephew and namesake, joined in the
family councils and advised the ensign to return to America.
Reluctantly young David yielded to the desires of his elders and,
with his father, crossed the Atlantic early in 1839. [15]

It was a fatal mistake—this uprooting of a British soldier in the making! If only the proud father could have looked into the future—if only he could have visioned the tragedy of this promising youth reverting to type, taking an Indian woman for his wife and passing his best years on an obscure Idaho farm—he would have returned to his empire alone. But there was no crystal into which the ambitious chief factor might gaze. He could see naught, just then, but a brilliant career for David in the service of the company, and that, in his mind, remained the noblest calling in Christendom.

It is apparent that Doctor John, while abroad, lived up to his reputation as a swift and thorough worker, for, by May, 1839, he and David were visiting in Montreal. There the returning chief factor attended various informal meetings of the company and acquainted Governor Simpson, Duncan Finlayson, and others with the details of what had been accomplished in London.[16] Hearing this impressive story from the lips of the man he had grown to dislike must have been a galling experience for the governor, but there is no hint of open friction between them on this occasion. George Simpson's hour to strike had not yet arrived. Just give this upstart from the West plenty of rope, he reasoned, and he would attend to his own hanging. But no such sinister thoughts were passing through the doctor's mind. He was highly pleased with the turn events had taken, and we can picture him enjoying the Montreal interlude to the utmost and reveling in the chance it gave him to demonstrate his rising power to the doubting David.

Resuming his westward journey, the chief factor attended a council of the Northern Department of Rupert's Land held on June 6 at the Red River Settlement. Here he was instrumental both in securing David's appointment to the position of apprenticed clerk in the Columbia department and in completing arrangements for a party to travel northward from Vancouver the following year to take possession of the Russian post at the mouth of the Stikine River in accordance with the terms of the London agreement.[17]

At another council held at Fort Garry on June 13, the doctor saw an opportunity to play politics. Avidly he seized it! A movement was started to elect George Simpson governor-in-chief of Rupert's Land, and Doctor John was among the first to climb aboard the band wagon. It was then decided to form a permanent council to assist the governor in the administration of his increased territory, and Vancouver's chief factor, in return for his support, was named one of the councilors.[18] This was a distinct promotion from the office of Councilor of the Governors of the Company's Territories which he had held since 1822.[19] Everywhere he was made conscious of the increased prestige he had attained. Indeed there was nothing in all this march to victory to indicate that he was riding for a fall.

Following the adjournment of the Fort Garry Council, the eagle and eaglet began their long trip overland for home. Once again they tarried at Lake Winnipeg to visit with John Tod, and it appears that, while there, the now thoroughly elated doctor engaged in a little boasting. At all events, Tod, in another of his gossipy letters to Edward Ermatinger, observed that "the big Doctor has again returned to the quarters with new power and fresh honours, their Honours at home having placed in him the most unbounded confidence in all affairs connected with the Columbia."[20] Obviously, Tod's source of information could only have been Doctor John himself!

At last, on his fifty-fifth birthday, October 19, 1839, the White-Headed Eagle reached his headquarters at Vancouver, having been sped down the Columbia by the trusty oars of his favorite boatman, Charlefoux. A great celebration was held at the post to honor the returning chief—voyageurs, Indians, traders, and officers all joining in the feast. Restrictions were momentarily cast aside, and liquor—good English rum—flowed freely. But in the quiet living room of the chief factor's house, the happiest woman in Oregon rejoiced that David—her youngest—had been safely brought back to her.

5

Upon his arrival at Fort Vancouver, Doctor John, though he had not as yet returned to the faith of his parents, was none the less gratified to learn how effectively the Catholic Church had begun its labors in Oregon. Having personally set in motion, on behalf of his French Canadian subjects, the machinery which at last had brought a pair of priests to the Columbia department, it pleased him not a little that two such able men as the Abbés Blanchet and Demers had come to work among his people.

In the original instance, the doctor's petitions had been addressed to Bishop Provencher of Juliopolis, who, in turn, had referred them to Archbishop Signay of Quebec. After a lengthy correspondence with Governor Simpson, intended to ascertain the views of the Hudson's Bay Company on the matter, the archbishop, in a letter dated April 17, 1838, had appointed the Abbé François Norbert Blanchet to the post of vicar general with jurisdiction over the territory "which is comprised between the Rocky Mountains on the east, the Pacific Ocean on the west, the Russian possessions on the north and the territory of the United States on the south." [21] Father Blanchet had proved his worth, both as a priest and as a man, by ministering heroically to the Acadians during a devastating epidemic of cholera which had broken out while he was in charge of the parish of St. Joseph de Soulange.[22] The archbishop had, of course, warned his vicar general against establishing missions in the territory south of the Columbia, "the possession whereof is contested by the United States." [23]

Traveling overland with the Hudson's Bay Company's annual

express, the Catholic missionaries had reached Vancouver on November 24, 1838, where "they were received with every demonstration of respect by James Douglas, Esq., who commanded that post during the absence of Mr. McLoughlin in England." [24] The effect of their coming upon both the whites and the natives appears to have been electric. From great distances Indians had flocked to Vancouver in awesome reverence to greet the Black-Robes, and the French Canadians had literally wept for joy at the scene. Their patience of years had been rewarded when, on the Sunday following the arrival of the priests, High Mass was celebrated in the schoolhouse at the fort. [25]

In line with the original orders of the company, the Abbés Blanchet and Demers had been directed to establish a mission in the Cowlitz valley north of Vancouver. In many respects this had appealed to them as a waste of energy because, at that time, there were but four French Canadian families living in the Cowlitz country as against some twenty-eight permanently domiciled in the Willamette valley. Father Blanchet, sincere and devout Catholic that he was, had not been able to abide the thought of depriving these simple people to the southward of a chance to practice their own religious faith. They had, he believed, waited long enough.

Accordingly, after having set up temporary missions both at Fort Vancouver and at the Cowlitz settlement, the courageous Abbé had set out for the Willamette valley with full knowledge that, technically, he was running counter to the company's wishes. Not only had James Douglas offered no objection, but by his cordial manner, he had openly encouraged the pastoral visit. On January 6, 1839, in the midst of the little colony near Champoeg, Father Blanchet had conducted the first Roman Catholic service in the present state of Oregon. Mass had been said in a rude log cabin which the enterprising French Canadians, living ever in hope, had built for a church shortly after Doctor

John had dispatched their first petition to Bishop Provencher. Before leaving the valley, the Abbé had taken possesion of a section of land surrounding the log church building because both he and the settlers had entertained every confidence that the White-Headed Eagle would secure permission in London for the establishment of a permanent mission.[26] But in the summer of 1839, several months prior to the doctor's return, James Douglas, on his own initiative, had officially sanctioned the project.[27]

Such was the situation that greeted the chief factor. We may be sure that both Father Blanchet and the faithful Douglas breathed more easily when they learned from the doctor himself that their bold actions in French Prairie had been regularized by the company's heads in London. Indeed Douglas had taken a grave risk, but his very taking of it indicated his abiding faith in the chief's ability to accomplish his entire program abroad.

6

At the Red River Settlement council, which Doctor John had attended on his way home from England, young Roderick Finlayson had been named as one of the party scheduled to carry the Hudson's Bay flag northward into erstwhile Russian territory during 1840.[28] Roderick, who was a nephew of Chief Factor Duncan Finlayson, was an ambitious and energetic apprenticed clerk with considerable enthusiasm for the fur trade but with very little actual experience to back it up. On the long journey overland, the doctor, ever on the lookout for promising new blood, took a fancy to the lad and, shortly after reaching Vancouver, placed him in charge of the company's gristmill, which was located some five miles above the fort. In addition to the responsibility of supervising twenty men, the new clerk was expected to render at Vancouver a weekly account of his operations each Saturday night.

On one occasion, Roderick, who had been detained at the mill until a late hour, was so determined to bring in his report on the day it was due that he tramped the full five miles on foot through a heavy rain. He was so late, in fact, that he was forced to hail the watchman and have the massive gate opened especially for him after hours—a serious infraction of the company's rules. The conscientious clerk had hoped to gain admittance without arousing the head of the post, but Doctor John, hearing the disturbance, upbraided him for his tardiness.

"We shall have to teach you young gentlemen from the East discipline," asserted the doctor, glancing across his table with a scowl. But when he learned the circumstances—how the lad had walked the full five miles through the cold and mud—he melted. In a second his temper had vanished. "You had better let him have a horse," he remarked to Douglas, who was with him at the time. "A horse," the doctor repeated, pounding on the table, "a horse, but mind you, no saddle; you must furnish your own saddle." Vastly relieved, Finlayson bowed his thanks and withdrew.

On the following Saturday evening, the ardent Roderick, proud of his new mount, dashed through the gate and reined his steed within the enclosure so that his friends might admire both his good fortune and his horsemanship. But alas, he had again broken the law!

Suddenly the peaceful Vancouver air was rent by a roar that came from the vicinity of the chief factor's house. "Who the devil is that daring to break the rules of the establishment by coming in the square in that fashion?" bellowed Doctor John, advancing belligerently. Completely taken aback, Roderick dismounted and stood at attention. This time there was no melting, and the angry chief factor, after delivering a spirited lecture on discipline for the benefit of those assembled, ordered the luckless clerk's horse back to the stables at the fort. Throughout the winter, the disillusioned Roderick was obliged to wade through the mud on foot, but he was careful, thereafter, to acquaint himself with all the rules of the post.[29] Apparently, London had not softened the chief factor!

It was a hard school, but discipline had to be maintained. As for Roderick Finlayson, he was to become one of the most trusted men on the Columbia, and, years later, in speaking of the White-Headed Eagle, he was to remark, "I cannot but express my utmost admiration of his character."

CHAPTER XVII

Local Politics

I

As the race between Great Britain and the United States for possession of the Oregon country quickened, Doctor John girded up his loins for battle. Indeed the issues upon which the struggle was eventually to be settled had, by 1840, assumed the semblance of a definite pattern, and the doctor, recognizing them with characteristic shrewdness, set about enthusiastically to carry forward his London-endorsed program.

We can readily believe that the mixed emotions which, for some years, had been assailing his peace of mind became further intensified upon his return from England. Still British to the core and still impeccably loyal to the company, he was hopeful of saving for Great Britain at least that part of Oregon which lay to the northward and westward of the Columbia River. Had he entertained serious doubts, he would scarcely have been so eager to place his two sons in the Hudson's Bay Company service. On the other hand, it is inconceivable that the possibility of failure, however remote, had not occurred to him. To most of his single-minded colleagues of the fur trade, such an eventuality would have meant disillusionment and almost certain withdrawal from the country, but not to the White-Headed Eagle. With the passage of the years there had grown up within him a passionate devotion to Oregon—a determination to end his days near the Columbia, come what might.

257

There is no doubt that the discerning mind of Governor Simpson had already fathomed this obsession on the part of his chief factor and put it down as a threat to the best interests of the company. Had not the good doctor, by his own words and deeds, supplied ample evidence for such suspicion?

At all events, Doctor John, with feverish energy, undertook to consolidate the gains he had achieved in London, and for him the early months of 1840 were busy ones. Simultaneously, plans for the two great projects—the Puget Sound Agricultural Company and the expedition into former Russian territory—were set in motion.

2

Under the chief factor's direction, a prospectus for the agricultural concern was issued by George B. Roberts, William Frazer Tolmie, and a newcomer to the Columbia, Forbes Barclay.[1] Since Barclay, a graduate of the Royal College of Surgery in London, did not reach Vancouver to assume his duties as post physician until the early spring of 1840, it is reasonable to conclude that most of the work of preparing this prospectus had been completed prior to his arrival. The document called for the establishment of two farms, at Cowlitz and Nisqually, along the lines which had been suggested by the doctor in Fenchurch Street. The proposed organization, under the auspices of the Hudson's Bay Company, provided for a capital stock of £200,000 in £100 shares. John Henry Pelly, Andrew Colville, and George Simpson were named directors, and stockholders' meetings were scheduled to be held in London each December beginning with 1840. Though the new concern was forbidden to deal in furs, the Hudson's Bay Company's general plan of organization was taken as a model.[2] Doctor John, as chief factor of the Columbia department, was named the first resident manager of the Puget Sound Agricultural Company, and, for his services, he was to receive a salary of £500 per year—sufficient reason, whispered some of his friends, to account for his untiring efforts abroad. That was in addition to his compensation as chief factor which amounted to £2,400 annually, assuring him of an income which, in those days, was not to be lightly regarded!

Toward the middle of 1840, the agricultural and grazing lands at Cowlitz and Nisqually, together with the Hudson's Bay Company's live stock and farm implements, were formally turned over to the Puget Sound enterprise. Unfortunately, the project was not destined to be a financial success. Uncertainty regarding the ultimate title to the Oregon country discouraged the company's officers from subscribing for shares to the extent which had been anticipated, and the inferior quality of the soil rendered all husbandry, except the herding of cattle and sheep, unprofitable.[3]

Even at that time, various of the doctor's fellow officers were not backward in expressing grave doubts regarding the feasibility of the plan. Archibald McDonald, to whom the idea for such an enterprise had originally occurred, cautioned his friend, Edward Ermatinger, not "to suppose that I am myself smitten with this colonization mania of ours,"[4] and John Work, with a touch of sarcasm, ventured the opinion that "for the Puget Sound Agricultural Association great expectations are held forth in fact so much so that in a short time furs will not be worth the trouble of looking for."[5]

It is unthinkable that the handicaps facing the concern, both natural and political, had not occurred to the prescient mind of Doctor John. Indeed his readiness to embrace a doomed cause, even if we concede the perfectly human temptation to add £500 a year to his salary, can be chalked up against a last determined effort on his part to hold the Puget Sound country for Great Britain.

Early in the spring, the chief factor was ready to dispatch

northward an expedition charged with the double responsibility of taking over Fort Stikine from the Russians and of founding a new post on the Taku River. He himself had arranged for this undertaking in London, and the Red River Council, which he had attended on his return, had set forth the details. "Either the ship to arrive at the Columbia next year from England," ran the minutes of this meeting, "or the ship 'Vancouver' accompanied by the 'Beaver', steam vessel, [shall] proceed with C. T. Douglas [chief trader], Mr. Wm. Glen Rae, Mr. John McLoughlin Junr. & Mr. Roderick Finlayson with a complement of 20 labouring servants and a sufficient outfit of goods and provisions to take possession of the Russian American Company's Establishment at the entrance to the River Stikine where Mr. Rae is to be left in charge assisted by the other clerks before mentioned [and] immediately after the Post at Stikine be taken possession of Mr. C. T. Douglas shall proceed to the River Tacou about 100 miles north of Stikine and select an eligible situation for establishing a post there."[6]

It was with supreme confidence that Doctor John, on the morning of April 22, 1840, bade the expedition Godspeed.[7] Not only was he counting heavily on the benefits which he hoped might result from the venture, but, entirely apart from business considerations, he was proud that, at last, one of his own flesh and blood was about to assume a post of major responsibility. Once again it is apparent that the doctor's unbounded ambition as a father transcended his sober judgment as an executive, for the thirty-year-old John was temperamentally unsuited for such hazardous service. Intelligent to a marked degree, active, and willing, the young man had nevertheless inherited from the gentle Margaret sufficient of the dark, inscrutable traits of the Indian to render him ruthless, inconsiderate, and resentful. Far too little of himself had the White-Headed Eagle been able to pass on to this unhappy heir. Little did he

dream, as he supervised the loading of the boats on that sunny
April forenoon, that the swarthy John, looking so manly in his
new outfit, would not return to Vancouver alive.

Certainly there was no portent of tragedy in the air as the
graceful flotilla swung majestically out onto the broad bosom
of the Columbia—no hint of the trials these brave adventurers
were to undergo in the north, the burning of Fort Langley,
the shortage of provisions, the incessant troubles with the Indians,
and all the rest.[8] It was just another leave-taking, and still it
was different from previous ones for not only was John, Jr.,
setting forth but the lovely Eloisa had chosen to accompany her
husband, William Glen Rae.[9] As the voyageurs struck up their
boat song, she waved her handkerchief in time with the wild
tempo of the music, and the doctor, standing proudly on the
shore, flourished his great cane in answer. Young David, not
yet reconciled to his lot, studied the scene with outward aloofness but with inward envy of the chance that had come to his
older brother. As the flotilla sped down the river, Doctor John
quieted the fears of his dark-skinned mate by reminding her
that Douglas—his most trusted officer—was in charge. No harm
would befall them, she was not to worry.

3

Toward the end of May, a lone canoe reached Fort Vancouver,
and Doctor John was not a little surprised when his old friend
Jason Lee was ushered into his presence. The missionary explained that he had returned with a large reinforcement for the
mission aboard the sailing ship *Lausanne,* which lay at anchor
near the river's mouth, and that further, impatient to complete
arrangements for the reception of the party in the Willamette,
he had come on ahead of the others.[10] With his customary cordiality, the doctor bade this Yankee comrade welcome; and,
while Margaret prepared tea, he listened to the missionary's story.

Though there was no trace of it in his genial manner, the White-Headed Eagle was not pleased. What possible need, he asked himself, could there be for fifty-two additional Americans in the Willamette valley? The soft-spoken Lee was quick to assure his host that this great party had been sent out exclusively to further the work of the mission, but the wise old doctor, who had kept in close touch with affairs south of the Columbia during the preceding two years, thought otherwise. Only too well did he know the true situation at the Methodist mission. Conversions had been few; sickness had been prevalent among the Indians and whites alike; a number, including Cyrus Shepard, the mainstay of the settlement, had died, and many of the others had become discouraged.[11] The Willamette valley, in truth, had not proved the fertile field for missionary activity that Lee and his original associates had hoped it might. Surely, reflected the doctor, Lee must have realized this prior to his departure for the East.

How, then, he wondered, had the bearded missionary been able to secure from his eastern church friends the $42,000 which had been required to outfit this great reinforcement?[12] Could it be that the fervent Mr. Lee had deliberately misrepresented the condition of affairs at the mission as well as the prospects for the future? The good doctor, who hesitated to think ill of anyone, shrank from such a thought, but he recalled the stirring petition the missionary had taken East to Congress—the same document which had been inspired by the visit of Lieutenant Slacum. Surely the gentle Jason Lee could not have forsaken the saving of souls in order to play the rôle of advance man for the American government! Were the recruits aboard the *Lausanne* sailing under false colors—were they merely so many colonists masquerading as missionaries? The chief factor shook his white head in bewilderment, but one thing he saw clearly —trouble lay ahead for his company with the advent of this sizable party. He was glad he had done what he could, through the Puget Sound Agricultural Company and the Russian treaty, to strengthen the Hudson's Bay hold on Oregon.

Pending the arrival of the *Lausanne,* Doctor John wisely held his suspicions in abeyance. While the missionary ship was slowly wending her way up the Columbia, her passengers were delighted to receive from Fort Vancouver a gift of fresh bread, butter, milk, and vegetables sent by the thoughtful chief factor.[13] At last, on the 1st of June, the *Lausanne* reached the headquarters post of the Columbia department after an exciting voyage around Cape Horn which had consumed eight months.[14] The doctor, still the genial host, entertained the vessel's skipper, Captain Spaulding, and a number of her passengers at tea, after which he went aboard and was presented to the entire party. The next day all the passengers visited the fort, and the chief factor was forced to admit that they were, on the whole, a splendid-looking company—alert, intelligent, and inspired by genuine religious fervor. For the moment, he breathed more easily.

Numbered among the *Lausanne's* recruits were the second Mrs. Jason Lee, Maria T. Ware, who was soon to become the bride of Daniel Lee, Chloe A. Clark, a school teacher from Connecticut whom the stalwart Dr. W. H. Willson was later to marry, the Reverend Gustavus Hines, George Abernethy, J. L. Parrish, and many others destined to become actively identified with the religious and political life of early Oregon. As Doctor John extended his hand in welcome to the Reverend Alvan F. Waller, he was happily unaware of the misery that courteous gentleman was shortly to cause him.

Forthwith the chief factor ordered rooms prepared for the entire company, and for several weeks they remained as his guests while the indefatigable Lee made arrangements to house them at various points throughout his district. During this period, the doctor invited several of the visiting ministers to preach at Vancouver's Sunday services. He even insisted that the marriage of Daniel Lee and Miss Ware take place in his own home with Jason Lee officiating.[15]

On the evening of June 3, Mr. Lee, who had returned from the valley mission whither he had gone following his conference with the doctor, held a large meeting in one of Vancouver's halls; and at this session the newly arrived workers were assigned to their respective posts in Oregon.

It became evident to Doctor John, as he listened to the proceedings, that the Methodists did, in truth, contemplate a vast expansion of their religious labors. Ministers and lay brothers were designated for Nisqually, for the Clatsop country near Fort George, for The Dalles, ninety miles up the Columbia, for the Willamette Falls, and for Chemeketa, some distance south of the original mission.[16] The chief factor took heart—perhaps these good people were not going to concern themselves with local politics after all. But if he entertained such hopes, he was to have a rude awakening not many months hence.

4

Hopeful that the Methodists would find their pretentious program sufficiently engrossing to keep them from dwelling on secular matters, the White-Headed Eagle dismissed, for the time being, the disquieting thoughts that had been troubling him. It is true that he experienced one passing flash of anger when he learned that the Reverend Mr. Waller proposed to erect a building on his Willamette Falls land claim. In order to place his own position squarely before Mr. Lee, he wrote that reverend gentleman, on July 21, a carefully worded letter.

"Yesterday," ran the communication, "I was informed that you intend to establish a mission at the Falls of the Wallamette. I beg to inform you that, in 1830, as is well known to most of

DR. JOHN McLOUGHLIN

From a daguerreotype made shortly after the doctor's retirement from the Hudson's Bay Company. Loaned through the courtesy of his great-grand-daughters, the Misses Elizabeth and Winifred Myrick.

the old settlers in the Wallamette, I took possession of the side of the Falls on which I got a mill race blasted, from the upper end of the Falls, across to the Clackamas River, and down to where the Clackamas falls into the Wallamette, including the whole point of land and the smaller Island in the Falls on which the portage is made, and which I intend to claim when the Boundary line is drawn."

It was merely a friendly warning for, in a postscript, the doctor hastened to add that "of course this is not to prevent your building the store, as my object is merely to establish my claim." [17]

Satisfied in his own mind that he had taken the necessary steps to prevent future misunderstandings, he generously proceeded to assist Mr. Waller by turning over to him a quantity of cut timber with which to construct the proposed building. Little did he dream that this small affair was but the prelude to a controversy which would soon rock Oregon, and which would bring sadness to his own last years.

It was a source of comfort to him, during the closing months of 1840, that the missionaries of other faiths represented in his empire were causing him no worry. The Catholic fathers were laboring quietly but with telling effect among the Indians and French Canadians at Vancouver, Nisqually, Cowlitz, French Prairie, and elsewhere. Only recently, their forces had been augmented by the arrival from St. Louis of the Reverend P. J. De Smet, a Jesuit priest of sterling character, who had chosen to work among the Flatheads.[18] It was but natural for the doctor, in his disturbed state of mind, to be deeply impressed by the zeal and piety of these holy men, who, it seemed, had neither the time nor the inclination for political activity. It is quite possible that from this time forward, Doctor John, remembering his unhappy experience with the Reverend Mr. Beaver and brooding over the secular aspirations of the

Methodists, found himself rapidly drifting back to the faith of his fathers.

Nor were the missionaries of the American Board causing him any concern except as he feared for their safety in territory that was admittedly hostile. Up to then, Whitman, Spalding, and Gray, brave men all, had been laboring patiently among the warlike Cayuses and Nez Percés with comparatively little to show for their efforts save the soul-satisfying knowledge that they had been devoting their entire energy to the difficult task of civilizing and Christianizing the red men. Their ranks had also been reinforced by the arrival of three ministers, Asa B. Smith, Elkanah Walker, and Cushing Eells, together with their wives and a number of lay workers.[19]

For the noble character of Narcissa Whitman, the White-Headed Eagle had long maintained a sincere admiration, and it pained him not a little that she continued to reside with her husband among the treacherous Cayuses. On more than one occasion he counseled Marcus Whitman to quit Waiilatpu, at least temporarily, on the theory that if he did so, his obstreperous charges would repent of their conduct and demand his return.[20] But Whitman, like the doctor, was a man of iron will. Had he but heeded this timely advice, he and his courageous wife might have been spared the ghastly fate that was destined to overtake them.

So, with the advance agents of three religious faiths competing for the souls of the perplexed natives, with the doctor's commercial plans coming on apace, and with the Oregon question rapidly heading for a crisis, the year 1840 passed into history.

5

For some little time, Doctor John, desirous of extending his trade into California, had been considering the feasibility of establishing a post on San Francisco Bay.[21] Before this dream could be realized, however, there remained certain routine matters to be ironed out with the none too friendly Mexican governor of California, Juan B. Alvarado; but the doctor decided against leaving Oregon at such a crucial period.

Very wisely he selected James Douglas, who had returned from Russian America late in 1840, as his personal envoy, and Douglas, now the proud possessor of a chief factor's commission,[22] left Vancouver on December 3 to try his luck at negotiating with the slippery Alvarado. The doctor could not have chosen a more fitting method of proving his faith in this protégé of the old Fort William days, for the mission was one of tremendous importance to the company.[23]

Douglas came out well in his dealings with the Mexican official. Not only did he secure permission for the establishment of a Hudson's Bay post on San Francisco Bay, but he succeeded in persuading the wily governor to set aside an official order which forbade the landing of foreign vessels except at a few stated ports. He also arranged for a substantial purchase of cattle from the Mexican government, and, though he objected to paying the exorbitant price of six dollars per head for choice cows and two dollars per head for ewes, he had no alternative. It was still a good bargain, everything considered, and the doctor's pupil had rendered a signal service. Leaving behind a sufficient number of men to drive the cattle northward, the youthful chief factor departed from California in February and reached the Columbia toward the end of May, 1841.[24] Doctor John's congratulations reflected both his deep admiration and his abiding gratitude.

It was near the middle of February when the doctor, anxiously awaiting some word of Douglas, received news of Ewing Young's death. The Yankee firebrand died as he had lived—a lone wolf and a man of mystery. Scarcely had he expired when it began to be noised about the valley that he had left no will, no mention of any heirs, and no means of disposing of his substantial estate, which included some six hundred head of cattle.[25] Had he been identified with either the Hudson's Bay Company or the Methodist mission, the settling of his affairs would have presented no serious difficulties, but he had never quite forgiven the chief factor nor had he, on the other hand, become intimate with the missionaries. Instantly it occurred to the alert mind of Doctor John that this unprecedented situation might suggest to the Willamette valley settlers the need for some sort of local government—a contingency for which he was scarcely prepared. As it turned out, his fears were not unfounded.

Ewing Young's funeral, which was held on February 17, was attended by a large number of Willamette valley residents. No sooner had the body been lowered into the ground than some one suggested the need of civil authority in the valley to administer the estate of the deceased cattle-man. Just as the doctor had surmised, the settlers were quick to seize the opportunity thus afforded, and a meeting was called for the next day at the Methodist mission. A few French Canadians joined their Yankee neighbors, and after some discussion a committee consisting of Father Blanchet, the Reverend Jason Lee, Gustavus Hines, J. L. Parrish, David Donpierre, M. Charlevaux, Robert Moore, Étienne Lucier, and William Johnson was named for the purpose of drawing up a simple code of laws.[26] Father Blanchet, without his knowledge, was drafted as chairman.

At this same session, the settlers selected a supreme judge, a clerk, a public recorder, a sheriff, and several constables—a sufficient staff, it would seem, to dispose of Ewing Young's effects. Before adjourning, they decided to reconvene at St. Paul, some miles to the northward, on June 1, at which time the law-making committee would make its report. Later, it was agreed that the election of a governor should be deferred until the wishes of the chief factor at Vancouver could be ascertained.[27] This was indeed significant. It meant that, for all their independence of spirit, these early pioneers still recognized the power of the White-Headed Eagle!

When Doctor John heard of these activities, he was profoundly disturbed. Here, at last, was a very definite threat to his sway in Oregon! It was patent to him that the Willamette valley people had chosen Father Blanchet as chairman of the committee and had included several French Canadians as members for the sole purpose of luring them away from the company's influence. It was masterful, this scheme—the doctor was forced to admit it—but it did not suit his book.

But he was not to be caught napping. After all, he reasoned, these French Canadians had no need of another government as they were already protected by the laws of Canada, and, furthermore, they were heavily indebted to the Hudson's Bay Company. Here, beyond a doubt, were two stout and deadly arrows for his quiver of opposition, and Father Blanchet himself shortly provided another. The Abbé, it seems, had been opposed to the project from the start and, upon learning of his appointment as chairman of the committee, promptly declined to serve.[28] Doubtless the good father was as loath to oppose the wishes of the company as he was to take any active part in temporal affairs. We can only surmise with what telling effect the White-Headed Eagle argued among his French Canadian subjects, but the fact remains that what little interest they professed in the Yankee plan soon vanished.

6

It was during this distressing period that another ally popped, providentially if unwittingly, into the doctor's fold. In 1838 the American government had dispatched the so-called United States Exploring Expedition under Lieutenant Charles Wilkes, an enterprising young officer who was later to become a national hero in the Civil War. Having completed the first leg of their journey around the world, the five ships comprising the squadron entered the Strait of Juan de Fuca on May 1, 1841, and the members of the party set out on foot to investigate the Northwest country. On May 29, after extensive travels through the Puget Sound region, Lieutenant Wilkes and a portion of his command reached Fort Vancouver, where they were courteously received by Doctor John.

The American naval officer was well pleased with his host, for, in his informative diary, he not only speaks well of the chief factor but provides a most valuable character sketch. "He is," runs the entry, "a fine looking person of robust frame, with a frank open countenance . . . of florid complexion his hair white . . . enthusiastic in disposition and I should think of great energy of character and well suited for the situation he occupies which requires no small talent and industry to fill." [29]

The seafaring visitor was royally entertained at Vancouver and was, in addition, afforded every facility for traveling safely through the country as well as for investigating the methods of the Hudson's Bay Company. Confident in the knowledge that he had nothing to conceal, Doctor John had become quite willing to expose his empire to the rigid scrutiny of sojourning Americans—particularly when they came as representatives of the United States government. He had not lost the subtle art of salesmanship.

Wilkes seemed pleased with everything. Commenting on the Indian boys cared for at Vancouver by the chief factor, he observes that "it was pleasing to see the interest that Dr. McL & Douglass took in them and much credit is due to them for their snatching as it were these castaway boys from the vices & idleness of the savage life. Much has been said about the disregard to morals & vices of this Company and I feel myself in justice to them to say that as far as my observation went to bear testimony to this and many other acts that will prove to the contrary." [30]

Then, with an eye to the interests of his own country, the lieutenant continues with the comment that "the officers of the Hon. Company have not only quieted the country but their operations have been so admirably conducted that they have opened the country to safe and secure emigration and rendered the task an easy one to its peaceful possession." [31]

Convinced that Lieutenant Wilkes had formed an excellent opinion of his régime in the Columbia department, the doctor looked forward to that officer's Willamette valley tour with no great apprehension. Departing from Vancouver on June 3, the observant Wilkes traveled southward in a large boat which had been bounteously provisioned by the chief factor.[32] He paid his respects at the Catholic and Methodist missions, dropped in on the predatory Mr. Waller at Willamette Falls, and traversed the valley in all directions with the reliable Michel La Framboise serving as guide. In the Willamette country his advice was eagerly sought by those who still entertained hopes for a local government. Lieutenant Wilkes offered them no encouragement. On the contrary, he suggested that laws not only were unnecessary but would be exceedingly difficult to enforce, that the religious differences among the settlers would make for political discord, and that the United States government, in its own time and in its own way, would inevitably spread its jurisdiction to them.[33] Guided by motives which differed widely from those of the doctor, Wilkes nevertheless proved a timely ally in the struggle to prevent a local government. Disheartened by the double opposition of the chief factor and the visiting Yankee officer, the valley settlers abandoned, for the time being, any efforts to organize themselves.

Back at Fort Vancouver, Wilkes had the pleasure of meeting Peter Skene Ogden, who had also been made a chief factor, and who was on leave from his own New Caledonia department. From the colorful Ogden, Lieutenant Wilkes gleaned considerable information of value regarding the northern country. At last, on June 17, having completed his pleasant visit at Vancouver, the head of the United States Exploring Expedition departed with Ogden's brigade for the north.

In his diary Wilkes describes the scene vividly and, in addition, furnishes his own private opinion of the missionaries. "On the morning of the 17th," he writes, "the Fort was in a stir at an early hour. . . . Now and then we saw a voyageur decked out in his ribband & feathers all attention to his duties. About 10 o'clock we were all summoned by Dr. McLoughlin to the Hall to take a parting cup. . . . All were present Missionaries and all the household. The former ought to have staid away for if they had been at my funeral instead of leave taking they could not have been so repugnant to good fellowship & feeling." [84]

So pleased and relieved was Doctor John with the turn events had taken that he gladly agreed to join the lieutenant at a Fourth of July celebration to be held near the Nisqually mission settlement. Although the chief factor was detained at the last minute by affairs at Vancouver and did not reach Nisqually until the 5th, his friendly gesture in coming was deeply appreciated by both the American settlers and Wilkes. During this significant visit he boarded the American sloop-of-war *Vincennes*—the first war vessel on which he had ever set foot—and received a lusty cheer from her crew. [85]

We can only guess what emotions the White-Headed Eagle must have experienced as he stood respectfully at attention and saluted the Stars and Stripes!

CHAPTER XVIII

GATHERING CLOUDS

1

FOR a time, Doctor John remained in the Puget Sound country. Undoubtedly he had important duties to perform as manager of the agricultural enterprise, but we suspect that he had an even stronger reason, just then, for delaying his return to Vancouver. He had been advised that Governor Simpson was due to arrive before long at the headquarters post, and he was not looking forward to the meeting with pleasure.

In this situation we discover a very human side of the doctor's character, and, oddly enough, it is reassuring to know that even he was subject to the foibles of lesser men. Although he was not the type of person to run away from difficult ordeals, we can imagine how gratifying it must have been to know that there was legitimate company business to hold him at Cowlitz and Nisqually. For one thing, business in the department had not been good, and, like a schoolboy reluctant to face his master with ill-prepared lessons, he was none too eager to subject himself to the governor's searching questions. He realized, too, that his friendly attitude toward the Willamette valley settlers, notwithstanding his success in subverting their fleeting dream of local government, would again come up for discussion. Furthermore, the governor had been knighted late in 1839 for his services to the crown during the Papineau rebellion,[1] and

Doctor John did not relish addressing as "Sir George" the man who had so violently opposed his one-time hero. Far better, he reasoned, to let the governor air his grievances to the faithful Douglas and to return when the atmosphere had cleared. He was aware, it would seem, of his own quick temper.

But Douglas, awaiting Sir George's arrival at Vancouver, was himself in a difficult position. Knowing the friction which had developed between his two chiefs and sympathizing, in the main, with the doctor, he was forced, nevertheless, to steer a middle course. With a nest of his own to feather, there was little else to do. It seems grossly unfair, in the circumstances, to accuse him, as some writers have done, of double dealing. His many acts of loyalty to his old benefactor prove the contrary. We know, for example, of a letter written by him to a subordinate who had penned a discourteous and ill-mannered note to Doctor John—an act, incidentally, which required no little courage.

"I have read your letter to Dr. McLoughlin," Douglas had written, "and do not approve of the warm expostulatory style, which I regret is neither proper nor respectful. It was never, my dear Sir, Dr. McLoughlin's intention to question the propriety of your general conduct, he merely inquired as a matter of justice equally to himself and to you, why certain specific orders had not been followed to the letter, and I certainly think you would have acted a much wiser part, had your reply to a requisition so simple, been given in a more courteous way." Then, as one who knew his chief's temperament intimately, Douglas added a parting admonition to this unknown upstart. "Dr. McLoughlin," he had concluded, "was greatly displeased with some passages of your letter, and intended to take a severe course with it, until a friend of yours suggested that the fault was evidently one of manner and not of intention, which induced him to drop the thing." [2]

There is every reason to believe that Douglas himself was the "friend" in question. At all events, with so trusted an associate at the helm in Vancouver, Doctor John could scarcely have entertained serious fears of being "sold out" to the knighted visitor.

2

Meanwhile Sir George, traveling in grand style, reached Fort Vancouver on the 25th of August, where, as he put it, "we were received by Mr. Douglas, as Mr. McLoughlin, the gentleman in charge, was absent at Puget Sound." [3] Having left London in March, the racing governor had made good time on the first half of his journey around the globe. Still the energetic field man, he had been sent out by their Honors in London to gather accurate information regarding the company's fortunes in all parts of the world, and it appears that the principal objects of his visit to the Northwest coast were to inspect the former Russian fort on the Stikine River and to arrange for the establishment of a post on San Francisco Bay. [4] Douglas was able to give him a complete account of what had recently occurred in California, as well as the further information that Doctor John, some months earlier, had sent his son-in-law, Chief Trader William Glen Rae, south to found the new Hudson's Bay settlement at Yerba Buena. [5]

Sir George carried with him a pretentious retinue. Indeed he seemed more like a powerful potentate visiting a neighboring kingdom than like the matter-of-fact representative of a great business organization. Included in his suite were, in addition to a secretary, named Hopkins, "four or five gentlemen connected with the Hudson's Bay Company's service and also a gentleman [Von Freeman] in the service of the Russian American Company, on his route from Petersburg to Sitka, which his superiors were thus preferring for him, as being shorter by thirty degrees of longitude, the breadth of all the rest of the world, to that of his native empire." [6]

Describing his approach to Vancouver, the governor noted that "being anxious to approach head-quarters in proper style, our men here exchanged the oar for the paddle, which, beside being more orthodox in itself, was better adapted to the quick notes of the voyageur songs." [7] Still a rigid observer of the amenities, Sir George had not changed since the days when, as plain George Simpson, he had crossed America with the budding chief factor, John McLoughlin. Nor had the seventeen-year interval robbed him of his sense of showmanship!

Though the chief executive tarried a week at Fort Vancouver, there was no word from Doctor John, whose duties at the Cowlitz and Nisqually farms were conveniently keeping him away. It was during this week that Lieutenant Wilkes, on his surveying trip up the Columbia, returned to Vancouver with three of his ships, the sloop-of-war *Porpoise,* the tender *Flying Fish,* and the recently acquired store ship *Oregon.* [8] The lieutenant was not in the best of spirits owing to the loss of one of his vessels, the *Peacock,* which had been wrecked in crossing the bar of the Columbia some weeks earlier. [9]

In honor of this second visitation, Sir George and Douglas tendered a formal banquet to Lieutenant Wilkes, Captain Hudson, and other members of the United States Exploring Expedition, but somehow the affair was not a success. [10] Even with his London drawing-room manners, the governor was not able to conceal a certain suspicion of the Americans, who, no doubt, felt keenly the absence of Vancouver's genial host.

3

With the arrival of September, it was high time for the industrious Sir George to be traveling. He had his inspection of the northern posts yet to make as well as his official visit to Sitka. Accordingly, on the first day of the new month, he set out from Fort Vancouver at the head of his impressive retinue. James Douglas, proud to be included in such a distinguished party, went along in the joint rôle of guide and traveling companion. A week was spent at the Cowlitz and Nisqually farms where the governor seemed pleased with the progress that had been made—at least one tribute from him to the wisdom and foresight of the department's chief factor.

If he encountered Doctor John at either place, he made no mention of the fact in the detailed narrative of his journey. Indeed the absence of any reference, by this meticulous diarist, to such an important meeting seems, in itself, sufficient proof that none took place. The doctor may well have decided that this was the psychological time to pick for his return to Vancouver.

The governor's party left Fort Nisqually "under a salute of seven guns" on September 6, and, comfortably settled aboard the stout little steamer *Beaver,* they started up the coast. As they rounded the southern end of Vancouver Island, Sir George and Douglas were favorably impressed by this site [11] as a possible haven for the company's headquarters if political exigencies should one day force them to withdraw from the Columbia. But it is not likely that either realized how soon their mutual inspiration was to result in the establishment of Fort Victoria.

Resuming the voyage, Governor Simpson called at Fort McLoughlin, where Charles Ross was in command, and at Fort Simpson, where Chief Trader John Work had been stationed since 1835. The governor, who had for years opposed Doctor John's insistence upon so many stations, decided that one of the two should be abandoned. He ruled against Fort McLoughlin, and, though that post was to struggle along for two years more, its fate was definitely sealed from the time of Sir George's personal inspection.[12]

Still farther to the northward, the party stopped at Fort Stikine where, for several months, the youthful John McLoughlin had been in charge, and at Fort Taku, which was manned at the time by John Kennedy.[13] Sir George was not at all pleased with the doctor's son, who impressed him with his utter lack of fitness for the position. Though his innermost thoughts were not to find expression until later, he doubtless formed, on the spot, a poor opinion of Doctor John's judgment in placing this headstrong and inexperienced clerk in charge of a post so vital to the company's progress.

Finally, at Sitka, the titled visitor was received in regal splendor by Governor Etholine and his charming wife. He was delighted to learn that business with the Russian American Fur Company had been good—so good, in fact, that the Czar himself had seen fit to renew its license for a "farther term of twenty years."[14] With the Hudson's Bay Company's tenure in Russian America dependent upon this grant, such news was more than welcome. After a merry—apparently very merry— round of entertainment provided by the hospitable Russians, the racing governor took leave of Sitka and reached Fort Vancouver on October 22.

Upon his return, he was cheered by the news that a party of Canadian emigrants, bound for the lands of the Puget Sound Agricultural Company, had arrived safely at Vancouver on October 4. These families, who had come from the Red River Settlement, had been compelled to abandon their carts and pack their goods on oxen over the Rockies.[15] Doctor John had received them with his accustomed cordiality and had sent them on to Nisqually where, owing to the inferior soil, only a few were to remain. Some years later, the governor was to blame the long-suffering chief factor for the desertion of these families to the inviting valley of the Willamette.[16] For the moment, however, the British fur traders in Oregon were encouraged by the addition to their ranks of this band of recruits who, they believed, would aid in strengthening John Bull's claim to the country.

At Vancouver, the long deferred meeting between Sir George and Doctor John finally took place. Determined to preserve the peace, each tactfully avoided unpleasant subjects. Though the explosion which was destined to disrupt their relationship once and for all was just around the corner, the fuse had not yet been ignited. Outwardly, everything appeared serene.

During this period of calm before the storm, the doctor actually found himself in agreement with not a few of his chief's ideas. For one thing, Sir George had taken a vigorous stand against the custom, generally practiced by the Russians, of using spirituous liquors in trade for furs with the northern Indians, and in this he had the enthusiastic backing of the resident chief factor. Though the two men did not see eye to eye in their attitude toward the Americans—the governor distrusting them cordially—they nevertheless agreed that the time had come for Great Britain to declare her claims to Oregon. Sir George made a minute of this in his bulging notebook as one of the matters to take up with his government in London, for, as he so aptly put it, "I feel assured that some step will very soon be taken, with like object, in favor of the United States." [17] There can be no doubt that his presentiment of such action on the part of the Yankees came direct from Doctor John, who was thoroughly familiar with Jason Lee's late political activities in Washington.

During this second Vancouver sojourn, the visiting chief made known to the doctor his desire to establish a post on the southern end of Vancouver Island. By that time, the project had assumed a double significance—the clinching of Great

Britain's claim to the island and the providing of a refuge for the company in the event things became too embarrassing on the Columbia. Doctor John readily assented to the plan. They also discussed the northern situation quite frankly, and the chief factor offered no objection when his superior officer recommended not only the abandonment of Fort McLoughlin but also the relinquishment of Forts Stikine and Taku for reasons of economy. The steamer *Beaver,* argued Sir George, could accomplish nearly as much, on an annual cruise to northern waters, as could these elaborate and expensive posts.[18]

What had come over the doctor? Why was he so willing to accept this drastic curtailment of his program? The answer lies not in any lessening of his ardor for the company but solely in his resignation to the current political puzzle. We may safely assume that Sir George was voicing his own sentiments as well as those of the doctor when, in his formal report to the Governor and Committee of the Hudson's Bay Company, he noted: "I am concerned to say the returns are gradually diminishing from year to year, this arises from no want of attention to the management of the district, but from the exhausted state of the country, which has been closely wrought for many years without any intermission. In the present unsettled state of the boundary line it would be impolitic to make any attempt to preserve or recruit this once valuable country, as it would attract the attention of the American trappers, so that there is little prospect of any amendment taking place in its affairs."[19]

Retrenchment was the order of the day, and if Doctor John grieved over the situation, he was at least thankful that the governor had given his régime a clean bill of health in point of efficiency. If Sir George's conversations, during his Vancouver sojourn, were as conciliatory as the language of his official report would seem to indicate, it is little wonder that the chief factor was able to keep his temper within bounds.

4

There was, however, one matter upon which the two adversaries crossed swords. During October, shortly after the governor's return from Sitka, there arrived at Fort Vancouver an engaging Frenchman named Mofras. Eugène Duflot de Mofras had come to the Northwest from California on the Hudson's Bay Company's bark *Cowlitz* by the roundabout Sandwich Islands route. Armed with a letter of introduction from Chief Trader Rae, who was then settled at Yerba Buena, and a passport from the Mexican foreign minister, the traveler had naturally expected to receive a friendly welcome.

Doctor John greeted the newcomer at the boat landing with his traditional good-fellowship, but Sir George, unable to conceal his suspicions, remained in his quarters at the chief factor's residence. Following a decidedly cool reception by the governor, which the doctor tried to soften with some timely witticisms in the French tongue, the visitor explained his errand. He spoke with the utmost frankness, cheerfully volunteering all the reasons for his journey.

Mofras, it developed, had been attached to the French embassy in Madrid until 1839, when, because of his interest in Spanish America, he had been transferred to his nation's legation at Mexico City. By reason of his proximity to the Northwest—a section about which the French people knew practically nothing—he had been sent by his government to ascertain "what advantages might accrue to France from commercial expeditions and the establishment of stations in these regions still so little known to France." [20]

Despite the Frenchman's candid manner and his repeated reassurances as to the purely commercial nature of his mission, Sir George remained openly hostile during the six weeks of the visitor's sojourn in Oregon. The doctor, on the other hand, could not abide the thought of a stranger within his gates receiving such treatment, so, goaded perhaps by his growing dislike of the governor, he set about to make his guest comfortable. The chief factor's ability to converse in fluent French, to say nothing of his inherent admiration for Napoleon and the French people, endeared him to the impressionable Mofras, who refers glowingly to his gracious host in the published recollections of his visit.[21]

During the time he allotted to Oregon, the representative of the French government traveled through the Willamette valley, down the Columbia to Fort George and northward to the farms at Cowlitz and Nisqually. As a good Catholic, he was impressed with Father Blanchet and a little puzzled by the Methodists; and, as a loyal Frenchman, he was deeply flattered by the reception the French Canadian settlers in the valley accorded him. To these honest people, many of whom spoke nothing but French, it was a decided novelty to meet and talk with a real Frenchman. Notwithstanding Sir George's cold reception and suspicious manner, Mofras was gracious enough to pronounce him an intelligent chief. If the governor could only have known that into the visitor's book would eventually go the positive opinion that Great Britain's claim to Oregon was stronger than that of the United States—despite a strong prejudice in favor of the Yankees—he might have felt differently.[22] But it was for Doctor John that the alert Frenchman reserved his most eloquent praise. Of his urbanity, erudition, and affable personality, Mofras could not say enough; but he was obviously inspired more by enthusiasm than by veracity when he observed that "with one accord, the colonists, English, American and French have offered him provisionally the government of all the territory."[23] But what did a little Gallic extravagance of statement matter between friends?

At about this time, Doctor John was again aroused by the

activities of the Methodists at his Willamette Falls land claim. Ever since he had dispatched his veiled warning to Jason Lee the previous year, he had considered the matter settled and had ceased to worry over the continued presence of the Reverend Mr. Waller at the Falls. But when word was brought to him that a certain Felix Hathaway, then connected with the Methodist mission, was, at that moment, building a house on another part of the claim, he hastened to the scene to remonstrate with the two men. Very adroitly, Mr. Waller quieted his fears by assuring him that he had taken a claim for himself on the Clackamas River below the Falls though he did not deny that the missionaries intended to hold the site they were then occupying solely as tenants by sufferance. The doctor was too trusting by nature to read any sinister motive into this dextrous omission, so, without comment, he turned his guns on Mr. Hathaway. That ambitious gentleman, wilting under the steadfast gaze of those piercing gray eyes, promised to abandon his building operations. Nevertheless he unwittingly reawakened the chief factor's suspicions by informing him that the house upon which he had been working was not intended for a milling company recently organized in the valley, as the doctor had been led to believe, but for himself. Puzzled and disillusioned but still hopeful that he had misread the motives of these Methodists, the White-Headed Eagle erected a small house of his own at the Falls merely as a precaution.[24]

During this same eventful year of 1841, the doctor was saddened by the death of two of his most capable officers—Chief Factor Samuel Black, who was shot by an Indian at the Thompsons River post, and Chief Trader Pierre C. Pambrun, who died following a fall from his horse at Fort Walla Walla.[25] Aside from the deep sense of personal loss, he felt the blow keenly from the business side, for Pambrun had proved himself a particularly able manager, and Black, an old North Wester, had been one of the company's mainstays in the West for many years. A colorful character to the last, Black had counted among his most cherished possessions a ring which had been presented to him at the time of the coalition of the two fur companies. On this ring was engraved the legend, "To the most worthy of the worthy North Westers." [26]

The year had nearly spent itself. At last, in December, the company's bark *Cowlitz* departed for California with a notable passenger list including Sir George, Doctor John, Hopkins, the governor's secretary, Mofras, a Mr. Hale of the United States Exploring Expedition, and Eloisa McLoughlin Rae, en route to join her husband at Yerba Buena. [27] Hale, who had been left behind by Lieutenant Wilkes to complete some details of the American expedition, was suspected of political intrigue by the governor, and, as for Mofras, he was so deeply wounded by Sir George's manner that he insisted upon paying for his passage— an unusual arrangement in those days of open-handed hospitality. With two such questionable foreigners aboard ship, we can imagine how relieved the Hudson's Bay Knight must have felt when the voyage was over.

It was Doctor John's first and last visit to California—a pleasant interlude before the tragic dénouement which was so soon to overtake him. He took genuine pleasure in looking over the Yerba Buena post which his son-in-law had founded for the company on San Francisco Bay, and he was happy to see his daughter settled, at last, in her own home. Already there were two grandchildren, John and Margaret Rae—the doctor's first as far as is known—and he literally worshiped this pair of healthy youngsters. Vancouver, he feared, would be dull without them.

Finally, after meeting Governor Alvarado, whom Simpson branded as "an ignorant, dissipated man, quite devoid of responsibility and character," [28] the White-Headed Eagle departed with Sir George for Honolulu, where the *Cowlitz* arrived on February 12.[29] The very next day, the doctor boarded the bark *Vancouver* for home.

5

Not long after his return to the Columbia, his second son, John, Jr., was brutally murdered by his own men at Fort Stikine. Because of the time required to convey news down the coast, the doctor went about his duties for several weeks in ignorance of the tragedy. When he did learn of it, he was overcome with grief. Indeed this killing did much to increase the anguish and heartache of the good man's closing years with the company.

Young John, as his father well knew, was not only a hot-head but entirely too inexperienced to be left in charge of twenty-two men in a wild and hostile country. The doctor had objected strenuously when Sir George, for reasons of economy, had insisted upon removing from Fort Stikine the only other commissioned officer stationed there, but the Knight had re-mained adamant.[30] Certain it is that conditions at this lonely outpost were diametrically opposed to what a youth of John's unstable temperament needed to bring out the best in him. "It was a miserable place," wrote Eloisa Rae, who had spent a year there with her husband. "There were only flat rocks and no trees around close. . . . The Indians were very troublesome. They never opened the gate to receive more than one Indian at a time to trade. . . . We had a trough made with two boards for half a mile to bring in water. When the Indians got drunk . . . they would destroy the trough so that we could not get water. . . . They were buying liquor and fighting all the time among themselves outside the Fort. . . . Of liquor a big hogs head four feet high was emptied in one day. It was on the occasion of a feast." [31] We need no more than this vivid descrip-tion of the place, coupled with our knowledge of young John's fondness for strong drink, his quick temper, his dominating manner, and his inexperience, to imagine the rest.

On the fateful evening of April 21, after several days of wild carousing during which the entire personnel of the establishment had become quite drunk, the hot-blooded clerk offended some of his French Canadian and Kanaka employees who promptly resolved to take his life. A general shooting mêlée ensued and, in the heat of the fracas, one of the Canadians killed John instantly.[32] That, in substance, was what took place.

Wild confusion followed the killing, and it is likely that the quarrelsome natives, unrestrained at last, would have captured and sacked the fort had not Governor Simpson, on his return from the Sandwich Islands by way of Sitka, arrived providentially on the *Cowlitz*. Four days having elapsed since the murder, Sir George was not able to ferret out a succinct account of what actually happened, but after a protracted inquisition, one of the Canadians confessed. The governor, puzzled as to what steps to take and anxious to end the miserable affair if possible, took the murderer to Sitka only to release him the next day. He later explained his action on the ground that, since "neither Canada nor Russia had any court of criminal jurisdiction in the country," there was nothing to do but let the guilty man go free.[33] The cultured Sir George was evidently unmindful of Peter Skene Ogden's legal code—the age-old law of an eye for an eye and a tooth for a tooth—and, whether for personal reasons or not, he was decidedly remiss in his handling of the affair.

Doctor John, when he learned the tragic news, was beside himself—torn between grief for his son and disgust with his chief. John Tod, in a lengthy letter to Edward Ermatinger, provides a startling account of the aftermath. Sir George, runs the communication, "also wrote to the Doctor requesting him to say as little as possible about the matter, which so incensed the latter that he immediately dispatched a vessel to Stikeen for the express purpose of carrying the whole establishment to England . . . to be brought to trial. He also wrote a thundering epistle to their Honors at home, concerning Sir Geo. ripping up old grievances and exposing the Knight's conduct thoroughly, particularly his amours since coalition." [34]

Poor, distracted doctor! Out in the open, at last, was the long smoldering quarrel. Henceforth, it was to be war to the knife! All the facts considered—even the despicable character of John, Jr.—one can scarcely blame the grief-stricken chief factor. Indeed, to him, it was not the question of an unworthy Hudson's Bay officer bringing about his own death—it was the loss of a son. Pathetic in the extreme is his defense of his ill-starred offspring. "Those fellows," he wrote to that perennial recipient of letters from Oregon, Edward Ermatinger, "wanted to impose on my son, to which he would not submit. They, finding they could not make him bend, conspired and murdered him. My son John was intelligent, active—had the faults of youth, was inconsiderate and thoughtless—at least had been so, but this was wearing away. At the same time he had the good qualities of youth—though I say it. He was frank, open, firm—but kind and generous—" [35] The subject was dropped abruptly—the tortured father could write no more, but, in that brief, unfinished statement, he penned a fitting epitaph for John McLoughlin the younger.

6

In the fall of 1842, there was valley talk of renewed activity at Willamette Falls on the part of Mr. Waller who, it was said, intended to press his claim in spite of all that had occurred. When this gossip reached the doctor, he again appealed to Jason Lee, who gave him only evasive answers or, at best, naïve assurances that he could not be responsible for Mr. Waller's personal aspirations. Waller himself proved equally difficult to pin down. Whenever Doctor John talked with him, he seemed reasonable—as soon as the chief factor was out of sight, he would either repudiate his previous agreements or come forward with new and fanciful proposals.

At length, his patience wearing thin, the doctor, in the hope of ending the ridiculous controversy, had his claim surveyed into building lots and officially named the settlement "Oregon City." He also erected a sawmill on the river bank and served notice that a gristmill would soon be built. Surely, he thought, he had heard the last of the affair.[36]

Instead of settling matters, however, the doctor's acts merely served to arouse certain members of the Methodist mission. Indignant over what they chose to term the arbitrary proceedings of the Hudson's Bay Company monopoly, they framed a petition to Congress which set forth, in minute detail, their fancied grievances against the White-Headed Eagle.[37] The fat was in the fire! It was some little time before the harassed chief factor was able to learn the exact contents of this unjust and, in many respects, untruthful document. When, during the following year, he was at last informed of the accusations which had been brought against him, he exclaimed, "Really, really, the citizens themselves are the best judges if we did so or not, and I am certain if they are so lost to a sense of what is due to truth as to make such an assertion, it is useless for me to say anything. I am astonished that there should be one person in the country to say such a thing of me." [38]

What a year it had been! Tortured in spirit by his various misfortunes, the weary doctor labored on through the closing months of 1842. It is at such times that men who have any religion in their souls turn to God. For some months, Doctor John had been quietly meditating upon the teachings of the faith into which he had been baptized; and while he was visit-

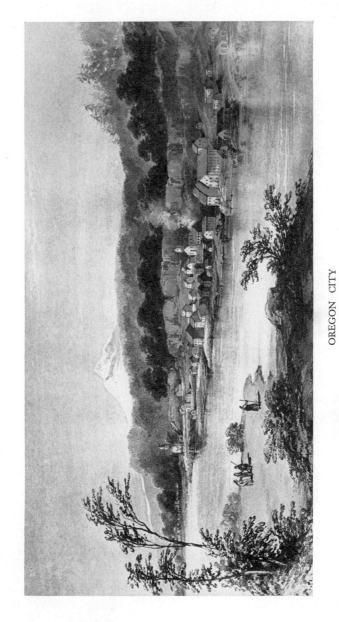

OREGON CITY

From an etching made by Lieutenant Warre of the Warre-Vavasour Expedition in 1845.

ing at Fort Nisqually he came upon a book entitled "The End of Controversy," which settled his troubled mind. Perhaps, in the circumstances, the title appealed to him for secular as well as spiritual reasons!

At all events, upon his return to Vancouver, he made his abjuration and profession of Faith at the hands of his good friend, Father Blanchet. On this same day, November 18, he made his confession, had his marriage to the loyal wife of many years blessed by the Church, and prepared himself for his first communion by fasting during the four weeks of Advent.[39] The thoughtful boy of Rivière du Loup had returned to the fold.

CHAPTER XIX

The Crisis

I

Numbered were the White-Headed Eagle's years of unchallenged authority. Enterprising citizens of New England and the Middle West had been stirred by accounts of his empire, and, in 1842, the stout wheels of covered wagons began to cut the long, weary trail to Oregon.

In that year the first real immigration of American settlers—about a hundred and twenty-five souls in all—reached the Willamette valley. Commanding this band of pioneers was Dr. Elijah White, a former member of the Methodist mission, who was now returning to the West as an Indian subagent of the United States government.[1] Leaving their wagons at Fort Hall, the immigrants, after splitting up into various factions, finally reached Oregon City on October 5 with the memory of a thrilling and precarious journey to carry to the end of their days. They did not pass through Vancouver—they were not to experience the White-Headed Eagle's generosity until later. Instead, they crossed overland from The Dalles to Oregon City on an Indian trail that carried them close by Mt. Hood.[2]

Dr. White, who, with a few ambitious pathfinders, had come ahead of the main body, addressed a mass meeting at Champoeg on September 23. This gathering had been assembled for the purpose of officially receiving the newly appointed agent's credentials.[3] In his maiden speech to the Willamette valley settlers, White conveyed the impression, perhaps unintentionally, that his commission carried with it substantial authority—authority far beyond that of an Indian subagent. Though this fiction could not long be maintained, his very manner, suggesting, as it did, Uncle Sam's interest in the welfare of the listening American settlers, served to rekindle in their hearts a desire for local government.[4]

One of the most colorful members of this first immigration to Oregon was Francis Xavier Matthieu, a young Canadian who, with six companions, had joined the overland company at Fort Laramie. He had grown up in the town of Terrebonne, Quebec, where he had known Doctor John's uncle, Dr. Simon Fraser. In the Papineau rebellion of 1837, he had cast his lot with the losing side and, as a result, had been forced to quit Canada. After a few years in the United States, young Matthieu had decided to try his luck in Oregon.

This picturesque pioneer, like most of the others, arrived in the Willamette valley practically destitute. Direly as he needed a new outfit, he had no means of paying for one. Money, had he possessed it, would have served no useful purpose, as furs, at a fixed valuation, constituted the first coin of the realm and wheat the second. In line with the policy Doctor John had established, the valley settlers were required to deliver their wheat to the Hudson's Bay Company's warehouse at Champoeg where they received receipts from the clerk in charge. These receipts were honored at Fort Vancouver for goods at their face value.

From Étienne Lucier the enterprising Francis Matthieu obtained a receipt, but when he attempted to cash it at Vancouver, he discovered, to his dismay, that Lucier's account had been overdrawn. In his extremity, the young man appealed to the solicitous chief factor, who, upon learning of his early days in Terrebonne and his acquaintance with old Dr. Fraser, gladly offered to help him. "You look honest," observed Doctor John, glancing up over his spectacles. "Go to the office and get this filled." With that he handed the astonished Canadian an order for $18. Matthieu, deeply moved by such unexpected generosity, mumbled his thanks and repaired to the window from which supplies were dispensed.

Behind the wicket stood none other than David, the doctor's youngest son, who, with a sly wink, invited the amazed pioneer to "take out all you need and never mind the old man." Francis Matthieu refused to accept more than his order permitted, but he must have wondered at David's business judgment in offering him unlimited credit. This Canadian immigrant was to become one of the most respected residents of early Oregon and one of Doctor John's warmest supporters.[5]

What the magnanimous White-Headed Eagle did for this straitened colonist, he was to do time and again for countless others, irrespective of creed or nationality. Once satisfied as to a man's honesty and genuine need, there was no limit to his largess. He advanced everything required and willingly furnished the use of boats to those who had no other means of transporting their modest possessions to the Willamette valley.

Not a few of these early immigrants to Oregon would have perished but for the good man's Christian charity, and many of them were to find his boats the only means of negotiating the last stage of their westward journey from The Dalles to Oregon City. For all these advances the doctor was held accountable by his company. Indeed he was obliged to assume complete responsibility for every cent not paid by the immigrants, a shocking number of whom were to repudiate their debts. It was this open-handed and often ill-advised liberality which was to become not only one of the main causes of his final break with the Hudson's Bay Company but also one of the principal reasons for the disillusionment of his last years.

Only a portion of the immigration of 1842 was destined to

remain in Oregon. Some of the people were of the roving type
who never stay long in one place, and others were frankly
disappointed in the new country, especially when they discovered that there was no substitute for good, honest work.
Doctor John engaged the more worthy among them to labor
at fair wages, but, in the spring of 1843, nearly half the original
party left for California. Again the doctor was overcome with
compassion, though the very fact that so many were looking
for a soft berth should have put him on his guard. Be that as
it may, he furnished these emigrants to California with supplies
upon their promise to pay for them at the company's Yerba
Buena post. Time would reveal how few of these obligations
were paid and how many had to be personally assumed by the
White-Headed Eagle.[6]

2

Doctor John now turned his attention to the political situation
more earnestly than ever before. In July, 1842, he had dispatched
James Douglas to Vancouver Island for the purpose of choosing
a favorable site for the new post. Douglas, after an extended
investigation, had returned with a lengthy report setting forth
the advantages and disadvantages of a number of situations. In
the meantime, the Council of the Northern Department of
Rupert's Land had officially sanctioned the project and had
passed a resolution to the effect that "an eligible site for such
a Depot be selected, and that measures be adopted for forming this Establishment with the least possible delay."[7]

The doctor appears to have left the final choice of a location
to Douglas, for, on March 1, 1843, that able officer left Fort
Vancouver at the head of a party of fifteen men with orders to
build the new station. Arriving at the island, he decided in
favor of Clover Point because of its excellent anchorage; and
on March 16, work was begun. As soon as operations were under

way, the junior chief factor, again acting under Doctor John's orders, proceeded northward on the *Beaver* to superintend the dismantling of Forts McLoughlin and Taku. The Stikine post, in accordance with instructions from the Council of 1842, was not to be abandoned until 1844.

By the 1st of June, Douglas was back on Vancouver Island with a substantial number of recruits from the defunct establishments to the northward. Leaving Charles Ross in charge of the now rapidly rising fort, with Roderick Finlayson as his assistant, he returned to Vancouver to receive the doctor's congratulations upon his able handling of the year's work.[8] In October, 1843, Fort Victoria was ready for occupancy, and the Hudson's Bay officers on the West coast were happy in the realization that at last they had built a stronghold from which the aggressive Yankees could scarcely hope to dislodge them.

We must go back a little in order to describe the condition prevailing in the White-Headed Eagle's empire at the commencement of 1843. It was such a situation as to try the patience of a less forbearing man than Doctor John. Neither Great Britain nor the United States could hope to set up a permanent government in the country with the boundary question unsettled. To the great disappointment of residents in Oregon, British and American alike, the Webster-Ashburton Treaty of 1842 had not attempted to solve this knotty problem.[9] Each faction was eager to see an end to the controversy—the British still hoping for the Columbia as their southern line, and the Yankees, at least the most enthusiastic among them, already beginning to clamor for everything up to the parallel of 54° 40'. It was not yet "Fifty-four forty or fight," but sentiment was crystallizing.

In this uncertain and, in many respects, unhealthy state of affairs, Great Britain looked to the Hudson's Bay Company to maintain law and order among her subjects in Oregon, whereas the United States, with no such adequate machinery set up,

seemed disposed to leave her citizens to their own resources.[10]
Up to 1842, Doctor John's word had been law. The Indians had
been quite generally subdued, the French Canadian settlers had
proved peaceable and law-abiding, and the company had ably
demonstrated its ability to discipline its own servants. Obviously, there had been no need for any other authority.

The immigration of 1842, however, had, by increasing the
American population in the Willamette valley, automatically
provided added opposition to the dominance of the Hudson's
Bay Company. There were, at that time, three distinct factions in Oregon. First stood the company itself with its well
stocked stores, its efficient personnel, its satellites, the French
Canadian ex-employees, and, perhaps most important of all,
its able chief factor. Next, in point of significance, came the
Methodists with their clergymen, their lay members, their
modest resources, and their mounting political aspirations.
Finally, there were the independent settlers—unattached missionaries, former mountain men, and free trappers. They were,
in a sense, the "common people" of Oregon.[11] Although there
were many differences of opinion between the Methodists and
the independent settlers, the fact that both factions were composed, for the most part, of American citizens, served to unite
them against the British in the struggle for some sort of regional
civil authority. It was not long before this feeling resolved itself into a definite demand for a provisional government.

As the local representative of the Hudson's Bay Company
and consequently of Great Britain, Doctor John was naturally
anxious to block such a movement in the valley. Any provisional government, he reasoned, in agreement with Governor
Simpson, would be dominated by Americans and would under-
take to assume authority over all the inhabitants of the district,
British subjects included. It is not difficult to understand why
one who had ruled wisely and well for so long a period would

hesitate to encourage his own loss of power. But until the arrival of the first substantial immigration, the influence of the company, through its French Canadian dependents, had been great enough to thwart the various attempts of the American settlers to organize. Such, in a nutshell, was the situation at the beginning of 1843.

3

An issue was needed to bring these people together, and one was soon found. Wild animals in the Willamette valley had been making serious inroads on the settlers' cattle. Early in 1843, in an effort to protect their live stock, the valley people called a series of conferences which were to go down in history as the "wolf meetings." A plan was at length devised to raise funds for the paying of bounties to those successful in killing wild beasts. At the close of one of these "wolf meetings," William H. Gray, who had come down from the Whitman mission to become secular agent for the Methodists, took advantage of the occasion to harangue the assembled crowd on the perennial question of a local government. Following his address, a resolution was passed "that a committee be appointed to take into consideration the propriety of taking measures for the civil and military protection of this colony." [12] A committee was then appointed and was asked to bring in its report at a general meeting of the settlers to be held on the second day of May at Champoeg.

The Americans had displayed sound judgment by inviting the French Canadians residing in the valley to attend the "wolf meetings," to which not a few had been lured by the common desire to protect their cattle. However, when the object of the gathering switched from bounties to politics, the ex-voyageurs began to lose interest. A small number, nevertheless, agreed with the Americans that some sort of government was advisable, and even Doctor John appears to have weakened in his opposition. "Tho some of the Canadians were present at the meeting," he wrote in a letter dated March 20, "still, though in no way inclined to join in the measure to erect a temporary government, yet they must admit the strength of the argument used by the Americans that they must, now that people are coming here from different countries, adopt some plan to keep peace in the country, and that while they, the Canadians, are bound, those who come from the states are amenable to no authority." [13]

This letter reveals the doctor in an unguarded moment. He had reasoned the matter out in his own mind and had apparently resigned himself to the inevitable. Indeed it is quite possible that he might have withdrawn his objections to the project even to the point of urging the French Canadians to support it, had not a certain bit of disquieting news reached him soon after he had put his thoughts into writing. It was then that he learned, for the first time, the exact contents of the petition which had been drawn up against the Hudson's Bay Company and himself in connection with the Willamette Falls land claim. As we have already noted, the good man was furious when he discovered the full extent of the calumny contained in this memorial. Further disillusionment came with the knowledge that the individuals who had drawn it were, in the main, the same ones who were pressing so persistently for a provisional government. [14]

The effect upon the doctor was electric! For a fleeting moment he had taken the larger view, even against the wishes of his company; but a personal affront had brought him back to realities with a vengeance. He allowed himself to visualize these people as archfiends. They were plotting to overthrow his empire, to turn his own French Canadians against him, to drive his company from Oregon. Well, they would not succeed! They would discover that the White-Headed Eagle

could still fight. He would send his loyal Canadians to the
Champoeg meeting en masse and they would blast the evil
design of these usurpers! Reason had given way to anger, but
the tide, in Oregon, had turned. The will of the king of the
Columbia was not to prevail.

Little dreaming that they were about to make history, an
approximately equal number of French Canadian and American
settlers assembled at Champoeg on May 2. Since there was no
building large enough to hold the crowd, the session was held
on the level ground near the bank of the Willamette. Ira L.
Babcock, of the Methodist mission, was elected chairman, and
William H. Willson, W. H. Gray, and George W. Le Breton,
secretaries. The preliminaries over, a motion was made to
adopt the committee's report, but, to the joy of the French
Canadians, it was defeated.

They were out in full force—these henchmen of the doctor
—and they had won the first round! It was a tense moment—
a moment in which anything could have happened. Some one
had the presence of mind to call for a division on the question
of proceeding to organize, and the final count revealed that the
proposal had carried by two votes. Two of the Canadians had
gone over to the American side.[15] The White-Headed Eagle
had lost, and Oregon's first government was at last a reality.

Out of this memorable gathering there has evolved a romantic
story to the effect that the picturesque Joe Meek, clad in the
ragged garb of a mountain man, strode forward when the
division was demanded and, in a loud, commanding voice,
called out, "Who's for a divide! All in favor of the report and
of an organization follow me!"[16] Truth or fiction, this story
has served to keep alive the memory of Champoeg.

Many were the cross currents of political thought dominating
the minds of those who voted that day. Half the Americans
residing in the valley, we are told, were either absent or opposed!

Eight men of British origin voted with the Yankees because of opposition to the Hudson's Bay Company, and two French Canadians deserted their compatriots on account of anti-British memories dating back to the Papineau rebellion of 1837.[17] How neatly the laws of chance had operated!

As soon as the outcome was known, the French Canadians— except those who had cast their lot with the winning side— withdrew. The election of a governor was deferred for the time being; but other officers were chosen, and a committee was appointed to draft a code of laws. These laws were formally adopted at a subsequent meeting held on July 5, and it is interesting to note that Joseph, the doctor's eldest son, who lived on a farm in the Willamette valley, moved the adoption of one of the articles.[18] So great was the dominance of the Methodists at this session that they were able to force the enactment of a statute which aimed—in one blow—to secure their claim to Willamette Falls and to oust Doctor John.[19] This, of course, served only to stiffen the opposition of the Hudson's Bay Company to the provisional government.

Almost immediately, the newly created governing body retaliated by passing an act which was designed to prohibit the doctor and his fellow Britishers residing north of the Columbia from participating in the benefits of the organization. Scarcely had this statute been adopted, however, when the sharper members of the provisional government realized that they had unwittingly fashioned a double-edged sword—that such action might well strengthen the British claims to the northward.[20] The doctor, we can imagine, found some little comfort in this situation, so embarrassing to his adversaries.

4

It was during the months of November and December that the great immigration of 1843, comprising about eight hundred and seventy-five persons, reached Oregon. They straggled into the valley by different routes, some crossing the mountains from The Dalles by the Indian trail, others traveling down the Columbia in boats, and still others transporting their wagons by water on improvised rafts. These people, like their predecessors, were generously treated by Doctor John, who provided boats for some, food and raiment for others, and hospital care at Fort Vancouver for the sick.[21]

When the canoes bearing the vanguard of this mighty company came into sight, the doctor hurried down to the river bank to greet them. Close by stood a little band of Indians, and, as the chief factor came nearer, he heard one of them cry out in a loud voice, "It is good for us to kill these Bostons!" Observing their warlike countenances and realizing from their manner that they were sounding him out in the hope of receiving some encouragement, the White-Headed Eagle rushed upon them. "Who is the dog that says it is a good thing to kill the Bostons?" he bellowed. The Indian who had made the remark was instantly cowed. "I spoke without meaning harm," he said, "but The Dalles Indians say so." "Well," retorted the doctor, his gray eyes flashing, "The Dalles Indians are dogs for saying so, and you also."[22]

Well did they know that the white-haired chief would punish any who dared harm the Americans, and they lost no time in conveying their fears to the neighboring tribe up the river. By taking this determined stand, the doctor was undoubtedly the means of preventing a wholesale slaughter of Yankees. Had such a catastrophe occurred, the further settlement of Oregon would have been delayed indefinitely, and the United States government would, in all probability, have dispatched troops to punish the red men. If this had happened, in the surcharged atmosphere of the disputed Oregon country, war with Great Britain would almost inevitably have followed. Indeed the

White-Headed Eagle had been instrumental in preventing a third armed clash between John Bull and Uncle Sam.[23]

With the advent of 1844, it became apparent that these newcomers were not pleased with the political situation they found in Oregon. Of the hardy pioneer type, they not only were disposed to be friendly with the French Canadian settlers but were inclined to resent the Methodist domination of the provisional government. Shortly they began to seek the means of creating a new controlling power which would be more representative of all factions in the Willamette valley.[24]

The doctor, delighted that his ex-employees were at last to be considered, tacitly withdrew his opposition to a local government and adopted, in its place, a neutral attitude. In a letter written some time later, he noted that "from the great additional numbers of immigrants who came in 1843, the Canadians considered it necessary to have an organization." [25] If he did not encourage the project openly, he at least did not stand in its way.

After a series of conferences in which they were assisted by Father Langlois, a French priest who had joined the local band of Catholic missionaries, these immigrants, with the aid of the French Canadians and some of the original American settlers, succeeded in forming a new government in March. Gradually the new order began to function. In May, officers were elected, taxes were levied, and a legislative committee was appointed for the purpose of drawing up new laws. The seat of government was established at Oregon City. Among other things, the highly partisan statute of the preceding government, which had been devised to deprive Doctor John of his Oregon City land claim, was repealed. So radical were the changes effected by this legislature of 1844 that its own members soon came to realize the necessity of calling a constitutional convention to ratify its acts.[26] This body, however, was not to meet until

1845. The White-Headed Eagle was thus given a year in which to ponder his course on behalf of the company. Forthwith he began to sound out his superiors, but, as the months drifted on, he was given scant satisfaction.

5

Meanwhile, the doctor's land claim case had been dragging along as a continual bone of contention between the mission and Hudson's Bay factions, its fortunes shifting with the vicissitudes of the ever changing local authority. Attorneys had been retained by each side, and enough evidence of one kind and another had been gathered to fill several volumes. As far as immediate results were concerned, the battle was futile because neither faction would have been satisfied with the rulings of a purely temporary government. From the first, it had been the purpose of each party to establish its claim so securely that when the United States finally extended its jurisdiction to the territory south of the Columbia, there could be no question as to the rightful ownership of the land in question.

To this end, Doctor John worked diligently. On April 4, 1844, he entered into a settlement with the Reverend A. F. Waller and David Leslie, acting superintendent of the Methodist mission, by which he paid Waller the sum of five hundred dollars and gave him, in addition, eight lots and three blocks in Oregon City. As a part of the same transaction, he gave the mission itself six lots and one full block. Surely, thought the doctor, he had done with the affair.

In truth, his troubles had scarcely begun, for, on July 15 of the same year, the Reverend George Gary, who had been sent to Oregon both to relieve Jason Lee, then on his way home, and to dispose of the mission's property, offered to sell the six lots and one block back to him for a total consideration of six thousand dollars! Though justly provoked by such brazen effrontery, the White-Headed Eagle held his temper—he had too much at stake, and the Methodists were still too strong in the valley to permit of any other course. After some futile dickering, he agreed to pay this extortionate sum for that which, by every moral right, he already owned.[27] That, in so far as the mission was concerned, closed the matter; but others, even less scrupulous, were soon to take up the battle, and Doctor John was not to receive anything even remotely resembling justice until long after his body had been lowered into the disputed ground.

In fairness to the Methodists, it should be mentioned that not all of them saw eye to eye with Mr. Waller, and a few openly disapproved of his tactics. Still others sincerely believed that the doctor had taken the claim not as an individual but as the recognized agent of the Hudson's Bay Company, which they regarded as a foreign monopoly seeking to gain control of the water privileges at Willamette Falls. While it is true that Governor Simpson visited the Falls with his chief factor in 1828 and urged him to establish a claim there, it is also true that, by 1828, the British had conceded the futility of attempting to hold any land south of the Columbia. In his last letter to his superiors, dated November 20, 1845, Doctor John made it very clear that, ever since he had come to realize that his company could not hold the site, he had been endeavoring to secure it in his own name. "I trust," he wrote, "that when the truth is known, it will be found that I have acted with as much zeal as if my life had been at stake, and justice will done me." [28] Though seventy-seven years have passed since his death, the last word on this affair has not yet been spoken. But at all events, the conscience of the White-Headed Eagle was at peace. One wonders about Mr. Waller's.

By the spring of 1844, the differences between the doctor and Sir George had come to a definite crisis. On March 20, he dispatched a long letter to the governor which, though respectful in tone, was nevertheless an ultimatum. Among other grievances, the chief factor complained about charges falsely brought against him by officers and servants in his department, about the type and number of men being sent to his district, about the governor's habit of failing to confirm rumors before relaying them to London, about the parsimonious tendencies of the company, about Sir George's handling of the Stikine affair, and about his lack of enthusiasm for the Yerba Buena post. In this same letter, the doctor set forth the returns of his department so fully as to nullify the extravagant statements some Americans were then making regarding the profits of the Hudson's Bay Company in the West, and he vigorously defended his many acts of charity on behalf of the destitute immigrants.[29] Indeed it was such an ultimatum as only a man prepared to face resignation would dare put on paper. Even as he penned it, Doctor John must have anticipated the outcome.

The immigration of 1844 brought no fewer than fourteen hundred settlers to Oregon. These people, like those who had come before them, experienced untold hardships on the journey, and they were given every assistance by the doctor. During the preceding year he had urged upon the colonists the raising of grain in anticipation of this great influx, for supplies, both at the fort and in the valley, were running low. There is no doubt that his forethought in this connection prevented widespread suffering.[30]

One of the members of this vast immigration, Joseph Hess, recalls that when the members of his particular party had eaten the last of their provisions, they were told that the old chief factor at Fort Vancouver would help them. Skeptical but desperate, they continued their journey to the fort. Greeting them in his office, Doctor John explained that he had befriended the immigrants from the States for several years past, and that he had established a store at Oregon City where they could procure needed supplies. With embarrassed looks, several of Hess's companions were forced to admit that they had no means of paying for food and clothing.

"Tut, tut, never mind that: you can't suffer," said the doctor, and then, in the very next breath, he commenced with the head-man, asking, "Your name, if you please. How many in the family, and what do you desire?" For each person he wrote out an order, explaining that the accounts were to be settled only after the colonists had taken claims and raised sufficient wheat to cover them.[31] Is it any wonder that hundreds of these travel-weary, hungry, and penniless incomers believed that they had met a saint on earth?

6

Striving valiantly to steer his course safely over the shoals of local politics, disillusioned by the attitude of his chief but encour-aged by the amicable manner of his new friends, the immigrants, the White-Headed Eagle entered upon the last year of his service with the Hudson's Bay Company. It was a feverish period for all concerned. In July, 1845, the people of Oregon gathered to ratify the government which had been formed the previous year. This accomplished, they elected, as Oregon's first pro-visional governor, George Abernethy, a merchant who had purchased the store once operated by the Methodist mission at Oregon City. Great must have been this man's popularity, for he was chosen against a field of candidates even though he was sojourning, at the time, in the Hawaiian Islands. Other officers were then selected, and the machinery of this primitive govern-ment was promptly set in motion.[32]

It was now high time for the doctor to face the issue squarely —whether to join the new government or remain aloof. In the minds of some, he stood between the powerful Hudson's Bay Company and the suffering immigrants as a great benefactor;

in the minds of others, he symbolized opposition to any authority but his own. In this ambiguous and altogether unenviable situation, which he appears clearly to have recognized, he was forced to make a difficult choice. He had good reason to be alarmed by the presence of so many Americans in his empire, many of whom were lawless and unruly, for, during the preceding year, one of them had brazenly started to build a cabin on land belonging to the company.[33] Though the doctor had pulled down the offending structure even before its completion, he had been made, thus forcibly, to realize the precariousness of his position.

Some time previously he had written to his company, requesting that the British government protect their holdings, but a satisfactory answer had not been received. Later, he had dispatched a similar plea to the British consul in Hawaii with the same result.[34] In June, 1845, he received orders to protect his interests as best he could. There could be no dodging of the issue.

In the meantime, the officers of the provisional government had been experiencing financial difficulties. Taxes, they had discovered, were not easy to collect, and they needed funds desperately. If only the Hudson's Bay Company could be induced to join them on a tax-paying basis, their coffers would be substantially replenished. Guided by this, as well as by other motives less selfish, the heads of the local constituted authority extended to the company, through Doctor John, a formal invitation to join their ranks. This overture was made on August 14, 1845.[35]

The doctor, after consulting with the ever faithful Douglas, accepted the offer the very next day and swore to "support the Organic Laws of the provisional government of Oregon as far as the said organic laws are consistent with my duties as a Citizen of the United States, or a Subject of Great Britain."[36]

In explanation of his step, he wrote: "We have yielded to the wishes of the respectable part of the people in the country, of British and American origin, by meeting with them in the formation of a temporary and provisional government designed to prevent disorders and maintain peace, until the settlement of the boundary question leaves that duty to the parent States. A crisis was evidently approaching, which would drive us to the painful necessity of yielding to the storm, or of taking field openly, arms in hand, with means so unequal compared with those arrayed against us, as to leave us no hope of success. . . . We decided on joining the association both for the security of the Company's property and the protection of its rights." [37] It was in this manner that the people residing north of the Columbia were brought under the sway of the struggling provisional government.

Aside from assuring themselves of additional protection under the rudimentary laws of Oregon, the Hudson's Bay leaders gained other advantages by their action. At that time, debts owing to the company from Willamette valley settlers amounted to nearly $30,000, and, as the company was to pay taxes only on amounts collected from these people, union with them was greatly to be desired. Although this aspect of the situation was not touched upon by Doctor John in his various communications to his superiors, he appears to have been less reticent about his own political aspirations. In a letter to J. H. Pelly, dated November 15, 1844, he hinted that, in the event the boundary squabble was not settled rather soon, the colonists might decide to form an independent state "of which I might be elected head were I to retire among them." [38] This confession stands out as further proof that the harassed chief factor had been considering retirement for some time.

Scarcely had he joined the provisional government on behalf of his company when there arrived, in the Straits of Juan de Fuca, a

British man-of-war, the *America,* commanded by Captain John Gordon. This vessel had come, quite obviously, for the double purpose of watching over the company's interests and of impressing the Yankees with the fact that Great Britain had not forgotten her claims to Oregon.[39] The arrival of the warship, at that particular time, doubtless caused the chief factor as much embarrassment as it caused the settlers alarm. Also, in 1845, two British agents, Lieutenants Warre and Vavasour, reached the Columbia department on a secret mission. Though they made extensive surveys in the interests of their government, the exact nature of their errand was not made public, nor is it yet fully understood. But Doctor John, highly incensed that he was not given an opportunity to inspect their report before it was dispatched to London, jumped to the conclusion that they had been sent by Governor Simpson to spy upon him.[40] Whatever his grounds for suspicion may have been, his reactions indicated clearly the distraught state of his nerves.

Earlier in this same troubled year, he had received a staggering blow in the form of a dispatch from San Francisco which told of the death, by his own hand, of Eloisa's husband, William Glen Rae. The chief trader in charge at Yerba Buena, it appeared, not only had become discouraged over business affairs at his post but had got himself hopelessly involved in a Mexican revolutionary plot.[41] Death had appealed to him as the only way out. It was a sad home-coming for Eloisa and her three small children when they reached Fort Vancouver aboard the *Cowlitz* some weeks later.

7

Doctor John had had enough. In the fall of 1845, he decided to sever his connections with the Hudson's Bay Company and to take pot luck with the growing community to the southward. His reasons were many, but the principal one was his long and bitter strife with Sir George. It is true that the doctor, now sixty-one years of age, had grown weary of the heavy responsibilities he had carried for so long a time, and that he was attracted by the pleasant prospect of spending his last years in his beloved Oregon. But the governor had never approved of his open-handed hospitality to the American immigrants and had objected strenuously to the substantial amounts of money he had advanced them. This appears to have been the main cause for Doctor John's dismissal—certainly, of all the others, it was the one bound to cut him most deeply. In his final answer, after defending his charitable acts on behalf of the colonists, he said, "Gentlemen, if such is your order, I will serve you no longer." [42]

It seems a safe assumption that somewhere, buried deep in the musty archives of the Hudson's Bay Company, there lies a demand, perhaps from Sir George himself, so arbitrary, so withering, and so final as to provoke this noble answer. Indeed the kindly old man's sincerity of purpose is magnificently set forth in his last official letter to the company, in which he said, "I beg to observe that I always thought that exerting myself zealously to promote the interests of the Hudson's Bay Company, to the best of my abilities, would at least assure me their approbation, if not their protection." [43]

There remained only the necessity of winding up his affairs with the company in preparation for beginning a new life in Oregon City. He was happy that his old friend Douglas would take his place—the company, at least, would not suffer. The White-Headed Eagle had relinquished his empire!

CHAPTER XX

SUNSET

I

DOCTOR JOHN's brilliant career as a leader ended abruptly with his resignation from the Hudson's Bay Company. True, he lived on for another eleven years, but they were years of anticlimax and disillusionment—a period we can pass over quickly. Strangely enough, these closing years, though closer to us in point of time, reveal him as an almost legendary figure. A few letters and public documents survive to chart, in broad outline, the troubled course of his old age, but, for the most part, we are dependent upon what early American pioneers recall of the "good old doctor."

In the spring of 1846, having bidden farewell to his successor, James Douglas, Doctor John moved to Oregon City.[1] He looked forward with eagerness to the approaching boundary settlement, which he believed would give him legal title to his long disputed land claim. With him came his loyal wife, Margaret, his widowed daughter, Eloisa, and his favorite son, David. All three were to remain faithfully by his side until the end. In the midst of the American settlers of this pioneer community, some of whom were to continue grateful for the many services he had rendered them while others were to turn against him, the sixty-two-year-old doctor embarked upon a new life with almost youthful enthusiasm.

Some time earlier, he had started work upon a home, pretentious for its day, which was completed during 1846. The lumber used in its construction had been cut from the nearby forests, but, since there were no mills on the Pacific Coast equipped to turn out doors and sashes, they had had to be brought from the East around Cape Horn. The former chief factor took as much pride in the rearing of this residence as he had taken in the building of his empire. His great work accomplished, he had become reconciled to the achieving of lesser tasks.

At first, everything seemed in his favor. From his earnings of many years, he had accumulated more than most men of the early West could ever hope to possess. He had had the foresight to stake a claim which, if only it could be secured, would make him wealthy. He had built a sawmill and a gristmill and had acquired a store. At one time or another, he had befriended most of the people among whom he had come to reside. He had willingly lent the support of his powerful company to the struggling provisional government at a time when that body sorely needed his backing. In a word, he had left nothing undone to insure his own prestige in a country he was certain would shortly belong to the United States. An impartial observer, back in 1846, would have rated high the doctor's chances of becoming Oregon's best loved and most influential resident.

Nevertheless, he was vulnerable. In a settlement so predominantly Protestant, the doctor's enthusiastic espousal of Catholicism had set the minds of many against him. Had he been thinking more of acquiring title to his land and less of his own religious convictions, he would never have permitted Father Blanchet to draw him back into the fold. Then, too, he was a British subject and, as such, the traditional enemy of those who were being roused to the heights of partisan ardor by the burning Oregon Question. But perhaps his greatest handicap was the fact that he was a man of means in a relatively poor community. Fresh in the minds of his fellow townsmen was the memory of his autocratic rule at Vancouver. Democratic America, argued these people, was no place for a British autocrat, even though he had been stripped of his authority.

Doctor John anticipated these objections and, in so far as his conscience would permit, took steps to meet them. He would not, of course, change his religion, nor could he alter his aristocratic nature. As a matter of fact, he had every reason to expect that his new neighbors, so extensively the recipients of his largess, would welcome him as a benefactor rather than spurn him as a fallen autocrat. He made the very human mistake of counting too heavily on the religious tolerance and anticipated gratitude of these people. Nevertheless, he made an honest effort to change his status as a British subject shortly after his resignation from the Hudson's Bay Company.

By the spring of 1846, the situation in Oregon had grown tense. President Polk's campaign slogan of "Fifty-four forty or fight" had become a live issue throughout America, and, on both sides of the Columbia, there were many who considered war with Great Britain inevitable. Doctor John, who had done everything in his power to prevent such a conflict, shared this belief. He found himself in a particularly awkward position. By changing his allegiance in time of war, he ran the double risk of being judged a traitor and of losing what little property he still retained in Canada. Nor could he, without declaring himself, hope to secure his extensive land claim at Oregon City.

In his dilemma, he appealed to Jesse Applegate, an immigrant of 1843 and a man for whom he entertained a high regard. Applegate urged him to lose no time in taking the oath of allegiance to the United States; so, acting upon this sound advice, he applied to Peter H. Burnett, the chief justice of the provisional government. Though Burnett thought highly of the former chief factor, he explained that he had no authority from the

DR. McLOUGHLIN'S HOME IN OREGON CITY

American government to administer the oath. But despite Doctor John's honest attempt to line up with the Yankees, his enemies seized upon this opportunity to capitalize on his British citizenship and to claim that he had made no move to relinquish it.[2]

Jesse Applegate criticized Burnett for standing on ceremony and intimated that the chief justice could have administered the oath had he chosen to do so—an inference scarcely warranted by the facts. "To Burnett's timidity," wrote Applegate, "was owing the doctor's subsequent troubles with individuals and the United States government."[3]

To the immense relief of all concerned, the boundary question was settled peacefully. After extended negotiations, which often threatened to end in war, a treaty fixing the northern line of the United States at the forty-ninth parallel was signed by President Polk on June 15, 1846, and was confirmed by the Senate four days later. The colonists, however, were kept on tenter-hooks until the following November, when the good news reached Vancouver by the British bark *Toulon*. Chief Factor Douglas promptly relayed this welcome information to Governor Abernethy.[4]

Peace reigned in Oregon, and Doctor John was saved from a most embarrassing predicament.

2

During his rule at Fort Vancouver, the White-Headed Eagle's influence had been so great that no tribe of Indians had dared to make war against the whites. It seems more than a coincidence, therefore, that in the very next year after his final withdrawal from the Hudson's Bay Company, the Cayuse Indians attacked the Waiilatpu mission and brutally murdered Marcus Whitman, his wife, and ten other persons. The tragedy occurred on November 29, 1847, but the first account of it did not reach

Oregon City until early in December.⁵ Immediately, the settlers prepared to chastise the natives.

From Vancouver, the doctor's old associate, Peter Skene Ogden, hastened to the scene with an armed party to rescue the surviving members of the mission. It was evident that the Hudson's Bay Company recognized the provisional government as the civil authority in the country, for Ogden made no move to punish the Indians. He merely summoned the Cayuse chiefs, rebuked them soundly, warned them that they had incurred the wrath of the Americans, and then returned the surviving women and children to Oregon City.⁶ Doctor John welcomed his old friend with enthusiasm and warmly applauded his prowess.

The period immediately following was one of great excitement. Faced with the necessity of waging punitive warfare against the murderous Cayuses, the provisional government, with neither an army nor the funds to equip one, found itself enormously embarrassed. Nevertheless, the local authority, under Governor Abernethy, undertook to negotiate loans for the purpose, confident that the United States government would eventually assume them. The settlers, both Americans and French Canadians, responded willingly to the cause, but Chief Factor Douglas insisted he had no authority to make advances on the Hudson's Bay Company's account.⁷

While these preliminary preparations were being made, Joe Meek, the colorful mountain man, started overland to carry news of the massacre to Washington and to intercede with the federal government on behalf of the settlers. Meek's vivid personality created a sensation in the national capital. Previously Governor Abernethy had dispatched to Washington the provisional government's new chief justice, J. Quinn Thornton. Largely as a result of the efforts of these two able emissaries, Oregon was admitted to the Union as a Territory. Naturally, all of this required time, and the desired objective was not obtained until 1849, when Joseph Lane of Indiana arrived in Oregon City to assume his duties as the new Territory's first governor.[8]

Meanwhile, the determined Oregon settlers fought and won the Cayuse War. That rough-and-tumble conflict claimed no more interested observer than Doctor John himself. How the old autocrat must have longed to be back at his post in Vancouver! It is safe to assume that his methods would not have been those of the cautious Douglas—he would doubtless have punished the murderers summarily only to be criticized later, both by Governor Simpson and by the Yankees, for having exceeded his authority! Indeed, when human life was at stake, he had never recognized any authority but his own. Such was his nature, and no provisional government on earth could have changed it. But an even more plausible conjecture is that the Cayuses would never have destroyed the Whitmans had they known beforehand that they would have to answer to the White-Headed Eagle.

Impatient in his impotency, the doctor had to be content with lending his support, both moral and financial, to the cause. He induced his talented stepson, Tom McKay, to lead a contingent of French Canadians and half-breeds against the Cayuses, and this little band rendered valiant service.[9] It must have brought keen satisfaction to the former chief factor to realize that his own policy of placing these former company servants in the Willamette valley had produced not renegades among the Indians, as Sir George had feared, but solid, dependable, and patriotic Americans.

When the confessed murderers of the Whitman party were brought to Oregon City for trial, Doctor John, of all persons, was called as a witness for the defense! He was merely asked by the court to relate his repeated attempts to induce Marcus

Whitman to leave Waiilatpu, but his testimony, as he hoped it
might, served only to strengthen the case against the culprits,
who were hanged on May 21, 1850.[10]

3

With Oregon safely inside the Union, the doctor hastened
to apply for citizenship. On May 13, 1849, the federal government assigned a judge to the newly created territory, and
on May 30 Doctor John took the oath of allegiance and made
his declaration to become an American. His goal was finally
achieved, after the passage of the two-year interval required
by law, on September 5, 1851.

Having declared himself, he believed that at last he could
legally claim his land; but he failed to reckon with the designs
of two of his enemies. One was W. P. Bryant, the first territorial chief justice in Oregon, and the other was Samuel R.
Thurston, a brilliant but misguided immigrant of 1847. In order
to understand the motives of these two schemers, we must go
back, for just a moment, to the period of joint occupancy.

In 1841, certain members of the Methodist mission had formed
the Oregon Milling Company and had concentrated their
activities on a part of the doctor's claim, an island in the Willamette. Then, in 1846, Governor Abernethy and his son had
become the sole owners of the Oregon Milling Company and
hence of "Abernethy's Island." Doctor John had protested in
vain. Finally, Judge Bryant, shortly after his arrival in 1849,
had purchased the Abernethy interests and had thus come to
regard himself as the rightful owner of that portion of the long
contested claim. Here, in truth, was one powerful adversary
lined up against the doctor.

Then there was Thurston—young, ambitious, and amazingly
lacking in scruple. By shrewdly enlisting the support of the
mission party against the Hudson's Bay faction, he had man-

aged to get himself elected to Congress in June, 1849, as Oregon's first territorial delegate. His campaign had been cleverly timed, for a good many of the French Canadians and independent Americans had been lured southward to the recently discovered gold fields in California. Doctor John had voted in this first general election, but not for Thurston!

No sooner did the delegate reach Washington than he began to work diligently for the passage of a law which would permit residents of Oregon to acquire land for themselves. Up to then, all of it had belonged either to the United States or to the missions. Coupled with Thurston's worthy objective was a sinister determination to despoil the former chief factor of his hard-fought-for land. The artful delegate deliberately misrepresented both the doctor's character and the history of his struggle to secure the Willamette Falls land claim in a circular letter which he mailed to the various members of Congress. But his task was not a simple one—he had to render his robbery palatable to the settlers back home, many of whom were Doctor John's friends. With consummate adroitness, he proposed, in one section of his bill, to award Abernethy's Island to the Oregon Milling Company, then owned by Judge Bryant, and to place the rest of the doctor's holdings "at the disposal of the legislative assembly, for the establishment and endowment of a university." Meanwhile, Bryant himself had arrived in Washington to take a hand in the fight. With two such able and unscrupulous advocates on the ground, the measure was assured of success.

But there was opposition out in Oregon. When, in September, 1850, news of the delegate's activities reached Oregon City, the doctor flew into a rage. The tribulations of many years had not improved his temper, but he calmed down sufficiently to pen a dignified and convincing answer to Thurston's groundless accusations. Indeed the fairness of his stand appealed so strongly to his friends that no fewer than fifty-six of them addressed a memorial to Congress, directing the attention of that body to the "severe, inequitable, unnecessary, and irremediable injustice" of the proposed bill. It was too late! Without the true facts at its command, Congress had already passed the Oregon Donation Land Law.

Thurston's predacious intentions were apparent from the skilful wording of his bill. With subtle malice, he had added a proviso which forbade any one claiming land under the Donation Land Law to claim it both under that statute and under the treaty of 1846, which clearly respected the possessory rights of British subjects. Either way, Doctor John was blocked. Having declared his intention to become an American citizen, he was no longer qualified under the treaty, and Congress having, on the representations of Thurston, taken from him what he claimed under the land law, he was left with no recourse whatsoever. The long, bitter fight had been lost. There can be no doubt that the rank injustice of Thurston's act saddened the old man's closing years and hastened his end.[11]

It remained for the Oregon legislature to make partial amends, but this was not done until the doctor had been five years in his grave. In 1862, the legislature passed an act which permitted the McLoughlin heirs to acquire all of the original claim, with the exception of Abernethy's Island, upon the payment of $1,000, and this modest sum was designated for the University Fund of Oregon.[12] If, during his lifetime, Doctor John could have had as able a champion as the late Frederick V. Holman, the whole course of his unhappy Oregon City years might have been different. But justice came too late. Holman's masterful brief for the "Father of Oregon" was not prepared until 1907.[13]

As for Thurston, he died at sea on April 9, 1851, while returning home from his first and only term in Congress.[14] His villainy against the former chief factor was the one blot on his career—in all other matters, he had rendered distinguished service. We may be sure that his sudden death at thirty-five made him a martyr in the eyes of his constituents and silenced Doctor John at a time when he would have preferred to reopen the fight. Fate had backed Thurston's design at every turn.

4

In the meantime, momentous events had taken place at Fort Vancouver. In 1849, James Douglas had transferred the Hudson's Bay Company western depot to Fort Victoria on Vancouver Island,[15] and, in the early spring of 1850, American troops under Major J. S. Hathaway had established a federal military post on the site of the old fort on the Columbia.[16]

How singularly alone the White-Headed Eagle must have felt! Douglas, Ogden, Work, McDonald, and all the rest of his former associates had forsaken the familiar Columbia for new fields. Sir George would trouble him no more. Of those who had pioneered the Oregon country with him, Whitman and Jedediah Smith had been murdered by Indians, and Jason Lee had died in the East.[17] Nathaniel Wyeth was many miles away in Boston, and Captain Dominis was somewhere on the Seven Seas. Of the Hudson's Bay men, only Forbes Barclay had followed his chief to Oregon City, where he had established himself as a practicing physician.[18] In a new and virile country, Doctor John was already a patriarch.

He labored bravely on through the early fifties, supervising his mills and store and struggling to collect the staggering amounts due him from settlers who either evaded their obligations or repudiated them entirely. The Hudson's Bay Company had held him accountable for every dollar, and this heavy burden gradually dissipated his accumulated savings. Between grieving over these losses and fretting over the despoilment of his land, he began to fail noticeably. A man of fortitude, he brooded in silence with only occasional outbursts when his sufferings became too intense. Not even the members of his own family were permitted to realize the full extent of his wretchedness.

In a pathetic document, penned toward the close of his career, he bared his soul. "By British demagogues," he wrote, "I have been represented as a traitor. For what? Because I acted as a Christian, saved American citizens, men, women and children from the Indian tomahawk and enabled them to take farms to support their families. American demagogues have been base enough to assert that I had caused American citizens to be massacred by hundreds by the savages. I, who saved all I could. . . . I could not have done more for the settlers if they had been my brothers and sisters. . . . But as I felt convinced that any disturbance between us here might lead to a war between Great Britain and the States, I felt it my bounden duty as a Christian, to act as I did, and which I think averted the evil, and which was so displeasing to some English demagogues that they represented me to the British government as a person so partial to American interests as selling the Hudson's Bay Company goods, in my charge, cheaper to American than I did to British subjects. . . . To be brief, I founded this settlement and prevented a war . . . and for doing this peaceably and quietly, I was treated by the British in such a manner that from self respect, I resigned my situation in the Hudson's Bay Company's service, by which I sacrificed $12,000 per annum, and the 'Oregon Land Bill' shows the treatment I received from the Americans." [19] A man without a country, the White-Headed Eagle, bowed with years and grief, maintained his kindly attitude to the last. We shrink from any further recital of the wrongs this noble benefactor received from those whose descendants were one day to revere him as the "Father of Oregon."

But these last years were not without their happy interludes.

When Father Blanchet returned from Rome in 1847 as an Archbishop, he brought a gift to Doctor John from the reigning Pope, Gregory XVI—a membership in the Order of St. Gregory the Great.[20] The doctor, in fact, was one of a very few Americans privileged to become a Knight of St. Gregory. In the original patent, his Holiness had written, "We have been informed on the highest authority that you are esteemed by all for your upright life, correct morals and zeal for religion, and that you are conspicuous for your allegiance to Ourselves and this Chair of Peter." [21] Tradition has it that the coveted insignia of this religious order remained the White-Headed Eagle's most cherished possession. Had Great Britain chosen to knight him, as she had done in the case of George Simpson, he could not have felt more highly honored.

Until the end, Margaret remained by the doctor's side, a loyal and helpful wife. In 1850, Eloisa, five years a widow, was married to Daniel Harvey, one of her father's employees,[22] and this new son-in-law, aided spasmodically by the roving David, assisted the old chief factor in looking after his dwindling interests. Of his once large family, only these were left. John, Jr., lay buried in the churchyard at Vancouver; Joseph had died in 1849, and Eliza had moved to England with her husband, Major Epps. Had it not been for the affectionate care of his own people, Doctor John's Oregon City years would have been well-nigh unbearable.

5

Many are the stories which have come down to us from old settlers who remember the White-Headed Eagle as a patriarchal figure in the early days of Oregon City. A stanch Catholic, he had, nevertheless, a most exacting conception of one's duty to one's own religion. When Daniel Harvey announced his wish to marry Eloisa, the old gentleman insisted that he first become a Catholic. Needless to add, the aspiring suitor promptly complied. On another occasion, a little orphan girl was brought to him by some destitute friends of her dead parents. After some investigation, he discovered that the waif's mother had been a Protestant, and straightway he arranged to have his ward brought up in that faith.

Toward the last it became difficult for him to curb his anger when he chanced to meet some settler who persistently refused to pay even though he could well afford to do so. Up would go his stout cane in righteous indignation, but, in a moment, he would catch himself, utter a scarcely audible "God forgive me," and hurry on his way. His granddaughter recalled that he used to segregate these old accounts into groups, according to their possibility of collection, and enter them in leather-bound blank books of various colors. He fell into the habit of spending long, weary hours over these grim reminders of his sorrow. Sometimes, after a whole evening of such torture, his massive white head would nod, and, leaning over his desk, he would sob loudly and unashamed.

Like most women of her race, Margaret became very stout as she grew older. The doctor continued to treat her with great deference, and he was quick to resent any slight shown her by the colonists. If one of them chanced to enter her presence without removing his hat, the chivalrous old gentleman would rebuke him severely, no matter who he happened to be. "Your manners, sir," he would blurt out, "your manners, before ladies!"

As long as he was able financially, he cared for the penniless immigrants who continued to flock into Oregon. Many a destitute family found food and shelter at his home, which was always open to strangers. There were two large couches in his reception room, and these, according to tradition, were seldom unoccupied at night.

For a number of years prior to his death, the doctor was an invalid. He lost so much weight that he appeared gaunt and grim, but his penetrating eyes, though deeply sunken, never lost their fire. Only his amazing vitality kept him at his daily tasks—his charities, his work for the Church, and his shrinking business activities. But there came a time, late in the summer of 1857, when the old fighter, dying by inches, was forced to his bed.

It was during this period that L. F. Grover, later a governor of Oregon, was requested to call at the doctor's home while passing through Oregon City on horseback. "I shall live but a little while," the patriarch greeted him from his bed, "and this is the reason I sent for you. I am an old man and just dying, and you are a young man and will live many years in this country, and will have something to do with affairs here. As for me, I might better have been shot forty years ago than to have lived here and tried to build up a family and an estate in this government. I became a citizen of the United States in good faith. I planted all I had here, and the government confiscated my property. Now what I want to ask of you is that you will give your influence after I am dead to have this property go to my children. I have earned it as other settlers have earned theirs, and it ought to be mine and my heirs'." [23]

Grover carried out his trust, for he was one of those who labored, in the Oregon legislature, to bring dilatory justice to the White-Headed Eagle.

6

The doctor was attended in his last illness by his old friend, Dr. Forbes Barclay, and by his nephew, Dr. Henri A. M. De Chesne, who had come to Oregon in 1850. In a letter written many years later, Dr. De Chesne recalled a visit paid to the dying chief factor by Henry G. Foote, a former United States

Senator from Mississippi. In the Senate, Foote had been a bitter enemy of Thomas H. Benton, one of the doctor's idols, but despite that, he gladly welcomed the distinguished southern statesman to his bedside. They chatted for a time, and then, when the sick man appeared to doze, Foote rose to leave. As he tiptoed out of the room, he whispered to De Chesne, "Your uncle is the picture of General Jackson." But Doctor John was not dozing. His withered face lighted, and, with a smile, he replied, "I thank you for the compliment." [24]

During those last few weeks, the doctor frequently conversed with his family in French. On the morning of his last day, September 3, 1857, with Margaret, David, Eloisa, and Daniel Harvey gathered around his deathbed, Dr. De Chesne greeted him with the familiar salutation, "Comment allez-vous?" The White-Headed Eagle, raising his eyes to heaven, chose to answer literally. "À Dieu," he replied softly, and, confident that he was going to God, he expired before evening.

THE END

NOTES BY CHAPTERS

CHAPTER I

[1] Holman, F. V., *Dr. John McLoughlin*, p. 23.
[2] From a Genealogy of the Fraser Family, supplied by M. Louis J. Pelletier of Rivière du Loup, Quebec.
[3] *History of the Ursulines* by a Member of the Community, Quebec, 1897, p. 357.
[4] *History of the Ursulines, loc. cit.*
[5] Merk, Frederick, *Fur Trade and Empire*, p. viii.
[6] Merk, *op. cit.*, p. ix.
[7] Allan, George T., *Reminiscences* (MS. #5, Bancroft Library).
[8] *History of the Ursulines, loc. cit.*

CHAPTER II

[1] Holman, F. V., *Dr. John McLoughlin*, p. 24. Fuller, George W., *A History of the Pacific Northwest*, p. 111. O'Hara, E. V., *Catholic History of Oregon*, p. 5.
[2] Larsell, Dr. O., "An Outline of the History of Medicine in the Pacific Northwest," *Northwest Medicine*, Sept., 1932, p. 440.
[3] Letter of David McLoughlin in the library of the Oregon Historical Society.
[4] Larsell, *loc. cit.*
[5] Letters exchanged between Malcolm Fraser of Murray Bay and James Ker of Leith Bank from 1809 to 1811. Loaned through the courtesy of Mr. J. A. Gray of Montreal.
[6] Skinner, Constance Lindsay, *Adventurers in Oregon*, p. 217.
[7] Coues, Dr. Elliott, *New Light on the Greater Northwest*, Vol. III, p. 981.
[8] Bancroft, H. H., *History of the Northwest Coast*, Vol. II, p. 432.
[9] Fuller, *loc. cit.*
[10] *Franchère's Voyage*, translated by J. V. Huntington, pp. 339–341.
[11] Skinner, *loc. cit.*
[12] Coues, *loc. cit.*
[13] Harmon, Daniel W., *A Journal of Voyages and Travels into the Interior of North America*, p. 158.
[14] Genealogy of the Fraser Family.
[15] Clarke, S. A., *Pioneer Days of Oregon History*, Vol. I, p. 189.

[16] Flavia, Sister Mary, of the Sisters of the Holy Names, MS. on Dr. McLoughlin.

[17] From the Parish Records of St. James Church, Vancouver, Washington.

[18] McLoughlin, David, Correspondence. Of these daughters of Margaret McKay, one married Lieutenant McCormack of the British Army; another, Captain McCargo, who ran a merchant freighter on Lake Superior; and the third, Chief Trader Sinclair of the Hudson's Bay Company.

[19] Elliott, T. C., "A Hudson's Bay Company's Marriage Certificate," *Oregon Historical Society Quarterly*, Vol. X, pp. 325–328.

[20] Clarke, *op. cit.*, Vol. I, p. 192.

[21] David McLoughlin, in his correspondence, stated that his father was married for the first time about 1808.

[22] Elliott, *op. cit.*, p. 325.

[23] Skinner, *op. cit.*, pp. 218–19.

[24] Bancroft, *op. cit.*, Vol. I, pp. 574–582.

[25] Sage, Walter N., *Sir James Douglas and British Columbia*, p. 55.

[26] Martin, *Lord Selkirk's Work in Canada*, Oxford, 1913, p. 126.

[27] Dye, Eva Emery, *McLoughlin and Old Oregon*, p. 68.

[28] Ermatinger Papers (Provincial Library, Victoria, B.C.), p. 240.

[29] Coues, *loc. cit.*

[30] Bancroft, *op. cit.*, Vol. II, p. 432.

CHAPTER III

[1] Bancroft, H. H., *History of the Northwest Coast*, Vol. I, p. 581.

[2] Laut, Agnes C., *Conquest of the Great Northwest*, Vol. II, pp. 203–204.

[3] Merk, Frederick, *Fur Trade and Empire*, p. xi.

[4] Laut, *op. cit.*, Vol. II, pp. 202–231.

[5] Bancroft, *op. cit.*, Vol. I, p. 583.

[6] Fuller, George W., *A History of the Pacific Northwest*, p. 111.

[7] Sage, Walter N., *Sir James Douglas and British Columbia*, p. 55.

[8] Fuller, *loc. cit.*

[9] Elliott, T. C., "Peter Skene Ogden, Fur Trader," *Oregon Historical Society Quarterly*, Vol. XI, No. 1, p. 241.

[10] Laut, *op. cit.*, Vol. II, pp. 230–31.

[11] Coues, Dr. Elliott, *Henry-Thompson Journals*, Vol. II, p. 900.

[12] Laut, *op. cit.*, Vol. II, p. 231.

[13] Newell, Aaron, "The Hudson's Bay Company's Merger," *Washington Historical Society Quarterly*, Vol. XV, pp. 201–203.

[14] Merk, *op. cit.*, pp. xiii–xiv.

[15] Sage, *op. cit.*, p. 56.

[16] Newell, *op. cit.*, p. 202.

[17] Merk, *op. cit.*, pp. xvii–xviii.

[18] Merk, *op. cit.*, p. xii.

[19] Newell, *op. cit.*, pp. 202–203.

[20] Sage, *op. cit.*, p. 56.

CHAPTER IV

[1] McLoughlin, David, Correspondence. Oregon Historical Society.
[2] Sage, Walter N., *Sir James Douglas and British Columbia*, p. 56.
[3] Gray, W. H., *History of Oregon*, p. 29. Sage, *loc. cit.*
[4] Holman, F. V., *Dr. John McLoughlin*, p. 26.
[5] Bancroft, H. H., *History of Oregon*, Vol. I, p. 30.
[6] Harvey, Eloisa McLoughlin, *Life of Dr. McLoughlin* (MS., Bancroft Library), p. 1.
[7] Bancroft, H. H., *History of the Northwest Coast*, Vol. I, p. 485.
[8] Merk, Frederick, *Fur Trade and Empire*, pp. 215–217.
[9] Merk, *op. cit.*, pp. xix, xx.
[10] Merk, *op. cit.*, Appendix A, p. 230.
[11] Clarke, S. A., *Pioneer Days of Oregon History*, Vol. I, pp. 66–83.
[12] Merk, *op. cit.*, pp. xxvi, xxvii.
[13] Merk, Frederick, *George Simpson's Journal*, p. 4.
[14] Merk, *op. cit.*, p.18.
[15] Merk, *op. cit.*, p. 23.
[16] Merk, *loc. cit.*
[17] Merk, *op. cit.*, p. 29.
[18] Merk, *op. cit.*, p. 31.
[19] Merk, *op. cit.*, p. 36.
[20] Merk, *op. cit.*, p. 42.
[21] Merk, *op. cit.*, p. 49.
[22] Merk, *op. cit.*, p. 65.
[23] Scouler, Dr. John, "Journal of a Voyage to Northwest America," *Oregon Historical Society Quarterly*, Vol. VI, p. 166.

CHAPTER V

[1] Merk, Frederick, *George Simpson's Journal*, p. 65.
[2] Merk, *loc. cit.*
[3] Bancroft, H. H., *History of the Northwest Coast*, Vol. II, p. 436.
[4] Merk, *op. cit.*, p. 73.
[5] Bancroft, *op. cit.*, Vol. II, p. 437.
[6] Merk, *op. cit.*, p. 75.
[7] Merk, *op. cit.*, p. 85 n.
[8] Bancroft, *op. cit.*, Vol. II, p. 323.
[9] Bancroft, *op. cit.*, Vol. I, p. 281.
[10] Fuller, George W., *A History of the Pacific Northwest*, p. 117.
[11] Dunn, John, *History of the Oregon Territory*, London, 1844, p. 143.
[12] Bancroft, *op. cit.*, Vol. II, p. 441.
[13] Holman, F. V., *Dr. John McLoughlin*, p. 27.
[14] Dunn, *op. cit.*, p. 120.
[15] Fuller, *op. cit.*, p. 107.
[16] Merk, *op. cit.*, p. 86.

[17] Clarke, S. A., *Pioneer Days of Oregon History*, Vol. I, p. 181.
[18] Skinner, Constance Lindsay, *Adventurers in Oregon*, p. 248.
[19] Merk, *op. cit.*, p. 92.
[20] Merk, *op. cit.*, pp. 104–105.
[21] Merk, *op. cit.*, p. 123.
[22] Merk, *op. cit.*, p. 124.
[23] Merk, *op. cit.*, p. 125.

CHAPTER VI

[1] McLoughlin, Dr. John, "Autobiographical Sketch," *Oregon Pioneer Association Proceedings*.
[2] Bancroft, H. H., *History of the Northwest Coast*, Vol. II, p. 438.
[3] *Oregon Pioneer Association Proceedings*.
[4] Bancroft, *op. cit.*, Vol. II, p. 440.
[5] Bancroft, *op. cit.*, Vol. II, p. 435.
[6] Bancroft, *loc. cit.*
[7] Merk, Frederick, *Fur Trade and Empire*, Appendix A: Letter of John McLoughlin to Governor and Committee, Aug. 10, 1825.
[8] Merk, *loc. cit.*: Letter of John McLoughlin to Governor and Committee, Oct. 6, 1825.
[9] Merk, Frederick, *George Simpson's Journal*, p. 66.
[10] Merk, *op. cit.*, p. 67.
[11] Merk, *Fur Trade and Empire*, Appendix A, pp. 229–230.
[12] Elliott, T. C., "Editorial Notes on the Peter Skene Ogden Journals," *Oregon Historical Society Quarterly*, Vol. X, p. 331.
[13] Cox, Ross, *Adventurers on the Columbia River*, Vol. II, pp. 212–213.
[14] Elliott, *op. cit.*, p. 332.
[15] From the correspondence of John McLoughlin and John McLeod, now in the Dominion Archives of Canada at Ottawa.
[16] Larsell, Dr. O., "An Outline of the History of Medicine in the Pacific Northwest," *Northwest Medicine*, Sept., 1932, p. 441.
[17] Larsell, *loc. cit.*
[18] *Douglas's Journal*, London, 1914, p. 106.
[19] Bancroft, *op. cit.*, Vol. II, p. 508.
[20] Scouler, Dr. John, "Journal of a Voyage to Northwest America," *Oregon Historical Society Quarterly*, Vol. VI, p. 168.
[21] Larsell, *op. cit.*, p. 439.
[22] *Douglas's Journal*, p. 107.
[23] *Douglas's Journal*, p. 152.
[24] McLoughlin, *loc. cit.*

CHAPTER VII

[1] Anderson, A. C., *Northwest Coast* (MS., Bancroft Library), pp. 6–7.
[2] *Journal of John Work*, ed. by Lewis and Phillips, p. 61.
[3] Allan, George T., *Reminiscences* (MS., Bancroft Library), p. 13.

[4] Merk, Frederick, *Fur Trade and Empire*, Appendix, pp. 205–206. Letter of Andrew Colville to George Simpson, Mar. 11, 1824.

[5] Bancroft, H. H., *History of the Northwest Coast*, Vol. II, p. 469.

[6] Elliott, T. C., "Dr. John McLoughlin and His Guests," *Washington Historical Society Quarterly*, Vol. III, p. 65.

[7] *Douglas's Journal*, London, 1914, p. 64.

[8] Elliott, T. C., "Journal of John Work," *Washington Historical Society Quarterly*, Vol. V, p. 99. Governor Simpson to John Work, Apr. 16, 1825.

[9] Elliott, "Dr. John McLoughlin and His Guests," *loc. cit.*

[10] Elliott, *loc. cit.*

[11] Merk, *op. cit.*, Appendix A, p. 281.

[12] Carey, Charles H., *History of Oregon*, pp. 286–287.

[13] Victor, Frances Fuller, *River of the West*, p. 33.

[14] Fuller, George W., *A History of the Pacific Northwest*, p. 113.

[15] Fuller, *loc. cit.*

[16] Victor, *loc. cit.*

[17] Elliott, T. C., "Peter Skene Ogden Journals," *Oregon Historical Society Quarterly*, Vol. X, p. 345.

[18] Elliott, *op. cit.*, p. 356.

[19] Elliott, *op. cit.*, p. 357.

[20] Elliott, *op. cit.*, p. 360.

[21] Elliott, *op. cit.*, p. 362.

[22] Elliott, *op. cit.*, p. 365.

[23] Elliott, "Journal of John Work," *Washington Historical Society Quarterly*, Vol. VI, p. 27.

[24] Harvey, Eloisa McLoughlin, *Life of John McLoughlin* (MS., Bancroft Library), p. 2.

[25] Elliott, "Journal of John Work," *loc. cit.*

[26] Bancroft, H. H., *History of Oregon*, Vol. I, p. 37.

[27] McLoughlin, David, *Correspondence*, Oregon Historical Society.

[28] Clarke, S. A., *Pioneer Days of Oregon History*, Vol. I, p. 182.

[29] Merk, *Fur Trade and Empire*, Appendix A, p. 287. John McLoughlin to Governor Simpson.

[30] Merk, *op. cit.*, Appendix A, p. 292. John McLoughlin to Governor Simpson.

[31] McLeod, John, *Journal* (Provincial Library, Victoria, B.C.), p. 123.

CHAPTER VIII

[1] Merk, Frederick, *Fur Trade and Empire*, Appendix A, p. 259. Gov. J. H. Pelly to Hon. George Canning.

[2] Merk, *op. cit.*, Appendix A, p. 287. John McLoughlin to Governor Simpson.

[3] Merk, *op. cit.*, Appendix A, p. 294.

[4] Merk, *op. cit.*, Appendix A, p. 266. Governor and Committee to Governor Simpson.

[5] Harvey, Eloisa McLoughlin, *Life of Dr. John McLoughlin* (MS., Bancroft Library), p. 5.

[6] *Douglas's Journal*, London, 1914, p. 242.

[7] *Douglas's Journal*, p. 247.

[8] Bancroft, H. H., *History of the Northwest Coast*, Vol. II, p. 476.

[9] Bancroft, *op. cit.*, Vol. II, p. 477.

[10] Harvey, Eloisa McLoughlin, *Life of Dr. John McLoughlin* (MS., Bancroft Library), p. 7.

[11] Harvey, *op. cit.*, p. 8.

[12] Bancroft, *op. cit.*, Vol. II, pp. 476–483.

[13] Bancroft, *op. cit.*, Vol. II, p. 483.

[14] Ermatinger, Frank, "Diary," *Washington Historical Society Quarterly*, Vol. I, No. 2, pp. 16–17.

[15] Bancroft, *loc. cit.*

[16] Ermatinger, C. O., *Washington Historical Society Quarterly*, Vol. V, pp. 197–198.

[17] Ermatinger, C. O., *Washington Historical Society Quarterly*, Vol. V, p. 198.

[18] McLoughlin, Dr. John, "Autobiographical Sketch," *Oregon Pioneer Association Proceedings*.

[19] Elliott, T. C., "Dr. John McLoughlin and His Guests," *Washington Historical Society Quarterly*, Vol. III, No. 1, p. 66.

[20] McLoughlin, *loc. cit.*

CHAPTER IX

[1] Elliott, T. C., "Dr. McLoughlin and His Guests," *Washington Historical Society Quarterly*, Vol. III, pp. 66–67.

[2] Elliott, *op. cit.*, Vol. III, p. 68.

[3] Merk, Frederick, *Fur Trade and Empire*, Appendix A, p. 299. Letter of Governor Simpson to William Smith.

[4] Merk, *op. cit.*, Appendix A, p. 300. Governor Simpson to William Smith.

[5] Merk, *op. cit.*, Appendix A, pp. 302–305. Governor Simpson to Jedediah S. Smith.

[6] Bancroft, H. H., *History of the Northwest Coast*, Vol. II, p. 442.

[7] Twombly, Alexander S., *Hawaii and Its People*, p. 328.

[8] Morison, Samuel E., *Oregon Historical Society Quarterly*, Vol. XXVIII, pp. 111–132.

[9] Morison, *loc. cit.*

[10] Victor, Frances Fuller, "Flotsam and Jetsam of the Pacific," *Oregon Historical Society Quarterly*, Vol. I, pp. 38–39.

[11] Bancroft, *op. cit.*, Vol. II, p. 443.

[12] Thompson, D. W., to Josiah Marshall, letter dated Mar. 26, 1829. *Oregon Historical Society Quarterly*, Vol. XXVIII, p. 126.

[13] Slacum's Report on Oregon, 1836–7, *Oregon Historical Society Quarterly*, Vol. XIII, pp. 189–190.

[14] Morison, *loc. cit.* Letter of John McLoughlin to John Rowand, July 29, 1830.

[15] Merk, *op. cit.*, Appendix A, pp. 330–331. Letter of John McLoughlin to the Governor & Committee, Oct. 11, 1830.

[16] Morison, *loc. cit.*

[17] Victor, *op. cit.*, Vol. II, pp. 39–40.

[18] Bancroft, *op. cit.*, Vol. II, pp. 502–503.

[19] Douglas, James, *Journal* (MS., Bancroft Library), 1840–41, pp. 3, 4.

[20] Merk, *op. cit.*, Appendix A, p. 331. Letter of Dr. John McLoughlin to the Governor & Committee, Oct. 11, 1830.

[21] Allan, George T., "Reminiscences of Fort Vancouver," *Oregon Pioneer Association Proceedings*, 1881.

[22] Allan, *loc. cit.*

[23] Merk, *op. cit.*, Appendix A, pp. 332–333. Letter of Dr. John McLoughlin to the Governor & Committee, Nov. 24, 1830.

[24] Scott, Leslie M., "Indian Diseases in the Northwest," *Oregon Historical Society Quarterly*, Vol. XXIX, p. 152.

[25] Scott, *loc. cit.* Quotation from Samuel Parker.

[26] Carey, Charles H., *History of Oregon*, p. 291.

[27] Merk, *op. cit.*, Appendix A, p. 294. Governor & Committee to Governor Simpson, London, Jan. 16, 1828.

[28] Merk, *op. cit.*, Appendix A, pp. 309–310. Letter of Governor Simpson to John McLoughlin, Fort Vancouver, Mar. 15, 1829.

[29] Bancroft, *op. cit.*, Vol. II, p. 505.

CHAPTER X

[1] Merk, Frederick, *Fur Trade and Empire*, Appendix A, p. 308. Governor Simpson to John McLoughlin, Fort Vancouver, Mar. 15, 1829.

[2] Merk, *op. cit.*, Appendix A, pp. 308–310. Governor Simpson to John McLoughlin, Fort Vancouver, Mar. 15, 1829.

[3] *Oregon Pioneer Association Proceedings*, 1880.

[4] Lyman, Horace S., *History of Oregon*, Vol. II, p. 382.

[5] *Oregon Pioneer Association Proceedings*, 1880.

[6] Roberts, George B., *Recollections* (MS. 15, Bancroft Library). Gray, W. H., *History of Oregon*, p. 21. Lyman, *op. cit.*, Vol. II, p. 380.

[7] Lyman, *loc. cit.*

[8] Lyman, *op. cit.*, Vol. II, p. 381.

[9] Lyman, *loc. cit.*

[10] Bancroft, H. H., *History of the Northwest Coast*, Vol. II, p. 499.

[11] Victor, Frances Fuller, *River of the West*, p. 30.

[12] Power of Attorney given by Dr. John McLoughlin to Jean Baptiste Taché before the Notary Thomas Casault of Kamouraska. From notes supplied by M. Louis J. Pelletier of Rivière du Loup.

[13] Power of Attorney given by Dr. John McLoughlin to M. Pierre Canac Marquis. From notes supplied by Mr. Louis J. Pelletier of Rivière du Loup.

[14] Sage, Walter N., *Sir James Douglas and British Columbia*, p. 51.

[15] Sage, Walter N., *Washington Historical Society Quarterly*, Vol. XXVII, p. 369.

[16] Bancroft, H. H., *History of Oregon*, Vol. I, p. 31.

[17] Roberts, G. B., *Recollections* (MS., Bancroft Library), p. 17.

[18] Sage, *Washington Historical Society Quarterly*, Vol. XXVII, p. 366.

[19] Bancroft, *History of the Northwest Coast*, Vol. II, pp. 473–475.

[20] Sage, *Sir James Douglas and British Columbia*, p. 48.

[21] Harvey, Eloisa McLoughlin, *Life of Dr. John McLoughlin* (MS., Bancroft Library), p. 13.

[22] Lyman, Horace S., "Reminiscences of Louis Labonte," *Oregon Historical Society Quarterly*, Vol. I, pp. 170–171.

[23] McLoughlin, Dr. John, "Autobiographical Sketch," *Oregon Pioneer Association Proceedings*.

[24] Holman, F. V., *Dr. John McLoughlin*, p. 33.

[25] Lyman, *History of Oregon*, Vol. II, p. 403.

[26] Lyman, *op. cit.*, Vol. II, p. 406.

[27] McLoughlin, *loc. cit.*

[28] McLoughlin, *loc. cit.*

CHAPTER XI

[1] Bancroft, H. H., *History of Oregon*, Vol. I, p. 38. George B. Roberts was the other apprentice.

[2] Dunn, John, *History of the Oregon Territory and British North-American Fur Trade*, London, 1846, pp. 41–45.

[3] *Washington Historical Society Quarterly*, Vol. V, pp. 260–261. Letter of J. E. Harriott to John McLeod, Feb. 21, 1831.

[4] Sage, Walter N., *Sir James Douglas and British Columbia*, p. 66.

[5] Letter of John McLoughlin to Edward Ermatinger, Feb. 1, 1835. Provincial Library, Victoria, B.C.

[6] *Washington Historical Society Quarterly*, Vol. V, pp. 260–261. Letter of J. E. Harriott to John McLeod, Feb. 21, 1831.

[7] Bancroft, H. H., *History of the Northwest Coast*, Vol. II, p. 622.

[8] Merk, Frederick, *Fur Trade and Empire*, Appendix A, pp. 329–330. Letter of Captain Simpson to John McLoughlin, September 23, 1830.

[9] Bancroft, *op. cit.*, Vol. II, p. 623.

[10] Merk, *op. cit.*, Appendix A, p. 331.

[11] Bancroft, *loc. cit.*

[12] Larsell, Dr. O., "An Outline of the History of Medicine in the Pacific Northwest," *Northwest Medicine*, Sept., 1932, p. 441.

[13] *Oregon Historical Society Quarterly*, Vol. XV, pp. 206–207. Letter of John McLoughlin to John McLeod, Fort Vancouver, Mar. 1, 1832.

[14] Bancroft, *op. cit.*, Vol. II, p. 520.

[15] Clarke, S. A., *Pioneer Days of Oregon History*, Vol. I, p. 199.

[16] Anderson, A. C., *History of the Northwest Coast* (MS., Bancroft Library), p. 70.

[17] Merk, *op. cit.*, Appendix A, p. 323. Letter of John McLoughlin to Governor Simpson, Fort Vancouver, Mar. 20, 1830.

[18] Bancroft, *loc. cit.*

Notes

[19] Irving, Washington, *Adventures of Captain Bonneville.*

[20] Victor, Frances Fuller, *River of the West,* p. 36.

[21] Wyeth, Nathaniel J., *Correspondence and Journals* (University of Oregon Press, 1899), p. xvii.

[22] Bancroft, *op. cit.,* Vol. II, p. 567.

[23] Wyeth, *op. cit.,* p. 176.

[24] Wyeth, *op. cit.,* p. 181.

[25] Harvey, Eloisa McLoughlin, *Life of Dr. John McLoughlin* (MS., Bancroft Library), pp. 16–19.

CHAPTER XII

[1] Powers, Kate N. B., "Across the Continent Seventy Years Ago," *Oregon Historical Society Quarterly,* Vol. III, p. 83.

[2] Ball, John, *Autobiography,* p. 93.

[3] Carey, Charles H., *History of Oregon,* p. 299.

[4] Ball, *loc. cit.*

[5] Evans, Elwood, *North Pacific History,* Vol. I, p. 123.

[6] Himes, George H., "Beginnings of Christianity in Oregon," *Oregon Historical Society Quarterly,* Vol. XX, p. 162.

[7] Harvey, Eloisa McLoughlin, *Life of Dr. John McLoughlin* (MS., Bancroft Library), pp. 10–11.

[8] Himes, *loc. cit.*

[9] O'Hara, E. V., *Catholic History of Oregon,* p. 17.

[10] O'Hara, *op. cit.,* pp. 18–19. Letter of George Simpson to the Bishop of Quebec, London, Feb. 17, 1838.

[11] Clarke, S. A., *Pioneer Days of Oregon History,* Vol. I, p. 187.

[12] McLoughlin, David, *Correspondence.* Oregon Historical Society.

[13] Larsell, Dr. O., "An Outline of the History of Medicine in the Pacific Northwest," *Northwest Medicine,* Sept., 1932, p. 440.

[14] Larsell, *op. cit.,* p. 442.

[15] Bancroft, H. H., *History of the Northwest Coast,* Vol. II, p. 525.

[16] Tolmie, William Frazer, "Journal," *Washington Historical Society Quarterly,* Vol. III, pp. 229–240.

[17] Tolmie, *loc. cit.*

[18] Tolmie, *loc. cit.*

[19] Bancroft, *op. cit.,* Vol. II, pp. 522–523.

[20] Bancroft, *op. cit.,* Vol. II, p. 522.

[21] Finlayson, Duncan, Letter to John McLeod, Fort Vancouver, Feb. 25, 1833, *Washington Historical Society Quarterly,* Vol. II, pp. 166–167.

[22] Finlayson, *loc. cit.*

[23] Bancroft, *op. cit.,* Vol. II, pp. 625–626.

[24] Bancroft, *op. cit.,* Vol. II, p. 628.

[25] Tolmie, *loc. cit.*

[26] Bancroft, *op. cit.,* Vol. II, p. 628 n.

[27] Lomax, Alfred L., "Pioneer Sheep Husbandry," *Oregon Historical Society Quarterly,* Vol. XXIX, pp. 111–113.

[28] McLoughlin, John, Letter to John McLeod, Fort Vancouver, Mar. 1, 1833, *Washington Historical Society Quarterly,* Vol. II, pp. 167–168.

[29] McDonald, Archibald, Letter to John McLeod, Fort Langley, Feb. 20, 1833, *Washington Historical Society Quarterly,* Vol. II, pp. 161–163.

[30] Bancroft, *op. cit.,* Vol. II, pp. 524–525.

CHAPTER XIII

[1] McLoughlin, Dr. John, Letter to John McLeod, Vancouver, Mar. 1, 1834, *Washington Historical Society Quarterly,* Vol. II, p. 165.

[2] The Bonaventura River was a mythical stream which was supposed to flow westward to the Pacific through the central part of the United States. It appears on many early maps.

[3] Work, John, *Journal,* ed. by Lewis and Phillips, p. 59.

[4] Work, John, Letter to Edward Ermatinger, Vancouver, Feb. 24, 1834, *Washington Historical Society Quarterly,* Vol. II, pp. 163–164.

[5] Bancroft, H. H., *History of the Northwest Coast,* Vol. II, pp. 526–527.

[6] Lee and Frost, *Ten Years in Oregon,* pp. 124–125.

[7] *Oregon Historical Society Quarterly,* Vol. XXIV, p. 239. Work, *Journal,* entry for May 22, 1834.

[8] Work, *Journal,* ed. by Lewis and Phillips, p. 59.

[9] Merk, Frederick, *Fur Trade and Empire,* Appendix A, p. 322. Letter of the Governor & Committee to Governor Simpson, London, Mar. 5, 1830.

[10] Brosnan, Cornelius J., *Jason Lee: Prophet of the New Oregon,* p. 2.

[11] Brosnan, *op. cit.,* p. 12.

[12] Lyman, H. S., *History of Oregon,* Vol. III, p. 144.

[13] Brosnan, *op. cit.,* p. 45.

[14] Gray, W. H., *History of Oregon,* p. 107.

[15] Wyeth, Nathaniel J., *Correspondence and Journals* (University of Oregon Press, 1899), p. 130.

[16] Wyeth, *op. cit.,* p. 117.

[17] Carey, Charles H., *History of Oregon,* p. 334.

[18] Brown, Jennie Broughton, *Fort Hall on the Oregon Trail,* pp. 139–140.

[19] Brosnan, *op. cit.,* p. 64.

[20] Lee, Jason, "Journal," *Oregon Historical Society Quarterly,* Vol. XVII, p. 262.

[21] Lee, *loc. cit.*

[22] McLoughlin, Dr. John, "Autobiographical Sketch," *Oregon Pioneer Association Proceedings.*

[23] Lee, *loc. cit.*

[24] Lee, *op. cit.,* Vol. XVII, p. 265.

[25] Lee, *op. cit.,* Vol. XVII, p. 266.

[26] Hines, Rev. Gustavus, *History of Oregon,* p. 76.

[27] McLoughlin, *loc. cit.*

[28] Brown, *op. cit.,* pp. 159–160.

[29] Wyeth, *op. cit.,* p. 147.

[30] Bancroft, *op. cit.,* Vol. II, p. 595.

[31] Brown, *op. cit.*, p. 229.

[32] Roberts, George B., *Recollections* (MS. 11, Bancroft Library).

[33] Lyman, H. S., *History of Oregon*, Vol. III, p. 77.

[34] Powell, Fred Wilbur, "Hall Jackson Kelley: Prophet of Oregon," *Oregon Historical Society Quarterly*, Vol. XVIII, p. 126.

[35] Powell, Fred Wilbur, *Hall J. Kelley on Oregon*, p. 180.

[36] Powell, *op. cit.*, p. 182.

[37] "A Narrative by Dr. McLoughlin," *Oregon Historical Society Quarterly*, Vol. I, p. 195.

[38] Lyman, *op. cit.*, Vol. III, p. 78.

[39] Lyman, *op. cit.*, Vol. III, p. 80.

CHAPTER XIV

[1] Bancroft, H. H., *History of Oregon*, Vol. I, p. 48.

[2] Dunn, John, *History of the Oregon Territory*, pp. 123–125.

[3] Bancroft, *op. cit.*, Vol. I, pp. 44–45.

[4] Allan, George T., "Reminiscences," *Proceedings of the Oregon Pioneer Association*, 1882.

[5] Crawford, Medorem, *Missionaries and Their Work* (MS.).

[6] Victor, Frances Fuller, *River of the West*, p. 31.

[7] McLoughlin, John, Letter to Edward Ermatinger, Fort Vancouver, Feb. 1, 1835, *Oregon Historical Society Quarterly*, Vol. XXIII, pp. 366–367.

[8] Gray, W. H., *History of Oregon*, p. 107.

[9] Blue, G. W., "Green's Missionary Report on Oregon," *Oregon Historical Society Quarterly*, Vol. XXX, p. 259.

[10] Fuller, George W., *A History of the Pacific Northwest*, p. 128.

[11] Elliott, T. C., "Dr. McLoughlin and His Guests," *Washington Historical Society Quarterly*, Vol. III, pp. 69–70.

[12] Fuller. *loc. cit.*

[13] Elliott, *loc. cit.*

[14] Carey, Charles H., *History of Oregon*, p. 413.

[15] Clarke, S. A., *Pioneer Days of Oregon History*, Vol. I, p. 205.

[16] Lee and Frost, *Ten Years in Oregon*, p. 137.

[17] Bancroft, *op. cit.*, Vol. I, p. 50.

[18] Ogden, Peter Skene, Letter to John McLeod, Feb. 25, 1837, *Washington Historical Society Quarterly*, Vol. XXXII, p. 332.

[19] Gray, *op. cit.*, p. 162.

[20] Gray, *loc. cit.*

[21] McLoughlin, John, Letter to Edward Ermatinger, Fort Vancouver, Feb. 1, 1836, *Oregon Historical Society Quarterly*, Vol. XXIII, p. 368.

[22] Brown, Jennie Broughton, *Fort Hall on the Oregon Trail*, p. 165.

[23] McLoughlin, *loc. cit.*

[24] Blossom, Robert H., "First Presbyterianism on the Pacific Coast," *Oregon Historical Society Quarterly*, Vol. XV, p. 83.

[25] Harvey, Eloisa McLoughlin, *Life of Dr. John McLoughlin* (MS., Bancroft Library), p. 13.

[26] Spalding, H. H., Letter to his brothers, Columbia River, Oct. 2, 1836, *Oregon Historical Society Quarterly*, Vol. XIII, p. 371.
[27] Himes, George H., "Beginnings of Christianity in Oregon," *Oregon Historical Society Quarterly*, Vol. XX, p. 168.
[28] Spalding, *op. cit.*, Vol. XIII, p. 377.
[29] Shippee, Lester Burrell, "Federal Relations of Oregon," *Oregon Historical Society Quarterly*, Vol. XIX, p. 22.
[30] Slacum, William A., "Report on Oregon, 1836–37," *Oregon Historical Society Quarterly*, Vol. XIII, p. 177.
[31] "A Narrative by Dr. McLoughlin," *Oregon Historical Society Quarterly*, Vol. II, p. 196.

CHAPTER XV

[1] "Slacum's Report on Oregon, 1836–37," *Oregon Historical Society Quarterly*, Vol. XIII, p. 192.
[2] "Slacum's Report," *loc. cit.*
[3] Beaver, Rev. Herbert, Letter to the Aborigines Protection Society of London, *Oregon Historical Society Quarterly*, Vol. XXXII, pp. 332–346.
[4] Merk, Frederick, *Fur Trade and Empire*, Appendix B, pp. 354–355. Letter of John McLoughlin to the Governor and Committee in London.
[5] Merk, *op. cit.*, Appendix B, p. 354. Letter of James Douglas to the Governor and Committee in London, Oct. 18, 1838.
[6] Meany, E. S., "First American Settlement on Puget Sound," *Washington Historical Society Quarterly*, Vol. VII, p. 137.
[7] Carey, Charles H., *History of Oregon*, p. 319.
[8] Fuller, George W., *A History of the Pacific Northwest*, p. 185.
[9] Lee and Frost, *Ten Years in Oregon*, p. 140.
[10] "Slacum's Report on Oregon, 1836–1837," *Oregon Historical Society Quarterly*, Vol. XIII, p. 213.
[11] "Slacum's Report on Oregon, 1836–37," *Oregon Historical Society Quarterly*, Vol. XIII, p. 196.
[12] Robertson, James R., "The Social Evolution of Oregon," *Oregon Historical Society Quarterly*, Vol. III, p. 16.
[13] "Slacum's Report," *loc. cit.*
[14] The doctor was in error. The correct year was 1837.
[15] McLoughlin, Dr. John, "Autobiographical Sketch," *Oregon Pioneer Association Proceedings*.
[16] "Slacum's Report," *loc. cit.*
[17] Lyman, H. S., *History of Oregon*, Vol. III, p. 178.
[18] Bancroft, H. H., *History of the Northwest Coast*, Vol. II, pp. 612–613.
[19] Merk, *op. cit.*, Appendix A, p. 339. Letter of Governor Simpson to Governor J. H. Pelly, London, Feb. 1, 1837.
[20] Bancroft, *op. cit.*, Vol. II, p. 616.
[21] Lee and Frost, *op. cit.*, p. 146.
[22] Bancroft, H. H., *History of Oregon*, Vol. I, p. 161.
[23] Lyman, *op. cit.*, Vol. III, p. 185.

[24] Sage, Walter N., *Sir James Douglas and British Columbia*, p. 87.

[25] Bancroft, *History of Oregon*, Vol. I, p. 52.

[26] Bancroft, *op. cit.*, Vol. I, p. 53.

[27] Bancroft, *op. cit.*, Vol. I, p. 36.

[28] Bagley, Clarence B., "Communication in Early Oregon," *Oregon Historical Society Quarterly*, Vol. XIII, p. 349.

[29] Jason Lee's Journal, North Fork of the Platte River, July 28, 1838, *Oregon Historical Society Quarterly*, Vol. VII, p. 232.

[30] *Washington Historical Society Quarterly*, Vol. VI, pp. 260–261.

CHAPTER XVI

[1] Oliver, E. H., *Canadian North-West*, Vol. II. Minutes of Council, Norway House, Feb., 1837.

[2] *Makers of Canada*, Vol. V, Part II (Papineau), p. 1.

[3] *Ermatinger Papers* (Provincial Library, Victoria, B.C.), p. 51. Letter from John Tod to Edward Ermatinger, Oxford House, July 12, 1838.

[4] Sage, Walter N., *Sir James Douglas and British Columbia*, p. 117.

[5] Guedalla, Philip, *Palmerston*, p. 393.

[6] McLoughlin, David, Correspondence (Oregon Historical Society).

[7] Oliver, E. H., *Canadian North-West*, Vol. II, pp. 791–796.

[8] Sage, *op. cit.*, p. 93.

[9] Carey, Charles H., *History of Oregon*, p. 277.

[10] Fuller, George W., *A History of the Pacific Northwest*, p. 137.

[11] Letter from Father Blanchet to Dr. McLoughlin (Oregon Historical Society).

[12] McLoughlin, *loc. cit.*

[13] Oliver, *op. cit.*, Vol. II, p. 772. From the Minutes of Council, 1837, Norway House, Northern Dept. of Rupert's Land.

[14] Genealogy of the Fraser Family. *History of the Ursulines*, by a member of the Community, Quebec, 1897, p. 361.

[15] McLoughlin, *loc. cit.*

[16] McLoughlin, *loc. cit.*

[17] Oliver, *op. cit.*, Vol. II, p. 785.

[18] Oliver, *op. cit.*, Vol. I, p. 283.

[19] Oliver, *op. cit.*, Vol. II, p. 722.

[20] *Ermatinger Papers*, p. 56. Letter of John Tod to Edward Ermatinger.

[21] O'Hara, E. V., *Catholic History of Oregon*, p. 19.

[22] Bagley, C. B., *Early Catholic Missions in Old Oregon*, p. 24.

[23] O'Hara, *loc. cit.*

[24] De Smet, P. J., *Oregon Missions and Travels over the Rocky Mountains in 1845–46*, p. 18.

[25] Bagley, *op. cit.*, p. 25.

[26] O'Hara, *op. cit.*, p. 25.

[27] Sage, *op. cit.*, p. 91.

[28] Oliver, *op. cit.*, Vol. II, p. 785.

[29] Bancroft, H. H., *History of the Northwest Coast*, Vol. II, pp. 619–621.

CHAPTER XVII

[1] Bancroft, H. H., *History of the Northwest Coast,* Vol. II, p. 615.

[2] Puget Sound Agricultural Company Prospectus, *Oregon Historical Society Quarterly,* Vol. XIX, pp. 345–349.

[3] Lyman, H. S., *History of Oregon,* Vol. III, p. 230.

[4] Letter of Archibald McDonald to Edward Ermatinger, Fort Colville, Apr. 2, 1840. Provincial Library, Victoria, B.C.

[5] Letter of John Work to Edward Ermatinger, Fort Simpson, Feb. 15, 1841. Provincial Library, Victoria, B.C.

[6] Oliver, E. H., *Canadian North-West,* Vol. II, pp. 791–796.

[7] Sage, Walter N., *Sir James Douglas and British Columbia,* p. 94.

[8] Sage, *op. cit.,* pp. 94–98.

[9] Harvey, Eloisa McLoughlin, *Life of Dr. John McLoughlin* (MS., Bancroft Library), p. 19.

[10] Brosnan, Cornelius J., *Jason Lee, Prophet of the New Oregon,* p. 162.

[11] Bancroft, H. H., *History of Oregon,* Vol. I, pp. 178–182.

[12] Bancroft, *op. cit.,* Vol. I, p. 171.

[13] Brosnan, *op. cit.,* p. 163.

[14] Lee and Frost, *Ten Years in Oregon,* p. 195.

[15] Brewer, Rev. Henry B., "Log of the Lausanne," *Oregon Historical Society Quarterly,* Vol. XXIX, p. 358.

[16] Brosnan, *op. cit.,* p. 164.

[17] McLoughlin, Dr. John, *Private Papers* (MS., Bancroft Library).

[18] Bagley, C. B., *Early Catholic Missions in Oregon,* p. 52.

[19] Bancroft, H. H., *History of Oregon,* Vol. I, pp. 136–138.

[20] Roberts, George B., *Reminiscences* (MS., Bancroft Library), p. 4.

[21] Sage, *op. cit.,* p. 103.

[22] Sage, *op. cit.,* p. 102.

[23] Douglas, James. Trading Expedition, *California Historical Society Quarterly,* Vol. VIII, p. 97.

[24] Bancroft, *History of the Northwest Coast,* Vol. II, p. 541.

[25] Fuller, George W., *A History of the Pacific Northwest,* p. 196.

[26] Lyman, *op. cit.,* Vol. III, pp. 235–236.

[27] Bancroft, *History of Oregon,* Vol. I, p. 295.

[28] O'Hara, E. V., *Catholic History of Oregon,* p. 71.

[29] "Diary of Wilkes in the Northwest," *Washington Historical Society Quarterly,* Vol. XVI, p. 218.

[30] "Diary of Wilkes in the Northwest," *Washington Historical Society Quarterly,* Vol. XVI, p. 299.

[31] "Diary of Wilkes in the Northwest," *loc. cit.*

[32] Bancroft, *History of the Northwest Coast,* Vol. II, p. 674.

[33] Bancroft, *History of Oregon,* Vol. I, pp. 295–296.

[34] "Diary of Wilkes in the Northwest," *Washington Historical Society Quarterly,* Vol. XVII, p. 64.

[35] Bancroft, *History of the Northwest Coast,* Vol. II, p. 677.

CHAPTER XVIII

[1] Sage, Walter N., *Sir James Douglas and British Columbia,* p. 49.
[2] Establishment of Servants, Columbia District, Outfit 1839 (Provincial Library, Victoria, B.C.).
[3] Simpson, Sir George, *Narrative of a Journey Round the World,* Vol. I, p. 172.
[4] Bancroft, H. H., *History of Oregon,* Vol. I, p. 250.
[5] Bancroft, H. H., *History of California,* Vol. IV, pp. 216–218.
[6] Simpson, *op. cit.,* Vol. I, p. 1.
[7] Simpson, *op. cit.,* Vol. I, p. 172.
[8] *American Historical Review,* Vol. XIV, p. 73.
[9] Sage, *op. cit.,* p. 115.
[10] Bancroft, H. H., *History of the Northwest Coast,* Vol. II, p. 681.
[11] Simpson, *op. cit.,* Vol. I, p. 182.
[12] Bancroft, *op. cit.,* Vol. II, p. 650.
[13] Bancroft, *op. cit.,* Vol. II, pp. 657–658.
[14] Simpson, *op. cit.,* Vol. I, p. 221.
[15] Holman, F. V., "Results from the Astor Expeditions," *Oregon Historical Society Quarterly,* Vol. XII, p. 216.
[16] McLoughlin, David, Correspondence (Oregon Historical Society).
[17] *American Historical Review,* Vol. XIV, p. 89.
[18] Sage, *op. cit.,* p. 119.
[19] "Report of George Simpson to Governor and Committee" (Fort Vancouver, Nov. 25, 1841), *American Historical Review,* Vol. XIV, p. 73.
[20] Pipes, Nellie B., "De Mofras Exploration of the Oregon Territory," *Oregon Historical Society Quarterly,* Vol. XXVI, p. 151.
[21] *Exploration de Territoire de l'Orégon, des Californies et de la Mer Vermeille.*
[22] Bancroft, *History of the Northwest Coast,* Vol. II, p. 666.
[23] Pipes, Nellie B., "De Mofras Exploration of the Oregon Territory," *Oregon Historical Society Quarterly,* Vol. XXVI, p. 151.
[24] McLoughlin, Dr. John, *Private Papers* (MS., Bancroft Library).
[25] Letter of Archibald McDonald to Edward Ermatinger, Mar. 30, 1842 (Provincial Library, Victoria, B.C.).
[26] Roberts, George B., *Recollections* (MS., Bancroft Library), p. 10.
[27] Bancroft, *op. cit.,* Vol. II, p. 658.
[28] *American Historical Review,* Vol. XIV, p. 88.
[29] Bancroft, *op. cit.,* Vol. II, p. 660.
[30] Letter of Dr. John McLoughlin to Edward Ermatinger, Feb. 1, 1843, *Oregon Historical Society Quarterly,* Vol. XV, p. 127.
[31] Harvey, Eloisa McLoughlin, *Life of Dr. John McLoughlin* (MS., Bancroft Library), pp. 19–20.
[32] Ermatinger, C. O., "A Tragedy on the Stikeen in '42," *Oregon Historical Society Quarterly,* Vol. XV, pp. 126–132.
[33] Simpson, *op. cit.,* Vol. II, p. 182.
[34] Letter of John Tod to Edward Ermatinger, Sept. 1, 1842 (Provincial Library, Victoria, B.C.).

[35] Letter of Dr. John McLoughlin to Edward Ermatinger, Feb. 1, 1843, *Oregon Historical Society Quarterly,* Vol. XV, p. 131.
[36] McLoughlin, Dr. John, *Private Papers* (Bancroft Library).
[37] Bancroft, *History of Oregon,* Vol. I, pp. 207–210.
[38] McLoughlin, *loc. cit.* Letter to L. W. Hastings.
[39] O'Hara, E. V., *Catholic History of Oregon,* p. 35.

CHAPTER XIX

[1] Thomas, Russell B., "Truth and Fiction of the Champoeg Meeting," *Oregon Historical Society Quarterly,* Vol. XXX, p. 230.
[2] Crawford, Medorem, *Oregon Pioneer Association Proceedings, 1881,* p. 14.
[3] Bancroft, H. H., *History of Oregon,* Vol. I, pp. 262–263.
[4] Clark, Robert C., "How British and American Subjects Unite," *Oregon Historical Society Quarterly,* Vol. XIII, pp. 144–146.
[5] Matthieu, F. X., "Reminiscences," *Oregon Historical Society Quarterly,* Vol. II, pp. 73–104.
[6] Holman, Frederick V., *Dr. John McLoughlin,* p. 69.
[7] Oliver, E. H., *Canadian North-West,* Vol. II, p. 847. Minutes of the Council of 1842.
[8] Sage, Walter N., *Sir James Douglas and British Columbia,* pp. 123–124.
[9] Carey, Charles H., *History of Oregon,* pp. 487–488.
[10] Fuller, George W., *A History of the Pacific Northwest,* p. 195.
[11] Clark, *op. cit.,* Vol. XIII, p. 147.
[12] Clark, *op. cit.,* Vol. XIII, p. 146.
[13] Clark, Robert C., *History of the Willamette Valley,* p. 793.
[14] Thomas, *op. cit.,* Vol. XXV, pp. 222–230.
[15] Thomas, *op. cit.,* Vol. XXX, p. 218.
[16] Carey, *op. cit.,* pp. 379–380.
[17] Scott, Leslie M., "Oregon's Provisional Government," *Oregon Historical Society Quarterly,* Vol. XXXI, p. 214.
[18] Bancroft, *op. cit.,* Vol. I, p. 307.
[19] Scott, *op. cit.,* Vol. XXXI, p. 213.
[20] Young, F. G., "Finances of Provisional Government," *Oregon Historical Society Quarterly,* Vol. VII, pp. 376–377.
[21] Bancroft, *op. cit.,* Vol. I, pp. 395–415.
[22] McLoughlin, Dr. John, "Autobiographical Sketch," *Oregon Pioneer Association Proceedings.*
[23] Holman, *op. cit.,* p. 71.
[24] Fuller, *op. cit.,* p. 200.
[25] Clark, "How British and American Subjects Unite," *Oregon Historical Society Quarterly,* Vol. XIII, p. 153.
[26] Fuller, *op. cit.,* p. 201.
[27] Holman, *op. cit.,* p. 108.
[28] *American Historical Review,* Vol. XXI, pp. 120–135.
[29] Letter of Dr. John McLoughlin to Sir George Simpson, Vancouver, Mar. 20, 1844, *Oregon Historical Society Quarterly,* Vol. XVII, pp. 215–239.

[30] Holman, *op. cit.*, p. 78.

[31] *Oregon Pioneer Association Proceedings, 1886*, pp. 24–27.

[32] Bancroft, *op. cit.*, Vol. I, pp. 471–472.

[33] Clark, Robert C., "Last Step in Provisional Government," *Oregon Historical Society Quarterly*, Vol. XVI, p. 323.

[34] Fuller, *op. cit.*, p. 201.

[35] Clark, *op. cit.*, Vol. XVI, p. 325.

[36] Oregon Archives.

[37] From two letters of Dr. John McLoughlin, one dated August 20, the other November 20, 1845.

[38] Clark, *op. cit.*, Vol. XVI, p. 321.

[39] Sage, Walter N., *Sir James Douglas and British Columbia*, p. 129.

[40] Schafer, Joseph, "Warre and Vavasour, 1845–6," *Oregon Historical Society Quarterly*, Vol. X, p. 1.

[41] From an original manuscript dealing with the death of William Glen Rae, Archives of the Provincial Library, Victoria, B.C.

[42] Holman, *op. cit.*, p. 90.

[43] *American Historical Review*, Vol. XXI, pp. 120–135.

CHAPTER XX

[1] Tolmie, William F., *Puget Sound* (MS., Bancroft Library), p. 47.

[2] Holman, Frederick V., *Dr. John McLoughlin*, p. 121.

[3] Bancroft, H. H., *History of Oregon*, Vol. I, p. 506.

[4] Lyman, H. S., *History of Oregon*, Vol. III, pp. 435–437.

[5] Lyman, *op. cit.*, Vol. IV, p. 43.

[6] Bancroft, *op. cit.*, Vol. I, pp. 685–697.

[7] Lyman, *op. cit.*, Vol. IV, pp. 45–46.

[8] Fuller, George W., *A History of the Pacific Northwest*, pp. 155–156.

[9] Carey, Charles H., *History of Oregon*, p. 547.

[10] Bancroft, *op. cit.*, Vol. II, p. 97.

[11] Holman, *op. cit.*, pp. 101–153.

[12] Fuller, *op. cit.*, p. 205.

[13] Holman, *op. cit.*

[14] Bancroft, *op. cit.*, Vol. II, p. 136.

[15] Sage, Walter N., *Sir James Douglas and British Columbia*, p. 149.

[16] Bancroft, H. H., *History of the Northwest Coast*, Vol. II, p. 710.

[17] Brosnan, Cornelius J., *Jason Lee: Prophet of the New Oregon*, pp. 274–275.

[18] Bancroft, *History of Oregon*, Vol. I, pp. 39–40.

[19] McLoughlin Document. Quoted in full in *Oregon Pioneer Association Proceedings, 1880*, pp. 46–55.

[20] O'Hara, E. V., *Catholic History of Oregon*, p. 90.

[21] From the English translation, a copy of which is in the archives of the Oregon Historical Society.

[22] From the Parish records of the Cathedral in Oregon City.

[23] Holman, *op. cit.*, p. 159.

[24] De Chesne, Dr. Henri A. M., Correspondence (Oregon Historical Society).

BIBLIOGRAPHY

Authorities Consulted

ALLAN, GEORGE T., *Reminiscences.* MS., Bancroft Library.

ANDERSON, A. C., *History of the Northwest Coast.* MS., Bancroft Library.

BAGLEY, CLARENCE B., *Early Catholic Missions in Old Oregon* (2 vols.). Also articles in *Oregon Historical Society Quarterly.*

BALL, JOHN, *Autobiography.*

BANCROFT, H. H., *History of California* (4 vols.).

————*History of Oregon* (2 vols.).

————*History of the Northwest Coast* (2 vols.).

BEAVER, REV. HERBERT, "Letters," in *Oregon Historical Society Quarterly.*

BLANCHET, ARCHBISHOP FRANCIS NORBERT, "Correspondence," in *Oregon Historical Society Quarterly.*

————*Historical Sketches of the Catholic Church in Oregon.*

BLOSSOM, ROBERT H., "First Presbyterianism on the Pacific Coast," *Oregon Historical Society Quarterly.*

BLUE, G. W., "Green's Missionary Report on Oregon," in *Oregon Historical Society Quarterly.*

BREWER, REV. HENRY B., "Log of the Lausanne," *Oregon Historical Society Quarterly.*

BROSNAN, CORNELIUS J., *Jason Lee, Prophet of the New Oregon.*

BROWN, JENNIE BROUGHTON, *Fort Hall on the Oregon Trail.*

CAREY, CHARLES H., *History of Oregon.* Also articles in the *Oregon Historical Society Quarterly.*

CLARK, ROBERT C., *History of the Willamette Valley.* Also articles in *Oregon Historical Society Quarterly.*

CLARKE, S. A., *Pioneer Days of Oregon History* (2 vols.).

COUES, DR. ELLIOTT, *New Light on the Greater Northwest* (3 vols.).

COX, ROSS, *Adventurers on the Columbia River* (2 vols.).

CRAWFORD, MEDOREM, *Missionaries and Their Work* (MS., Bancroft

343

344   *Bibliography*

Library). Also articles in *Oregon Pioneer Association Proceedings*.

DE CHESNE, HENRI A. M., *Correspondence*. Oregon Historical Society, Portland.

DE SMET, P. J., *Oregon Missions and Travels over the Rocky Mountains, 1845-46*.

DOBBS, CAROLINE C., *Men of Champoeg*.

DOUGLAS, DAVID, *Journal*.

DOUGLAS, JAMES, *Journal*.

———"Trading Expedition," in *California Historical Society Quarterly*.

DUNN, JOHN, *History of the Pacific Northwest*.

DYE, EVA EMERY, *McLoughlin and Old Oregon*.

ELLIOTT, T. C., various articles in *Oregon Historical Society Quarterly* and *Washington Historical Society Quarterly*.

ERMATINGER, C. O., articles in *Washington Historical Society Quarterly*.

ERMATINGER, EDWARD, *Papers*. Provincial Library, Victoria, B.C.

ERMATINGER, FRANK, "Diary," in *Washington Historical Society Quarterly*.

EVANS, ELWOOD, *North Pacific History*. MS., Bancroft Library.

FARNHAM, THOMAS J., *History of the Oregon Territory*.

FINLAYSON, DUNCAN, "Correspondence," in *Washington Historical Society Quarterly*.

FLAVIA, SISTER MARY (of Sisters of the Holy Names, Marylhurst, Oregon), MS. on Dr. McLoughlin.

FRANCHÈRE, GABRIEL, *Franchère's Voyage* (translated by J. V. Huntington).

FRASER, MALCOLM, original letters (loaned by J. A. Gray of Montreal, Canada).

FULLER, GEORGE W., *A History of the Pacific Northwest*.

GEER, T. T., *Fifty Years in Oregon*.

GHENT, W. J., *The Road to Oregon*.

GRAY, W. H., *History of Oregon*.

GREENHOW, ROBERT, *History of Oregon and California*.

GUEDALLA, PHILIP, *Palmerston*.

HARMON, DANIEL WILLIAMS, *A Journal of Voyages and Travels into the Interior of North America*.

HARRIOTT, J. E., "Correspondence," in *Washington Historical Society Quarterly*.

HARVEY, ELOISA MCLOUGHLIN, *Life of Dr. John McLoughlin.* MS., Bancroft Library.

HIMES, GEORGE H., various articles in *Oregon Historical Society Quarterly.*

HINES, GUSTAVUS, *Oregon and Its Institutions.*

———*Voyage Round the World.*

History of the Ursulines, by a Member of the Community (Quebec, 1897).

HOLMAN, FREDERICK V., *Dr. John McLoughlin.* Also articles in *Oregon Historical Society Quarterly.*

HORNER, JOHN B., *History of Oregon.*

IRVING, WASHINGTON, *Adventures of Captain Bonneville.*

JOHNSON, SIDONA V., *A Short History of Oregon.*

JUDSON, KATHERINE B., *Early Days in Old Oregon.* Also articles in *Oregon Historical Society Quarterly.*

KER, JAMES, original letters to Malcolm Fraser (loaned by J. A. Gray of Montreal, Canada).

LARSELL, DR. O., "An Outline of the History of Medicine in the Pacific Northwest." *Northwest Medicine,* Sept., Oct., Nov., 1932.

LAUT, AGNES C., *Conquest of the Great Northwest* (2 vols.).

———*The Overland Trail.*

LEE AND FROST, *Ten Years in Oregon.*

LEE, JASON, "Journal," in *Oregon Historical Society Quarterly.*

LOMAX, ALFRED L., articles in *Oregon Historical Society Quarterly.*

LYMAN, HORACE SUMNER, *History of Oregon* (4 vols.).

MCARTHUR, LEWIS A., *Oregon Geographic Names.*

MCDONALD, ARCHIBALD, *Correspondence.* Provincial Library, Victoria, B.C. Also in *Washington Historical Society Quarterly.*

MCLEOD, JOHN, *Journal.* Provincial Library, Victoria, B.C.

MCLOUGHLIN, DAVID, *Correspondence.* Oregon Historical Society, Portland.

MCLOUGHLIN, DR. JOHN, "Autobiographical Sketch," in *Oregon Pioneer Association Proceedings.*

———*Private Papers.* Bancroft Library.

———"Last Letter," *American Historical Review.*

———material on, in files of the *Morning Oregonian;* and correspondence in many of the references listed in this bibliography.

Makers of Canada Series, Vol. V, Pt. II: "Papineau, Cartier," by Alfred D. De Celles.

MARTIN, CHESTER, *Lord Selkirk's Work in Canada.*

MATTHIEU, FRANCIS X., "Reminiscences," in *Oregon Historical Society Quarterly.*

MEANY, EDMOND S., *History of the State of Washington.* Also articles in *Washington Historical Society Quarterly.*

MERK, FREDERICK, *Fur Trade and Empire.*

MOFRAS, EUGÈNE DUFLOT DE, *Exploration du Territorie de l'Orégon, des Californies et de la Mer Vermeille.*

MORISON, SAMUEL E., articles in *Oregon Historical Society Quarterly.*

MORROW, HONORÉ WILLSIE, *On to Oregon.*

———*We Must March.*

NEWELL, AARON, articles in *Washington Historical Society Quarterly.*

OGDEN, PETER SKENE, "Correspondence and Journal," in *Washington Historical Society Quarterly.*

O'HARA, BISHOP E. V., *Catholic History of Oregon.*

OLIVER, E. H., *Canadian North-West* (2 vols.).

Oregon Archives. Salem, Oregon.

Parish Records, St. James Church, Vancouver; the Cathedral, Oregon City; and St. Paul's Church, St. Paul, Oregon.

PARKER, SAMUEL, *Journal of an Exploring Tour.*

———"Letters," in *Oregon Historical Society Quarterly.*

PARRISH, PHILIP H., *Before the Covered Wagon.*

PELLETIER, LOUIS J. (Rivière du Loup, Quebec), genealogy of the Fraser family and other invaluable source material on Dr. McLoughlin's early life.

PIPES, NELLIE B., "De Mofras Exploration of the Oregon Territory," *Oregon Historical Society Quarterly.*

POWELL, FRANK WILBUR, *Hall Jackson Kelley on Oregon.* Also articles in *Oregon Historical Society Quarterly.*

POWERS, KATE N. B., articles in *Oregon Historical Society Quarterly.*

RAE, WILLIAM GLEN, MS. dealing with Rae's suicide. Provincial Library, Victoria, B.C.

ROBERTS, GEORGE B., *Recollections.* MS., Bancroft Library.

ROBERTSON, JAMES R., articles in *Oregon Historical Society Quarterly.*

ROSS, ALEXANDER, *Adventures of the First Settlers on the Oregon or Columbia River.*

SAGE, WALTER N., *Sir James Douglas and British Columbia.* Also articles in *Oregon Historical Society Quarterly* and *Washington Historical Society Quarterly.*

SCHAFER, JOSEPH, *History of the Pacific Northwest*. Also articles in *Oregon Historical Society Quarterly*.

SCOTT, HARVEY W., *History of the Oregon Country* (6 vols.).

SCOTT, LESLIE M., various articles in *Oregon Historical Society Quarterly*.

SCOULER, DR. JOHN, "Journal of a Voyage to Northwest America," *Oregon Historical Society Quarterly*.

SHIPPEE, LESTER BURRELL, articles in *Oregon Historical Society Quarterly*.

SIMPSON, SIR GEORGE, *Narrative of a Journey Round the World* (2 vols.). Also "Correspondence," in *Oregon Historical Society Quarterly* and *Washington Historical Society Quarterly*.

SKINNER, CONSTANCE LINDSAY, *Adventurers in Oregon*.

SLACUM, LIEUT. WILLIAM A., "Report on Oregon," *Oregon Historical Society Quarterly*.

SPALDING, H. H., "Correspondence," in *Oregon Historical Society Quarterly*.

THOMAS, RUSSELL B., articles in *Oregon Historical Society Quarterly*.

THOMPSON, CAPT. D. W., "Correspondence," in *Oregon Historical Society Quarterly*.

TOD, JOHN, *Correspondence*. Provincial Library, Victoria, B.C.

TOLMIE, WILLIAM FRAZER, "Journal," in *Washington Historical Society Quarterly*.

——*Puget Sound*. MS., Bancroft Library.

TOWNSEND, JOHN KIRK, *Narrative of a Journey Across the Rocky Mountains*.

TWOMBLY, ALEXANDER S., *Hawaii and Its People*.

VICTOR, FRANCES FULLER, *River of the West*.

WALLACE, W. S. (Librarian, University of Toronto Library), valuable information on the Fraser family and early life of Dr. McLoughlin.

WHITMAN, NARCISSA, *Letters*. Oregon Historical Society, Portland.

WILKES, CHARLES, "Diary of Wilkes in the Northwest," in *Washington Historical Society Quarterly*.

WORK, JOHN, *Correspondence*. Provincial Library, Victoria, B.C. (also in *Washington Historical Society Quarterly*).

——*Journal*, ed. by Lewis and Phillips.

WYETH, NATHANIEL J., *Correspondence and Journals*.

YOUNG, F. G., articles in *Oregon Historical Society Quarterly*.

Index

349